Swiss Democracy

Swiss Democracy

Possible Solutions to Conflict in Multicultural Societies

Third Edition, Revised and Updated

Wolf Linder
Professor Emeritus of Political Science, Institute of Political Science, University of Bern, Switzerland

First published 2010 by
PALGRAVE MACMILLAN

Palgrave Macmillan in the UK is an imprint of Macmillan Publishers Limited,
registered in England, company number 785998, of Houndmills, Basingstoke,
Hampshire RG21 6XS.

Palgrave Macmillan in the US is a division of St Martin's Press LLC,
175 Fifth Avenue, New York, NY 10010.

Palgrave Macmillan is the global academic imprint of the above companies
and has companies and representatives throughout the world.

Palgrave® and Macmillan® are registered trademarks in the United States,
the United Kingdom, Europe and other countries

ISBN 978-0-230-23188-7   hardback
ISBN 978-0-230-23189-4   paperback

This book is printed on paper suitable for recycling and made from fully
managed and sustained forest sources. Logging, pulping and manufacturing
processes are expected to conform to the environmental regulations of the
country of origin.

A catalogue record for this book is available from the British Library.

A catalogue record for this book is available from the Library of Congress.

10   9   8   7   6   5   4   3   2   1
19   18   17   16   15   14   13   12   11   10

Printed and bound in Great Britain by
CPI Antony Rowe, Chippenham and Eastbourne

Contents

List of Boxes

List of Figures and Tables

Figures

Tables

Preface to the Third Edition

Since the first edition of this book in 1994, Switzerland's political system has seen many gradual changes: a soft total revision of its constitution and federalism, the strengthening of its parliament, or the unattended fusion of many of its communes. The political party system is in a state of profound transformation: In three consecutive elections, the national-conservative People's Party became the biggest party. A rather polarised system with three forces – green-left, centre and right – sees the former bourgeois alliance split on many occasions. The composition of the all-party government coalition, which had been the same for decades, changed in 2003 and will see further alterations in the future. The spirit of accommodation in Swiss *Konkordanz* or consensus democracy has partly diminished. The majority of the Swiss people have chosen to stay outside the European Union but have approved the policy of its government to be selectively integrated into the common market by bilateral treaties with Brussels. As a small and export-oriented country, Switzerland is fully exposed to the dynamics of globalisation and Europeanisation. They are accelerating the government's political decision-making, pushing towards privatisation and liberalisation which leave new winners and new losers behind. Lone-standing, more vulnerable to external pressures, more divided by social cleavages than two decades ago, Switzerland has lost many advantages of the former *Sonderfall* (special case). Despite the dynamics of internationalisation and social divides which have become deeper, the basic structures of the political system have not changed: the combination of federalism, direct participation of the people and political power-sharing still make the originality of Swiss democracy.

It is obvious, therefore, that the text of *Swiss Democracy* needed thorough revision. Besides the updating of all statistics, great parts of the original text have been rewritten. Moreover, political science research on the Swiss polity and especially on the functioning of direct democracy has strongly developed. As in the first edition, the challenge was to integrate the state of the art of this research, but in a way accessible to non-specialists. Despite all reworking, the basic structure rests the same. The main focus of the book is on the three main institutions of Swiss democracy: federalism, direct democracy and power-sharing, including a final chapter that presents these institutions in a comparative perspective. And the message of *Swiss Democracy* is the same: Switzerland, thanks to its political institutions, has found ways to build up the unity of a multicultural society, to integrate its minorities, and to overcome social divides by way of accommodation through consensus democracy. The Swiss way of integration and policy-making has developed in a specific historical and socioeconomic context. It has its dark sides too, and I have tried to emphasise this in my account. This is one of the reasons why I consider Swiss democracy not a model to be exported but a historical experience. As a possible solution to multicultural conflict, others may draw from it, considering their own cultural and institutional heritage.

Fortunately, English-speakers today are offered more academic publications on the Swiss political institutions than at the beginning of the 1990s. I particularly mention Michael Butler *et al.*'s *The Making of Modern Switzerland, 1848–1998*, Clive Church's *The Politics and Government of Switzerland* with many historical details, or Kriesi and Trechsel's more policy-oriented *The Politics of Switzerland*. For readers interested in an in-depth academic account on institutions and policies, I refer to Ulrich Klöti *et al.* (eds) *Handbook of Swiss Politics* or to Jan Erik Lane's (ed.) *Swiss Labyrinth*. They all provide complementary views and information from which the new edition of *Swiss Democracy* is drawing and which allowed me to keep its text focused and appealing to a larger public. For scholars interested in the formal institutions, Walter Haller's *The Swiss Constitution* with comparative comments may be of particular interest.

Many statistics used in this book to give proportions will soon be out-dated, and the reader may be interested in the continuation of narratives of political processes mentioned in the text. Thanks to many online databases, this has become less a problem, and readers interested in doing so may keep up-dated. I particularly mention the following internet platforms: the yearly chronicle on events in Swiss politics, including data on elections and votations is online under: http://www.anneepolitique.ch. For the data on all federal votations since 1874 with links to official documents, see: 'Swissvotes', http://www.swissvotes.ch; for the statistical analysis of elections and votations: http://www.bfs.admin.ch under the keyword 'Politik', as well as the VOX-surveys under http://www.polittrends.ch/vox-analysen.

Last but not least, I would like to thank all those who have helped me to prepare this 3rd edition, particularly Franziska Ehrler for updating the statistics, Michael Sutter for the bibliographical research, Hans Hirter for many hints, Andrea Iff for many advices in the chapter on federalism, Mirko Wittwar for professional proof reading of the new parts of the text, and Monika Spinatsch, once more, for all secretarial help.

W.L. (2009)

Preface to the Second Edition (1999)

The positive reception the publication of *Swiss Democracy* received two years ago demonstrated the large public interest in Switzerland. As few English publications on Swiss polity and politics exist, political science colleagues use the book as a basic reference and a concise introduction, mainly to explain the sense and the functioning of consensus democracy, power-sharing or federalism. Several hundred copies have been distributed to official visitors by the Swiss foreign ministry, and to libraries by the Swiss arts foundation 'Pro Helvetia' via Swiss embassies. I welcome the many questions and suggestions from constitutionalists as well as politicians from India, Canada, USA, South Africa, Bosnia, Belarus, Slovenia and Poland, all eager to know more about power-sharing, minority protection, decentralised implementation, designs of federalism, or local autonomy in Switzerland. The book will be translated into Serbo-Croat and has already been published in Polish.

I was glad to learn that the most important message of the book came through: that Switzerland's organisation of democracy, shaped by the history of the nineteenth century, is a stimulating model for solutions to conflict in multicultural societies today. We say 'model' not in the sense of an ideal polity, but in the institutional design of 'consensus' democracy that differs from the prevailing Westminster model of majoritarian democracy. Moreover, the experience of the last two years has confirmed my view that it is not the formal design of the institutions alone but the political culture that makes consensus democracy work. Swiss democracy, therefore, is not an export blueprint but an experience, which shows that democracy can work in a different way than in most other countries. I hope that the second edition of *Swiss Democracy* will continue to spread this idea.

In order to keep the second edition of the book as slim as the first one, I concentrated on adding and integrating into the text references important recent publications, and updating statistics. The revised final conclusions deal with the issue of European integration and take into account Switzerland's situation of both isolation and integration after the vote of 6 December 1992 when the Swiss people turned down membership of the European Economic Area.

Many thanks go to Marina Delgrande, Reto Wiesli, Thomas Holzer and, once more, to Monika Spinatsch.

W.L. (1998)

Foreword to the First Edition

The late Stein Rokkan once called Switzerland a microcosm of Europe because of its cultural, linguistic, religious and regional diversity. Rokkan recommended that anyone wishing to study the dynamics of European politics should immerse themselves in the study of Switzerland. Today this advice seems even more justified. With the continuing process of European integration, it becomes increasingly clear how difficult it is to bring together different cultures into a single political system. With the fall of the iron curtain, cultural identities have gained greater importance, certainly in Central and Eastern Europe, but to a certain extent also in Western Europe.

Under these conditions, this present study by Wolf Linder is a welcome contribution to the discussion of European politics. He enlightens us about the lessons to be drawn from the Swiss experience. These lessons are far from naively optimistic. Linder is too critical of his own country to simply offer its history and institutions as a blueprint for Europe. Linder's approach is institutionally-oriented, which fits in nicely with the trend in political science towards a 'new institutionalism'. For Linder, however, there is nothing new in this emphasis on institutions. Before becoming a political scientist he received a thorough legal training. This background has made him doubly aware of the importance of institutions in the political process.

Linder stresses three institutional features in the political system of Switzerland: power-sharing, federalism and direct democracy. From this perspective, Switzerland is the exact opposite of the classical Westminster model. In the United Kingdom power is concentrated in the majority party in the House of Commons. In contrast Switzerland has developed a system of dispersed power. The cantons and the local communities enjoy much autonomy; at all levels the major political parties participate in the executive; and the citizens themselves are, in many important issues, the ultimate decision-makers. This dispersion of power is the Swiss way of handling the problem of cultural diversity.

As Linder points out, the dispersion of power also has a negative side, namely a certain immobility in the system. With accelerated development now in so many fields, this immobility is increasingly felt in the daily life of Swiss politics. The most prominent example relates to relations with the European Community. Switzerland has great difficulty in deciding what exactly this relationship should be. Thus it is lagging behind in the construction of a new Europe, instead of letting Europe profit from its multicultural experience.

Linder's analysis is a very differentiated one. On the one hand he recognises that federalism, the referendum and power-sharing are very important tools for the practice of democracy in an increasingly multicultural world. On the other hand he tries to sharpen these tools in such a way that the danger of immobility can be reduced. In this way much can be learned from Linder's study about the future of European politics. The lesson is certainly not: do it like the Swiss, and everything will be fine. Rather: study the history and the institutions of Switzerland, adopt what seems to work and avoid the many pitfalls.

The major part of this study was written when Wolf Linder, during sabbatical leave, stayed at our house in Chapel Hill. Thus my wife Ruth and I had the intellectual pleasure of following day by day the emergence of his analysis.

Jürg Steiner
University of North Carolina at
Chapel Hill and University of Bern (1994)

Introduction to the First Edition

In 1991 Switzerland celebrated its 700th year of existence. For its inhabitants this was an occasion to reflect on its history, to think about inherited values and to be grateful to be living in a country that is well
known for its stable democracy, for remaining unscathed and independent through two world wars, and for its wealth. Yet the 700th anniver-
sary of Switzerland was not just a year of celebration. It was also a time
of doubts about Swiss identity.

The Swiss, proud to be living in one of the oldest European democracies, learned that the intelligence service of their government had
snooped not only on criminals and spies from other countries, but also
on hundreds of thousands of their fellow citizens, and this often for
ridiculous reasons. Moreover, at the beginning of the 1990s the Swiss
economy seemed to be less competitive and less efficient than in previous
decades. And then there were fundamental questions about Switzerland's
future: when the Soviet Union disintegrated Switzerland's political neutrality lost much of its significance. In 1991–2 the European integration
process reached a new stage when the countries of the European Free
Trade Association signed the European Economic Area treaty with the
European Community. The Swiss government, which was in favour of
integration, not only signed the treaty but was willing to negotiate on the
eventual EC membership of Switzerland. At the end of 1992, however, a
popular vote rejected the EEA treaty. This halted the government's plan to
integrate and left the country politically divided. Will Switzerland really
remain on its own, proud of the independence it has defended so vigor-
ously in the past, or will it join the integration process in Europe in a few
years time? Switzerland seems to be in a state of transition, with outside
and inside pressure for fundamental changes. Even if the things that so
impress visitors – mountains, cleanness, wealth, reliable public transport
– will remain, there are changes of mentality in the country. At the end
of 1991 the editor-in-chief of the newspaper *Le Nouveau Quotidien* in
Lausanne, Jacques Pilet, wrote:

> Switzerland has changed.... We shall never think again that our
> country will be the eternal innocent-girl model of democracy. Swiss
> democracy, like other democracies, can be led into wrong or even
> stupid ways of behaving. We shall never believe again that, by

nature, we are more capable of behaving more economically, more proficiently than our neighbours, from whom we actually learned so many lessons in the past. We shall never believe again that our wealth will last for ever. Recent economic problems remind us of the fact that, in order to maintain our standard of living, we have to try harder than ever and must renounce many comfortable and soporific privileges. We shall never believe again that it will be wise for our small country, for eternity, to take its political decisions proudly and solitarily without regard for its friends and partners. So much exaggerated pride has been dashed that we shall have to develop new reasons to be proud.... The Swiss have a somewhat irritating and, at the same time, seductive quality: a certain inclination to take the opposite course to predominant fashions and modes, and a certain resistance to go where everybody is going. Let's cultivate this quality.[1]

In some ways, this book is written in this spirit. First, it describes a 'deviant case' of democracy: a democracy where citizens participate not only in the election of its parliament and its government, but also vote on and ratify parliamentary decisions of major importance. Since this type of direct democracy has remained unique, it runs the risk of being doubly misunderstood: being rejected out of hand or giving rise to uncritical mystification. My intention is to provide a critical account that avoids both fallacies. Moreover this book will focus on those questions of political history and modern political life that are important beyond the borders of Switzerland, asking how it was possible to create and integrate a political nation out of four different linguistic regions with a religious division between Protestants and Catholics. And why it was that Switzerland – a small country whose population of 6.9 million inhabitants makes up only about 2 per cent of Western Europe – did not fall apart when faced with the class struggles arising from modern industrialisation, and furthermore, managed to hold on to its independence and democracy in times of war and totalitarism in Europe. Finally I ask: how can a small democracy like Switzerland ensure political stability yet innovate at the same time?

These questions are of paramount importance today. First, multicultural coexistence, integration and peace are crucial, and too often unresolved in many parts of the world. Conflicts between different ethnic, language, religious and cultural groups are a main reason behind the failure of social modernisation in the Third World, of war in the Middle East and the Balkans as well as in many other nations where different ethnic groups coexist. The oppression of cultural minorities through-out its many decades of existence played a major role in the internal collapse of the Soviet Union, and in producing the outbreak of a new nationalism in the now independent republics. But how will this new nationalism – focusing as it does on cultural or ethnic identity – deal with the problem of other minorities who remain inside the boundaries of newly created states in Eastern Europe?

Problems of cultural minorities also constitute persistent and serious political problems in developed industrial societies, as we see with blacks in the USA, Catholics in Northern Ireland and French-speakers in Belgium and Canada. Industrialisation and market-oriented economies have led to a worldwide exchange of goods, services and capital. But this situation has also led to confrontation between different cultures and produced millions of refugees, especially among and from the Third World. In the new order of worldwide liberalisation and open markets, if the money does not go to the poor, the poor go where the money is. A large majority of the 170 nations considered as sovereign states nowadays constitute multi-cultural societies. However it seems that the real problems of integrating different ethnic and cultural traditions, and of dealing with religious and linguistic minorities within the boundaries of existing nations, have remained politically unresolved, despite promises of self-determination and democracy.

Switzerland has been fortunate in finding political ways of achieving multicultural understanding over the past 150 years. The solution was based on two concepts. First, Switzerland renounced – or was forced to renounce – the idea of creating a one-culture, one-language nation-state. Instead, from the very beginning of its modern existence it has been an 'artificial' multicultural nation, depending only on the con-straints of history and on the political will of inhabitants with different cultures. This was, and still is, fundamentally different from other ideas of nationalism in the middle of the nineteenth century as well as of those at the end of the twentieth century. Second, the Swiss were able to develop a type of democracy that favours – and enforces – political power-sharing between Protestants and Catholics, between the German-speaking majority and French-, Italian- and Romansch-speaking minor-ities, and between organised employers and trade unions. This has led to social integration, peaceful conflict-resolution by negotiation, and national consensus amongst a once fragmented and heterogeneous population.

If Switzerland is considered to be a 'paradigmatic case of political integration',[2] this has been helped by historical circumstances. The problems of Swiss integration may not be comparable with the much greater difficulties of multicultural integration in many young nations of today. Political scientists have observed many models of political integration through power-sharing that are different from those found in Switzerland.[3] Nevertheless, I believe that it may be helpful to illustrate in this book a successful case of political integration. The creation of a multicultural state, and the political integration of different religions and languages without destroying particular cultural identities, is probably the most precious legacy of Switzerland's democracy, and it may be the most precious message it can leave for others.

Because of this message, the focus of this book may differ slightly from earlier monographs on Switzerland in English.[4] Besides the peculiarities of direct democracy, it focuses on different aspects of political power-sharing, sometimes called 'consociational democracy'. In Chapter 1 the historical process of Swiss nation-building is described. It includes not only the creation of the Swiss federation, but the process of achieving the participation of the most important minority groups and the different social classes through proportional representation. The latter is considered a first element of power-sharing, the common notion of many comparative political scientists to describe the characteristics of democracies that renounce majority and 'winner takes all' rules.

In Chapter 2, we focus on the characteristics of Swiss federalism. Federalism allows the division of power between central and regional government and is therefore a widely used institutional arrangement in multicultural societies. In the Swiss case, it allows not only the protection of various minorities, it has also served to preserve different regional identities, themselves multicultural. In Chapter 3 I turn to direct democracy – how it works in modern Switzerland, and how it works despite the claim of many theorists that it is too demanding for people in a highly developed industrial society. I try to define the limits of direct democracy, and consider why it has led to political conservatism rather than to social innovation. Many other countries use a variety of institutional forms of plebiscite, referenda and popular initiative in order to influence parliamentary and governmental policies. Switzerland, however, is the only country where direct democracy has become an important – perhaps also the most constraining – element of power-sharing. In fact the referendum has enabled minorities successfully to challenge parliamentary proposals that did not take into account their group interests. Consequently lawmaking in Switzerland has become impossible without the participation of various interest groups. Thus the referendum has profoundly changed the Swiss political system, which initially intended to follow the winner-takes-all pattern of Anglo-Saxon democracy. Instead it has developed patterns of political pluralism. In its structures of consociational democracy, all political parties and interest groups are permanently represented in the political institutions, and lawmaking has become a process of negotiation and mutual adjustment involving all political forces.

In the final chapter I try to develop three perspectives, based on the previous chapters, that go beyond the case of Switzerland, beginning with direct democracy. In a theoretical perspective, democracy is not a definitive concept, but one which changes with the passage of time. Thus enhancing the participation of the people by direct democracy as in Switzerland – considered revolutionary in the nineteenth century – may still be considered a very progressive form of democracy. But can the principle of utmost participation of the greatest possible number of people be applied to the whole spectrum of political issues and decision-making? And are increased political rights, offering the people not only a voice in the election of their representatives but a chance to vote on major decisions, an efficient way forward to better democracy? The second perspective is that of federalism. Traditionally federalism has been a means for the sub-national division of institutional power. But could it also play a role in the supranational division of power and the participation of minorities? Despite the fact that federalism is an old and well-known institutional arrangement, it seems that not all of its possibilities are exploited today. Finally, I discuss different institutional arrangements for political power-sharing and their effectiveness in settling conflicts, especially in multicultural societies. I end by stressing that power-sharing is not just an institutional arrangement, it has to be based on the specific culture of the society that intends to introduce it.

Thus, I would like to give a first response to the subtitle of this book: Switzerland provides a model example because of its enduring will to constitute an independent political nation based on the mutual respect of its minorities. It provides a model for finding political institutions and patterns of behaviour that enable peaceful conflict-resolution in a multicultural society. While the model cannot be copied in its entirety, some of its basic elements can be noted, adapted and used by others. Renouncing a 'nation-state' of one culture, one religion and one language was essential for the success of the Swiss model. The option of political integration and democratic pluralism could be an alternative to today's new nationalism. Elements of political power-sharing – such as federalism, proportional participation of minorities, lawmaking by negotiation – can be helpful in any country that is faced with problems of multicultural conflict. Properly adapted, direct democracy can enhance the quality of citizens' participation in parliamentary systems. Democracy and peaceful conflict-resolution, however, not only depend on adequate political institutions. They also need the social development of a political culture. Unlike technical innovation, this takes a long time to develop. This may be the last, but not the least important lesson offered by the Swiss experience: successfully overcoming cultural conflicts is a political process requiring decades rather than years.

I am indebted to a number of persons who assisted me during the research and writing of this book.

The first is George W. Jones from the London School of Economics, whom I met at an international congress on local government at Germany in 1988. He not only inspired me to write a book on Swiss government but got things started by looking for a publisher for the project. Later he gave invaluable advice on revisions of earlier versions of the text. Similar help came from Clive Church of the University of Kent at Canterbury. As a specialist in Swiss contemporary history, Clive made particularly well-informed suggestions on how to explain the specificities of Swiss political institutions to an English-speaking public. I am also very grateful to both of them for their help in improving my 'Swiss English'.

As mentioned in the Foreword, the first draft of the book was written during my sabbatical at the University of Chapel Hill. I am grateful to Ruth and Jürg Steiner; their kind hospitality made my work at Chapel Hill pleasant in every respect.

The focus of the book is on Swiss political institutions and democracy. In many respects, however, it goes beyond the perspective of political science. I am particularly thankful, therefore, to a number of colleagues from other disciplines for their support during the writing of the book. Jean-François Aubert from the University of Neuchatel, Peter Saladin and Walter Kälin from the University of Bern, all of whom are specialists in constitutional or international law, and peace-researcher Johan Galtung from the University of Honolulu, were critical readers of the manuscript and gave invaluable advice as well as encouragement.

Hans Hirter, Lorenz Kummer, Martin Senti and Adrian Vatter, assistants at the Political Science Institute in Bern, indulged me in various versions of my argument. Daniel Hug undertook the bibliographical research, collected economic and sociological data and prepared some of the information boxes. Visiting scholar Peter Stettler helped to improve the English and provided historical advice. I am most grateful to Monika Spinatsch for her excellent editorial work on all the drafts of the manuscript. Last but not least, I thank my partner Ursula Nordmann for many discussions on the book, and for all her personal encouragement.

W.L. (1994)

Notes

1 Jacques Pilet, 'Voeux au bout d'une année folle', *Nouveau Quotidien*, January 1/2 1992.
2 Karl Deutsch, *Die Schweiz als paradigmatischer Fall politischer Integration* (Bern: Haupt, 1975).
3 Arend Lijphart, *Democracy in Plural Societies* (New Haven and London: Yale University Press, 1977); Kenneth D. McRae (ed.), *Consociational Democracy* (Toronto: McClelland and Stewart, 1974).
4 For instance André Siegfried, La Suisse, démocratie-témoin (Neuchâtel: La Baconnière, 1948); George A. Codding, *The Federal Government of Switzerland* (Cambridge Mass: Riverside Press, 1962); Christopher Hughes, *Switzerland* (London: Praeger/Benn, 1975); Jonathan Steinberg, *Why Switzerland* (London/ New York: Cambridge University Press, 1976); Oswald Sigg, *Switzerland's Political Institutions* (Zurich and Bern: Pro Helvetia, 1983); Kenneth D. McRae, *Conflict and Compromise in Multilingual Societies*, vol. 1, *Switzerland* (Waterloo, Ontario: Wilfred Lauder University Press, 1983); Clive, H. Church *et al. Aspects of Switzerland: Sources and Reflections* (Canterbury: University of Kent, 1986); Nicholas Gilett, *The Swiss Constitution – Can it be Exported?* (Bristol: Yes Publications, 1989); J.E. Hilowitz, 'Switzerland in Perspective', *Contributions in Sociology* no. 92 (1990) (Praeger/Greenwood).

1
Building a Multicultural Society by Political Integration

1.1   Introduction

Switzerland today seems to be one of the most privileged countries in the world. When its direct neighbours were engaged in the destructive conflicts of the First and Second World Wars, Switzerland survived as a successfully neutral and independent small nation in the heart of war-torn Europe. At the beginning of this century its inhabitants are enjoying one of the highest living standards among industrialised countries. Switzerland lacks natural resources, but Swiss industry produces high-quality goods: precision machines and tools, watches, electronic devices, pharmaceutical and chemical products, and services such as banking, insurance and tourism, which are appreciated all over the world. With high import and export rates Switzerland is strongly dependent on the European and world markets yet has maintained its ability to compete in many fields. Although Switzerland's population is small, the country can compete in exports and foreign investments with the largest of industrialised nations. In exported goods Switzerland ranks tenth in the world and among foreign investors it lies fifth. If we consider bank credits to foreign countries, we find that Switzerland ranks as high as third. Once a poor region of mountain farmers, it has become a rich nation and is seen as a model case of successfully finding a profitable niche in world markets (Boxes 1.1 and 1.2).

Moreover, the Swiss people pay relatively low taxes for the many benefits they receive from their government. There are high-quality, reliable public transport systems which not only link cities but also extend up to small mountain villages. The infrastructure of roads, energy supply and telecommunications is comprehensive and well maintained. Public education is of a high standard, especially in professional schools. In some

1

Box 1.1 Characteristics of Switzerland

A. *Geography*	
Area	41 293 km^2
Jura (per cent)	10.0
Mittelland (per cent)	30.0
Alpine regions (per cent)	60.0
Land-use (in per cent)	
Residential/industrial	4.3
Meadow/arable	28.3
Pasture	20.6
Forestry	25.5
Wasteland, rivers, lakes	21.3
B. *Population*	
Resident population (2007, in millions)	7.59 (100.0%)
Foreigners	1.70 (23.0%)
Urban population	5.64 (74.3%)
Rural population	1.95 (25.7%)
Density of population (2004, inhabitants/km^2)	
Switzerland	180
Urban regions	609
Rural regions	69
Population by language (2000, in per cent)	
German	63.7
French	20.4
Italian	6.5
Romansh	0.5
Others	9.0
Population by religion (2000, in per cent)	
Protestant	35.3
Roman Catholic	41.8
Christ- and orthodox Catholic	2.0
Jewish	0.2
Muslim	4.3
Others or no religion	16.4
C. *Economy (2006)*	
GDP (billion US Dollars)	285.3
GDP per capita (US Dollars)	37 747
Unemployment rate (per cent)	4.5
Inflation rate	0.8
Average annual growth rate in real GDP (1985–2006, in per cent)	1.5
Exported goods and services (billion USD)	206.2
Imported goods and services (billion USD)	174.3
Trade balance: Exports minus imports (billion USD, percent of GDP)	31.9 (11 per cent)

Box 1.2   Development of various sectors of the economy, 1800–1990

Employed persons according to economic sectors, 1850–2006 (per cent of persons in employment)*

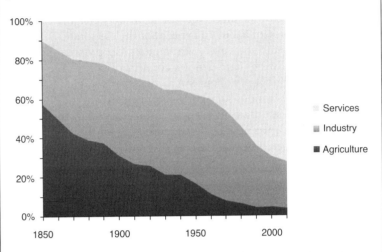

*1850–1960 Full-time employment; 1970–2006 full- and part-time employment

Employment	total	male	female
Persons in employment (2005, millions)	4.2		
Employment rate (2006, per cent)	77.9	84.7	71.1
Unemployment rate (2006, per cent)	4		
Working hours per week (2005, mean)	41.6		
Gross wage per month (2004, mean, CHF)	5548	5953	4781

Strikes (2005)			
Number	5		
Workers involved	338		
Working days lost	1392		

Size of firms (2005)	Share of total employees (per cent)	Number of companies	per cent
Companies with 1–9 employees	26.4	261 582	87.6
Companies with 10–49 employees	21.7	30 638	10.3
Companies with 50–249 employees	19.4	5 472	1.8
Companies with +249 employees	32.5	1 028	0.3

Sources: Statistisches Jahrbuch der Schweiz 2007, OECD Factbook 2008: Economic, Environmental and Social Statistics, Bundesamt für Statistik. For latest data, see: www.bfs.admin.ch/

fields of research, the federal institutes of technology have a world-wide reputation. Health services and social security are available to everybody.

The political stability of Switzerland is outstanding. For almost 50 years the Federal Council, the seven-member head of the Swiss government, has been composed of a successful coalition between the same four parties, which represent about 70 per cent of the electorate. Despite the fact that the electorate votes every year on up to six proposals to change the constitution, Switzerland is not a country of political revolution. Outsiders wonder not only about Swiss conservatism, but also about a seeming absence of serious social or economic conflict.

Switzerland, in maintaining its own interpretation of the principle of neutrality, has until now played a lesser role on the stage of international politics than other neutral countries such as Sweden and Austria. In doing so it has avoided many of the conflicts and complications in international affairs in the past that could have been dangerous, perhaps even catastrophic, for a small, young nation.

It would be fundamentally wrong, however, to think of Switzerland as a country without historical conflicts. Modern Switzerland was not created by one homogeneous ethnic people, but by different ethnic groups speaking different languages and following different religions. Nation-building was a bottom-up process and right from the beginning led to a multicultural nation-state. Nation-building and the processes of urbanisation, industrialisation and modernisation were accompanied by societal conflicts just as in other countries. Moreover, they were in many ways comparable with processes in developing countries today. At the beginning of the political federation of Switzerland there was a civil war between conservative Catholics and progressive Protestants. Thereafter, despite its political neutrality, in the First World War Switzerland almost broke apart when the political elites opted for different sides in the conflict between its neighbours: the majority of German-speaking Swiss identified with the German side whereas the French-speaking population sympathised with France.[1] During industrial development there were economic inequalities and a class struggle developed between workers and capitalist entrepreneurs which culminated in a nationwide strike and intervention by federal government troops in 1918. The workers whose claims were all denied by the bourgeois government became a radicalised opposition group during the following decade. After the Second World War an important minority conflict broke out in the canton of Bern when the French-speaking population of the Jura region denied the legitimacy of the state government.

After a long political struggle they succeeded in creating a canton of their own. Today, the Swiss people are deeply divided on the question of European integration. Geographically situated in the centre of Europe, Switzerland is not a member of the EU, and in a popular vote in 1992 the majority of the Swiss refused to become a member of the European Economic Area. Switzerland, at the beginning of the twenty-first century, faces the challenges of globalisation and *Europeanisation* on its own. Being a small state, it runs the risk that many of its traditional comparative economic advantages turn into disadvantages. Thus, the question of European integration is still controversial: 'Traditionalists' see Switzerland's best future in continuing its long standing policy of neutrality and utmost sovereignty, while 'modernists' want Switzerland to become a member of the European Union.[2]

So how has the Swiss nation-state, once Utopian idea, become a reality? How was Switzerland able to keep its independence as a political nation and deal with its economic, social and cultural conflicts? And finally, how was Switzerland able to turn itself into a modern, industrialised nation, and develop a form of democracy that in the nineteenth century went further than in all other European countries?

In saying that Switzerland represents a 'paradigmatic case of political integration', I echo the view of Karl Deutsch, a scholar looking at Switzerland from the outside.[3] Indeed Switzerland has become a society with its own identity only through and because of its political institutions. The role of the political institutions was fundamental in uniting a people with four languages, two religions and different regional cultures and in turning these disadvantages into advantages. The key to this process was integration and a particular way of dealing with conflicts and problems in a peaceful manner. In this chapter as well as in many other parts of the book, I shall illustrate, using specific examples, what integration meant and how it worked.

1.2 The origins of modern Switzerland

After the Vienna Congress in 1815, when much of the prerevolutionary old order was restored in Europe, nobody could have foreseen that Switzerland would become one of the first democracies and a small nation-state.

Three tiny alpine regions had declared themselves independent of the Habsburgs in the thirteenth century. Other regions and cities then followed suit and by the time of the French Revolution 13 Swiss cantons had formed a loose confederation. However, what had once been a product of peasant revolution transformed itself into a feudalist regime of privileges, in which the old cantons exploited the resources and people of newly acquired regions. This moribund 'old regime' broke down when troops of the French Revolution, promising to bring democracy, invaded Switzerland as they had other European countries. While France was successful in breaking the privileges of the old cantons, it failed, not surprisingly, to merge the cantons into a united *Helvetic Republic* in 1798. Five years later, on the order of Napoleon Bonaparte, part of the autonomy of the cantons was restored in the so-called *Mediation Act*, but in 1815 the Swiss chose to return to the old system. A loose confederation of 25 independent cantons, who considered themselves sovereign states, was reestablished. The 'eternal' treaty guaranteed collective security by mutual assistance. A conference of canton delegates was empowered to implement common decisions. But the delegates were bound by the instructions of their cantonal governments. Agreements and decisions were difficult to reach. Thus, the Swiss confederation did not have a real parliament, let alone an executive body. In other words, Switzerland was not yet a true nation-state.[4]

There is often confusion about the meaning of the term *confederation*. Here it is used to describe a treaty-based system of independent states, whereas the term 'federation' designates a state wherein power is shared between one central government and a number of non-centralised governments having the status of constituent or member states. Thus, Switzerland will be called a confederation for the period 1815–48, and thereafter a federation.

In the decades after 1815 the Swiss confederation lived through a period of internal polarisation between two forces, the Conservatives and the Radicals. The Conservatives were Catholics from mainly rural regions. Being a minority, they insisted that decisions taken at the Conference of Delegates should be unanimous. They were sceptical about the idea of strengthening the authority of central government – just as the anti-federalist forces in the United States had been a few decades before. In a time of early democratisation in the cantons the Conservatives wanted to preserve the traditional cultural and political roles of the Catholic Church. The Radicals, on the other hand, were rooted in mainly Protestant, industrialising cantons. The Radicals strove foremost for democracy under the slogan *people's sovereignty* with the aim of public control of all authorities. The democratic revolutions in many cantons sought not only political rights for all people, the division of power, and publicity for the debates of the elected parliament, but also the separation of state and church. Radicals denied the

Catholic minority the old social privileges of their church. From the sixteenth to the eighteenth century, the old confederation suffered four internal religious wars – but it also achieved agreements between Catholics and Protestants that led to periods of peaceful coexistence. With the arrival of democracy religious differences again led to conflict (Box 1.3).

Religion was not the only conflict between Radicals and Conservatives, but it was the one that concentrated many other political issues within and among the cantons. It led to rebellions and repression by military force, as when armed volunteers (*Freikorps*) of Radicals from other cantons wanted to 'liberate' the Lucerne canton from its Catholic government. In 1845 the Catholic cantons signed a separate treaty (the *Sonderbund*) to defend their common interests. They also demanded a revision of the treaty setting up the confederation and tried to obtain diplomatic help (and more) from Austria, France and Sardinia to defend their cause. In 1847 the Catholic cantons left the Conference of Delegates, or *Tagsatzung*. This was interpreted by the Protestant cantons as secession. The differences over religion, culture and secession then escalated into a short civil war, which ended – after 26 days and with only about a hundred casualties – with the defeat of the secessionists.[5]

Box 1.3   Religious conflicts between Protestant and Catholic cantons from the sixteenth to the eighteenth century

---

1529: A military conflict between Protestant Zurich and the five Catholic cantons was prevented by the first *Kappeler Landfriede* which contained the promise of confessional tolerance.

1531: Battles between Catholic and Protestant troops from Zurich and Bern were won by the Catholics. The second *Kappeler Landfriede* was therefore in favour of the Catholics: Protestant confession was acknowledged but the Catholics conserved some prerogatives. This second *Kappeler Landfriede* regulated the balance until 1656.

1656: Zurich and Bern tried to improve their position against the Catholic cantons but lost the first battle of Villmergen, which confirmed Catholic dominance.

1712: The second battle of Villmergen was won by the Protestants. The victory eliminated Catholic hegemony in the old confederation and gave Protestant Zurich and Bern political influence appropriate to their economic power.

The way was then free for the creation of a nation-state fundamentally different from that established by the confederative treaty of 1815. The victorious Radicals were the leading force in drafting a constitutional framework that involved:

- The *transition from a loose confederation to a federation*: The 25 cantons (today 26) were willing to establish a national government, and, upon becoming member states of the federation, agreed to give up some of their rights as sovereign states. Switzerland therefore represents one of the cases in which bottom-up nation-building power is divided between the cantons and their communes on the one hand and central government on the other;
- The *creation of a multicultural state*: According to the constitution of 1848, the Federation consisted 'of the peoples of the cantons'. In contrast to the unification of Germany or Italy at that time, the concept of the state was not based on the same culture, religion or language of its people but on the same citizenship of the different peoples of the cantons. Switzerland therefore represents a political, not a cultural nation;
- The *transition to a constitutional democracy* with an executive authority and a parliament of its own. Moreover, the constitution granted minimum standards of democratic institutions for the member states, including guarantees of political and basic rights, the division of power and free elections to parliament, with the people as the supreme authority when it came to changing the constitution.

The draft was submitted to a popular vote in 1848. The votation did not conform to the same standard in all cantons because there was no common procedure. In Freiburg and Graubünden it was the cantonal parliament which decided 'in the name of the people', and there were some doubts about the results obtained in the canton of Lucerne: its radical government declared that the people had accepted a federal constitution when in fact the government had counted the 30 per cent of non-voters as yes-voters. Despite these irregularities, two thirds of the cantons accepted the project, and on 12 September 1848 the *Tagsatzung* declared that the federal constitution had been accepted by a large majority of the people and the cantons.[6]

Revised in 1874 and 1999, the constitution of 1848 contained most of the organisational framework of today's polity (Boxes 1.4 to 1.6). Table 1.1 shows that the Swiss federal system consists of legislative, executive and judicial organs at each level. Note, however, that the

Table 1.1 The Swiss federal system and the executive, legislative and judicial powers at each level

	Executive Power	Legislative Power	Judicial Power
	Federal Council:	Federal Assembly:	Federal Supreme Court:
Federation	Seven federal councillors elected by the Federal Assembly. The councillors are the heads of the seven government departments.	National Council: 200 national councillors elected by the people directly using proportional rule. The number of cantonal representatives depends on population size. Council of States: 46 state councillors, two for each canton. Popular election according to cantonal rules.	35–48 full-time and additional substitute supreme judges elected by the Federal Assembly.
	Cantonal Council:	Cantonal Parliament:	Cantonal Court:
Canton	Election by the people every four to five years. The Council consists of five to seven members.	Election by the people using proportional rule.	Election by the cantonal council or cantonal parliament.
	Communal Council:	Communal assembly:	District Court:
Commune	Election by the people.	In small communes usually formed of all citizens in the commune. In larger communes: parliaments elected by the people.	Election by the people of a number of communes forming a district, or appointed by cantonal authorities.

Box 1.4 Main authorities of the federation: Power-sharing and proportional representation among representatives of different cultures, languages and parties

---

Federal Assembly: Bicameral parliamentary body representing the people (National Council) and the cantons (Council of States). Both chambers have equal powers. The Federal Assembly exercises the supreme authority of the federation, having the legislative power to make all federal laws, and appointing the members of the Federal Council and the Federal Court, the Commander-in-Chief (in times of war) and other major federal bodies. It supervises all authorities of the Swiss federal government, and approves the annual budget prepared by the Federal Council.

Federal Council: Supreme executive and governing authority of the Swiss federation. Its composition minors power-sharing between different parties and cultures: The seven members of the Federal Council are representatives of four different political parties (in the same composition since 1959: three bourgeois centre-right and one left party). An unwritten law requires that at least two members should come from French- or Italian-speaking regions. The Council acts as a collegiate body. There is no role of prime minister with prerogatives over the other members of the Cabinet; thus most decisions come from and are underwritten by the Council as a whole. One of the seven councillors serves as president of the federation. By custom this function is carried out by a different member each year. The president has no special political privileges, only formal duties. Each federal councillor heads one of the seven ministries (called departments): Foreign Affairs; Interior; Justice and Police; National Defence; Finance; Public Economy; Transport, Communication and Energy. The federal administration, located mostly in Bern, has a staff of about 36,000 civil servants and employees, rail and postal services not included.

Federal Supreme Court: The Federal Supreme Court acts as the final court of appeal in cases coming from cantonal courts and involving federal law. Thus the Court acts in all areas of Swiss law but in very different functions, depending on the specificity of the case. The Court decides on conflicts between the federation and the member states and on conflicts among the cantons. It is empowered to review legislative and executive acts of the cantons and guarantees the constitutional rights of the citizens. However, the Court does not have the power, either directly or by implication, to rule on the constitutionality of federal laws.

Box 1.4 Main authorities of the federation: Power-sharing and proportional representation among representatives of different cultures, languages and parties – *continued*

> The seat of the Supreme Court is located in Lausanne and in Lucerne. A number of federal affairs in public administration and crime are dealt with in first instance at the Federal Court of Administration in St. Gallen and at the Federal Criminal Court in Bellinzona. Appeal can be made to the Supreme Court. The Federal Assembly elects the judges for a term of office of six years. The composition of the Supreme Court and the Federal Courts reflect two dimensional power-sharing: all three official languages and the political factions of the Federal Assembly are represented in all three Courts.

Box 1.5 Direct democracy

> Besides electing their parliament, the Swiss voters are provided with two important instruments of direct democracy: the popular initiative and the referendum allow them to influence parliamentary decisions.
>
> *The popular initiative* is a formal proposition which demands a constitutional amendment. It must be submitted to the vote of the people and cantons if the proposition is signed by at least 100,000 citizens within 18 months. Before the vote, the Federal Council and the Federal Assembly give non-binding advice on whether the proposal should be accepted or rejected and occasionally formulate a counterproposal.
>
> *The referendum* is a constitutional right of the people, which obliges the parliament to submit every amendment of the constitution, a major legislation or an important international treaty for popular approval. For the different types of referenda see Chapter 3.

Swiss system conforms less with the classical concept of separation of powers than with an idea of mutual cooperation and control that is partly comparable with the checks and balances of the US constitution.

Box 1.6 Political parties

The social cleavages and antagonistic political interests in the second half of the nineteenth century led to three main tendencies in Swiss political life: liberalism, conservatism and socialism. These tendencies crystallised in the four governmental political parties of Radicals, Christian Democrats, Social Democrats and the People's Party. Federalism and proportional representation, however, led to a highly fragmented multi-party system. Since there are no quotas, sometimes more than ten different parties were represented in the Federal Assembly.

An important distinction has to be made between governmental and non-governmental parties. The development of political power-sharing in the twentieth century has led to a multi-party government. From 1959 to 2007 there has been a stable coalition of the four biggest parties forming the Federal Council (the 'magic formula', according to which the seats in the executive are distributed proportionally to the electoral strength of the Radicals, Christian Democrats, Social Democrats and the People's Party.). The rest of the parties occupy less than 30 per cent of the seats in the Federal Assembly and do not form a coherent opposition. The profiles of governmental and non-governmental parties and their share of votes (in the 2007 national elections) are as follows:

A. Governmental parties

Radical Party (15.8 per cent): regards itself as the heir to nineteenth century liberal ideas; it enjoys close relations with business and industry and is highly influential in economic matters. It is the political representative of independent professionals, entrepreneurs and the middle class.

Christian Democrats (14.5 per cent): successor to the Catholic conservative movement. Still the preferred party of the Catholics. With a bourgeois and a trade-union wing, it thus tries to integrate the opposing interests of entrepreneurs and employees.

Social Democrats (19.5 per cent): in former times it was periodically a radical-left movement. Today it is a moderate party standing for social, ecological and economic reforms. Enjoys close relations with trade unions. Most of its supporters are in urban, industrialised regions, but it draws on all social groups.

Box 1.6   Political parties – *continued*

Swiss People's Party ('farmer's party'; 28.9 per cent): once a conservative party appealing mainly to farmers, craftsmen and independent professionals, it has more than doubled its electoral force in the last 15 years and become the biggest political party. Defending Swiss sovereignty and neutrality, it is today situated at the national-conservative right. The success of the People's Party was the result of several factors: Take-over of smaller right-wing parties, strong mobilisation of anti-European, anti-immigration oriented parts of the electorate, partly populist strategies, stronger professional organisation, charismatic and authoritative party leadership.

B. Non-governmental parties

Small parties, sometimes represented in just a few cantons, of heterogeneous ideological orientation:

Green Party (9.8 per cent): Party of the ecology movement; has drawn from left parties as well as from new social movements.

Green Liberals (1.4): Split from the Green Party in 2007 to address centre-oriented ecologists.

Liberals (1.9 per cent): Dates back to the nineteenth century; represents a right-wing secession from the radicals. Most affinity of all Swiss parties to neo-liberal ideas. Represents the upper middle class and independent professionals, mostly in Protestant, French-speaking cantons. In 2009 merger with the Radicals.

Protestant party (2.4 per cent): counterpart of the Christian democrats, but without its electoral success.

Freedom Party (former Automobile Party) (0.1 per cent): single-issue party once defending interests of car owners and small craftsmen; with populist and xenophobic tendencies.

Swiss Democrats (0.5 per cent): party of the national extremist right with a bluntly xenophobic outlook. Successor to former anti-immigration movements (Republicans, National Action).

Alternative Left (1.1 per cent): Successor of former radical left parties (mainly the Communist Labour Party and progressive organisations) that have almost disappeared. Non-dogmatic, social and ecological orientation.

Box 1.6 Political parties – *continued*

> *Bourgeois-Democratic Party:* Split from the Swiss People's Party in
> 2008, with five members of parliament and one member of the
> Federal Council, which was elected in 2007 against the official can-
> didate of the People's Party. Will participate in national elections in
> 2011 for the first time.

1.3 Turning poor odds to good, or factors that made Swiss nation-building a success

As the short historical account in the previous section suggests, the
transition from confederation to federation was not an easy one. First,
the Conservatives' desire to maintain key elements of the old order
made them directly opposed to giving away the sovereign rights of
their cantons, preferring instead to maintain the *status quo*. The innovating forces, on the other hand, were firmly opposed to this. Second,
there was the problem of cultural differences. Besides the issue of religion there was the question of language. German was, and is, the language of more than 70 per cent of the population. Those in the French-
and Italian-speaking regions feared that, as minorities, they would be
made worse off by yielding their political power to a central government. Third, economic structures differed from canton to canton, as
did preferences for trade regulations protecting the interests of farmers,
craftsmen and traders. Fourth, nationalism, at the beginning, was a
kind of abstract Utopia. What is called nationalism today in East
European countries, for instance, is an appeal to a common cultural
heritage or ethnic group when striving for independence from a central
government. In Switzerland, the reverse applied: the people of the
cantons represented different languages, ethnic groups and religions
and had to be convinced that they should form a common nation,
which to them was artificial in every respect. Certainly the people of
the cantons were known as 'the Swiss', but they really felt themselves
to be from Zurich, Uri, Geneva or Tessin, with little in common with
people from other cantons. Last but not least, some cantons had
serious internal conflicts. In Basel, for instance, the city was not willing
to give up its political control over the surrounding regions. When a
compromise failed to be reached, Basel city and Basel county separated
to form two independent semi-cantons.[7] Thus, it was not easy to push
the idea of a nation-state when political perspectives and horizons were

shrinking rather than widening in many cantons. Instead of forming a single territorial state, the cantons could have been stuck with their internal quarrels and disappeared from the map of Europe.

So what did bring Switzerland together?

1.3.1   Economy

By the middle of the nineteenth century, early industrialisation had reached many cantons. New elites, whose status was based on industrial wealth and capital rather than on family standing, entered the public arena. The harnessing of power from rivers led to a pattern of decentralised industry, reaching far up into the valleys of the Alps. The first railroad between Baden and Zurich opened in 1847 and from then on it became evident that the boundaries of cantonal markets were obstacles to growing industrial activities. The federal constitution promised not only to remove those obstacles but also to create a common economic market. It banned cantonal toll barriers and empowered the federal government to issue a Swiss currency as well as introduce a federal postal service. Moreover, the constitution aimed to promote 'common wealth', and it promised equal rights as well as the freedom to reside in any canton to all those who became Swiss citizens. One historian has gone so far as to say that the economic necessity of creating a common market was more important than political ideas of Swiss nationalism.[8]

1.3.2   Pressure from the outside

When the great powers, at the Vienna Congress of 1815, restored the patterns of Old Europe, Metternich and the delegates of the other countries were not unhappy about the presence of a neutral zone between Austria, Sardinia-Piemont and France. The Swiss confederation thus gained some recognition of its political neutrality (see Box 1.7), which the cantons had begun to observe from 1648. During the period 1815–48, however, the cantons learned that they were somewhat dependent on the good, or bad, will of their powerful immediate neighbours. The latter were far from thinking of annexing the cantons, but this did not make them refrain from diplomatic intervention in Swiss affairs. This situation was exacerbated by some of the cantons seeking diplomatic help from outside, as did the members of the *Sonderbund*.

In the middle of the nineteenth century the cantons witnessed important experiments in nation-building when the small neighbouring kingdoms of Sardinia-Piemont, Lombardy-Venetia, Baden, Wurttemberg and Bavaria became parts of Italy and Germany. What would be the future

Box 1.7   Neutrality: A necessary aid in building up the Swiss nation

Political neutrality has long been a tradition in Switzerland. After a disastrous defeat in a battle at Marignano (near Milan, Italy) in 1515, the Swiss cantons slowly grew aware of the advantages of neutrality, which turned out to be the only way to maintain the integrity and independence of a confederation consisting of small cantons surrounded by larger and belligerent powers. Subsequently, the Swiss avoided becoming involved in conflicts between surrounding states, especially during the 30 years of religious war in Europe which ended in 1648. It took a long time, however, for the unilateral declaration of neutrality to be recognised by neighbours. It, therefore, did not prevent the Swiss cantons from being occupied by the French during the years 1798–1802. Things changed after the Vienna Congress of 1815, when the European powers at last recognised the neutrality of the confederation, realising that it was in their interest to use it to preserve the political equilibrium sought by them. After the creation of the federation Switzerland became able to defend efficiently its neutrality with armed forces. This was particularly important in the twentieth century, when Switzerland was one of the very few European nations not to be involved in the First and Second World Wars.[9]

Neutrality, historically, has had two main functions: *internal integration* and *external independence*: integration through neutrality prevented the cantons of the old confederation from becoming divided by the conflicts of their neighbours or from being broken up into antagonistic religious and cultural parts. Later, armed neutrality helped to preserve the independence of the Swiss federation.[10]

Today the Swiss idea of neutrality is based on notions of the law of nations formulated in the 'Hague treaty on the rights and duties of neutral powers and persons' of 1907. 'Neutrality in the sense of the law of nations' means nothing more than the neutral nation's non-participation in a war involving other nations. In fulfilling this, first, Swiss neutrality is permanent and defended by an army. Second, Switzerland pursues a policy of doing everything to ensure neutrality in a future war. But Switzerland's policy goes far beyond this. After the Second World War its extensive interpretation of 'neutrality' even meant non-participation in the European Community, the United Nations and other multilateral organisations. The reason for this was given as the wish not to participate

Box 1.7 Neutrality: A necessary aid in building up the Swiss nation
– *continued*

---

in economic sanctions or peace-enforcing measures, which were considered to present a threat to Switzerland's neutrality.

After the end of the East-West conflict and the Cold War, the government's policy has changed. In the 1990s, it participated in peace-keeping missions of the EU and the UN in the Balkans. In 2002, Switzerland decided by a popular vote to become a member of the UN. Neutrality no longer is an obstacle for participation in economic sanctions or peace-keeping operations, decided by a universal organisation such as the UN.[11]

---

of the small cantons when their neighbours developed as members of larger and more powerful nation-states? In fact, the process of Swiss unification developed a strong momentum by assuring a better collective security for all the cantons. Indeed the Swiss constitution of 1848 speaks of federal responsibilities to guarantee the independence of the Swiss nation in 'unity, force and honour', as well as to uphold internal security and order.

1.3.3 Democracy and social values

Enthusiastic nineteenth-century writers praised the Swiss for their 'innate taste for democracy'. The Swiss were certainly not the inventors of democracy – such ideas were brought to Switzerland through the French revolution – and while finding their modern form of democratic government, the Swiss and the US constitutionalists were mutually influenced.[12] However, Switzerland did have a cultural heritage that had prepared its people both to learn about democracy and to live with it. For centuries the Swiss cantons were independent of monarchial rule. Their old regimes were elitist, but they were still very much part of their own community. As small societies, the cantons were not able to develop complex regimes. Most lacked the resources, for instance, to build up bureaucracies, the modern form of 'rational power'. Especially in rural regions, public works – such as road-building and the construction of aqueducts in the Alps in the Valais canton – were done on a community basis: every adult man was obliged to work for several days or weeks a year for the common good.[13] In addition, many other economic activities – for example farming in rural regions and crafts in the cities – were bound up in organisations which required collective decision-making. This, and the mutual dependence of people in small societies, promoted communalism.

This was reflected in the slogans used in the democratic revolution in the cantons and the calls for 'sovereignty of the people'. It is difficult to say whether Swiss democratisation came from 'above' or from 'below'. Certainly the democratic revolutions, which began in 1831 and swept through many cantons, involved more than just the elites. In the small canton of Thurgau, which then had less than 80,000 inhabitants, more than 100 petitions with 3000 propositions for a new democratic constitution were collected and discussed in the communes.[14] Some scholars however say that democratisation did not eliminate power elites, but rather redistributed the cards for a new game under the same rules. Democratic revolution neither took away inherited economic wealth from old patrician families nor prevented the concentration of industrial capital in the hands of a few.[15] And it is true that the rules of these democracies were – by the standards of today – less than perfect: women were denied political rights, while some cantons established electoral rules that excluded poor or unmarried men from the vote. The citizens elected a parliament, but were denied the right to elect its executive. Yet at the same time political rights were extended to allow the people to participate in the current decisions of parliament. This was the beginning of semi-direct democracy, which will be described in Chapter 3.

After 1831, the concept of democracy – implying equality and an equal right to vote – spread among all cantons and their different cultures. When it succeeded at canton level the experience of democracy helped the process of unification: sovereignty of the people was one of the few things that almost all the different cantons had in common, and what they wanted and agreed upon (see Box 1.8).

1.3.4   The combining of democracy with federalism

Democracy is founded on the principle of 'one person, one vote' and on the rule of the majority, which makes collective decisions binding on all. But is it defensible that a minority with different opinions and interests should have to comply with the decisions of the majority? One of the answers to this controversial question of political theory is that no majority decision is final. The minority has the right to propose a reconsideration of the decision, and if its arguments are convincing a new majority will be found for a revised decision. Whereas this may hold good for different opinions on common interests, it would not satisfy minority groups with religious beliefs or values inherently different from those of the majority. French ethnics cannot become German ethnics and Catholics do not become Protestants because of democracy. If a society is deeply divided by such cultural or religious cleavages, democracy cannot help the problem of 'frozen' or 'eternal' minority or majority positions. For the eternal majority, who can afford not to learn, power can become pathological.[16] The minority, which has no chance to win, is likely to be frustrated and discriminated against.

This was the exact problem when the Swiss cantons were ready to set up their central government. For good reasons Catholic and non-German-speaking cantons were fearful of being systematically over-ruled on questions of religion, language and culture. Thus, if a popular desire for government by the people gave momentum to unification, democracy was at the same time disadvantageous to the prospects of the creation of a Swiss nation-state. It threatened minorities, especially those in the Catholic and the French-speaking cantons.

Combining democracy with federalism provided the answer. Federalism allowed the sharing of power between central government and the cantons. In all matters that were the responsibility of the cantons, different answers to the same questions were possible – answers that corresponded to the preferences of different ethnic or religious group. Thus, federalism permitted – and permits – cultural differences to coexist, and it protects minorities. As we shall see when discussing federalism in the next chapter, the division of power between the federation and the cantons was in favour of the latter, providing the utmost autonomy for the cantons and their ethnic or cultural particularities. In 1848 the division of power in favour of the cantons also meant a concession to the Catholic conservative minority, which gave the project a better chance of succeeding in the forthcoming referendum on the new constitution.

Federalism also allowed the cantons to become participants in central-government decision-making. The constitution provides for a system of parliamentary bicameralism similar to that in the US. The National Council – representing the people – is complemented by a Council of the States, where the cantons are equally represented regardless of the size of their population. Moreover, the cantons participate in the popular vote on constitutional amendments. The popular majority for such a decision has to be matched by a majority amongst the cantons for it to become effective. In both mechanisms, therefore, the democratic majority rule of 'one person, one vote' has to match a federal majority rule of an 'equal vote for every canton'. As we shall see in Chapter 2 the requirement for a cantonal majority has become very important.

Box 1.8   Developing a collective identity

Successful nation-building also needed some kind of cultural cement: the development of collective identity.

Unlike nations as France, Germany and Italy, Switzerland could not rely on one common culture, language or ethnicity, which were the prevailing bases of European nation-building in the nineteenth century. Therefore, it may have been difficult to find a common thread to bind together people from different cantons and thus identify themselves as 'Swiss'. The development of patterns of collective identity therefore relied on such different elements as national symbols, history and myths, and federal polity.

After 1848 one can observe a search for identity, for a common denominator.[17] Historians offered an integrating view of the past. The many local battles in the old peasant cantons to defend their independence against invasions by the 'Habsburg hordes' were part of a glorious heritage that all Swiss could be proud of. Historians told that the Swiss elites went back as far as 1291. Three local leaders swore an oath of political independence and mutual help – an act of *will* was especially emphasised – and this is thought to have been the birth of Switzerland. In 1891 this contract of 1291 was for the first time celebrated on a national basis on 1 August. History was personalised so as to improve the opportunity for identification. Legendary and symbolic figures such as William Tell (a hero killing a foreign tyrant) and Helvetia (the mother of the nation) were omnipresent on postal stamps, on popular pictures and on hundreds of pub and inn signs. Today, historians give a much more sober account of Swiss history when trying to distinguish between the facts and the myths. Some of them claim that William Tell never existed, and that the events in 1291 are fictions. From the point of national identification, this misses the point. Symbolic figures and myths gave life to the idea of a common Swiss culture probably more than actual events because they were independent of a particular social structure and allowed people with different backgrounds to identify with them.

The Alps were another element of national identification. The picture of a nation – consisting mainly of farmers and shepherds living in isolated mountain chalets or small villages – was drawn to distinguish Switzerland from other countries, despite the fact that large parts of Switzerland had already been industrialised by the nineteenth century.

Box 1.8 Developing a collective identity – *continued*

From the very beginning, therefore, Swiss identity relied not only on what its people shared together, but on Swiss specificities[18] – things that allowed the Swiss to feel different from their neighbours in other countries. Most important in this respect was the Swiss polity itself. Swiss direct democracy is different from others, and it has also become the most precious element of its common culture. The fact that all men are legally bound to serve in the army is not only a means of social integration. Until 1971, when voting was the privilege of male citizens only, duty of serving in the army was considered to be correlative with having political rights – and was also used as an argument against women's suffrage. The ideology of all male citizens defending their country, and identifying with this task, was said to be the 'cement' of Swiss male society, especially in the time of World War II.

1.4 Religious and ethnic minorities from coexistence to pluralism

The constitution of 1848 provided an institutional framework able to give unity to the nation. It promised peacefully to resolve conflicts between minorities and majorities. A constitution, however, is only a legal document at first; later it is a framework for political life, not political life itself. In this section we turn from the framework to the picture and ask: how did formal political unity further develop the integration and identity of Swiss society? Instead of treating this subject in a general form, I prefer to concentrate on the two minorities which were most important at the time, and for whom the success or failure of integration was crucial: the Catholics and the linguistic minority.

1.4.1 Political Catholicism: From segmentation to integration

In the middle of the nineteenth century the Catholic minority comprised about 40 per cent of the Swiss population. The cantons more or less represented religious boundary lines. In 1860 ten cantons were over 75 per cent Protestant and 11, rather smaller, cantons were over 75 per cent Catholic. Only four cantons (Geneva, Graubünden, Aargau and St Gall) had a more even distribution of religions. Despite the fact that Catholic conservatives eventually achieved a good constitutional compromise, history first led to segregation of the Catholic minority rather than to integration. Politically they retired to the strongholds of 'their' cantons and let the radical majority take the initiative in forging the national projects of the young federation.

The Catholic regions were mostly rural, cut off from the industrialisation that was the main concern of the political elites of their progressive Protestant counterparts. The First Vatican Council of the Catholic Church, held in Rome in 1871, was hostile to the modernisation of society and scientific progress, as well as to the separation of religion and state, and tried to enforce the position of the Pope as the binding authority in all respects of Catholic life. All this led to segregation. Many Catholic cantons entrusted the Catholic church with the task of public education or maintained segregated public primary and secondary schools. Even in a few mixed cantons, religious segregation in schools was continued up to the second half of the twentieth century. In Fribourg a Catholic university was founded. A tight web of social and semi-political organisations kept Catholics together and close to the church both in the home cantons and in the diaspora regions where Catholics were a minority. Catholics not only had their own party, they also had their own trade unions, newspapers and bookshops. In mixed regions they remained loyal to the Catholic butcher, café, plumber and carpenter, even when the quality of a Protestant competitor was said to be better.[19] This kind of segmentation was also to be found on the other side, but to a lesser extent as Protestant Switzerland lacked the political leadership of a confessional party able to integrate all social classes on a continuing basis. No wonder that conflict over religious issues became acute, especially in the mixed cantons. Swiss history books speak of 'the cultural struggle' (*Kulturkampf*) because the issue went beyond religion to different views of society and state.

The revision of the Federal Constitution in 1873–74 was influenced by this cultural struggle, which reached its culminating point around 1870. The constitution of 1874 aimed at a fully secularised state and led to the elimination of public functions of the church. Several articles of the constitution confirmed the anti-clerical character of the federation and the isolation of the Catholics. Some examples of this were:

– A prohibition on Jesuit activities,
– A prohibition on founding and restoring monasteries,

- New episcopates could be created only with the permission of the federation,
- Federal control of citizenship and protection of marriage by the State,
- A prohibition on clerical courts and jurisdictions,
- An obligation on the cantons to establish confessionally neutral schools under the direction of the state,
- Full freedom of religion without privilege for one of the Christian confessions.

Insofar as these provisions were discriminating against Catholics, they have been eliminated from the constitution in the second half of the twentieth century. Today, the regulation of the relationship between the Church and the state is in the sole responsibility of the cantons. These relations vary from canton to canton. Usually there is no complete separation of state and Church: the Protestant, Roman Catholic and the small Christ-Catholic Churches are acknowledged as public institutions, called *Landeskirchen*. Some cantons – for instance Zurich – have given a similar status to the Jewish community, but not (yet) to the 20 times larger Muslim community which has grown rapidly in the last two decades.

The historic cultural conflicts between Catholics and Protestants have now faded away. Many of the issues were settled by the establishment of a modern, liberal democracy, which reduced the direct influence of religious organisations on the state. However, the more than four generations in which federalism permitted 'in between' solutions to these conflicts needs to be noted. Thus, cultural issues were less 'settled' than given time to cool down.

This cooling down and the decline of the confessional schism was helped by several factors. First, the separation of Catholic and Protestant societies was overcome by the modernisation process. Geographically, a strong and steady migration between Catholic and Protestant regions opened 'ghetto-oriented minds' to religious tolerance and cooperation. Migration led to desegregation, which helped lead to integration. The declining influence of religion on people's lives opened the way to pragmatic solutions: smaller communities, instead of building two churches, constructed one that was used by both Catholics and Protestants. Marriage between Protestants and Catholics became common. Industrialisation and the modern economy did not distinguish between Catholic and Protestant money. Divisions also disappeared as more and more Catholics gained equal access to those economic and social activities which had once been seen as typically Protestant. Cultural and political Catholicism itself developed pluralist attitudes towards the state. At the beginning of the 1970s the former Catholic Conservative Party renamed itself the Christian Democratic Party. The new label suggested the promotion of more general values of Christian belief and culture and acceptance of the separation of state and religion. This was similar to the programmes of Christian democrats in Germany and Italy after the end of the Second World War.

This brings us to the second, political, factor. Federalism permitted Catholics to maintain the particularities of their culture in their 'own' cantons during the first decades of the nation-state. But later the devices of direct democracy permitted the Catholic minority to participate, with considerable success, in federal decision-making. After the introduction of the referendum in 1874 the Catholic conservatives were able successfully to challenge the proposals of the radical-dominated parliament. Majority politics became impossible – the Catholics had to be integrated through participation in the government. Moreover, in 1918 a coalition of Catholic conservatives and social democrats succeeded in breaking the majority rule for elections to the National Council. The introduction of proportional rule meant the end of the absolute majority of the radical democrats in parliament. For the Catholics at least it was the beginning of power-sharing. The Catholic opponent of the nineteenth century became the closest government partner of the radicals in the twentieth century.

Power-sharing, beyond participation in the Federal Council and in key positions within the federal administrative services, meant compromises on legislative issues between radicals and Catholic conservatives. It brought political influence, recognition and success to the Catholic part of society – and that success is enduring. Despite the fact that religious cleavages have gone, the Christian democrats still constitute one of the four governmental parties. Economically, they have become advocates of business almost as much as their radical partners in government but often defend social policies together with the left. Christian Democrats, therefore, have become a pragmatic centrist party. Even so, it should be noted that some crucial questions of cultural schism – such as the prohibition on the activities of Jesuits who in the nineteenth century were regarded by Protestants as advocates and conspiratorial actors of counter reformation – were only resolved long after the practical relevance of the issue had disappeared. Questions of fundamental values and religious belief take time to be settled – or even a long period of voluntary non-decision which avoids the reawakening of old cultural conflicts.

1.4.2   Multilingualism: Understandings and misunderstandings

Multilingualism constitutes the second aspect of the historical integration of cultural minorities into Swiss society.[20] Today, about 73 per cent of Swiss citizens speak German, 21 per cent French, 4 per cent Italian and 0.6 per cent Romansh, a minor language largely descended from Latin and spoken in a few Alpine regions in south-eastern Switzerland.[21] The issue of multilingualism, however, differs in two ways from the subject previously discussed. Multilingualism – with the important exception of the Jura problem, which is discussed below – never became as crucial as the question of religious minorities. And, as we shall see, societal segmentation by language played, and plays a different role.

Let us consider the institutional arrangements that protect linguistic minorities. Federalism, first, lets Romansh-, Italian- and French-speaking minorities live within their own culture inside the boundaries of 'their' cantons. Moreover, as cantons, the minorities have a political voice in the decision-making of central government. The historical importance of this voice may be illustrated by the fact that for decades the members of the National Council were seated in linguistic and not partisan blocs. Second, there are statutory rights for linguistic minorities. Linguistic autonomy is guaranteed by the principle of 'territoriality': the cantons are authorised or even charged to guarantee the traditional language of their regions, so that no commune can be forced to change its language for official use. German, French, Italian and Romansh are all defined as national languages.[22] Hence federal-government documents or banknotes are worded in four languages. The Romansh language is spoken by less than 50,000 inhabitants. So, for practical reasons most legal texts are translated only into German, French and Italian, even though the constitution today recognises Romansh as an official language.

Third, we find a strongly enforced proportional rule that leads to political quotas. An unwritten rule says that two of the members of the Federal Council should be of French or Italian-speaking origin, and over time, this has been well observed. In federal commissions of experts, or in parliamentary committees, linguistic proportions are observed more than any other proportional rule. Complaints about 'German predominance' – more common among the French- than the Italian-speaking community – are not well founded when looking at federal personnel statistics: at all levels of government proportionality is observed to a high degree (Table 1.2).

In contrast to quota in many other countries, Swiss quota are not defined as hard legal rules. While some of them are written as general

Table 1.2 Proportional representation of linguistic groups (percentages)

Representation	German	French	Italian	Romansh
Population (Swiss citizens only)	72.5	21.0	4.3	0.6
Federal Council	71.4	28.6	0	
Federal Court	60.0	30.0	6.6	3.3
National Council	72.0	24.0	4.0	
Council of States	73.9	21.7	4.3	
Expert Committees	76.9	20.0	3.1	
Federal Administration:				
All personnel	71.5	20.7	6.5	
Senior staff	73.5	21.6	3.8	
Top management	71.9	22.9	4.3	

Sources: BfS (Volkszählung 2000); Eidgenössisches Personalamt: Bericht an den Bundesrat über die erste Umsetzungsperiode der Weisungen über die Förderung der Mehrsprachigkeit in der allgemeinen Bundesverwaltung 1996–1999, Bern. Basic data for the councils are from 2004 (www.parlament.ch), own calculations for the percentages.

regulations in the law, most quota are informal, that is, they are obeyed as a political custom. This allows for flexibility under concrete circumstances. As can be seen from Table 1.2, general regulations and informal quota can have astonishing results for the fair representation of different cultural minorities. This does not necessarily mean, however, that proportional influence is guaranteed. If we imagine a table of ten Swiss with seven German-speakers, two French-speakers and one Italian-speaker, the proportional *rule* is well observed, even in favour of the smallest minority. However, the seven German-speakers can provide a two thirds majority decision without even speaking or listening to the French- and Italian-speakers. Moreover, the latter are forced to learn German in order to understand what the discussion is about. Of course the minority has the right to speak French or Italian. But knowing that the majority would not understand all the subtleties of those languages, it would probably, for the sake of the argument, be better to hold the discussion in German. If this were not enough, the French- and Italian-speaking members may also have to face a situation where the German majority, at the end of the formal session, begins to converse in their regional dialects, which are very different from standard or 'high' German and therefore barely understandable by French- and Italian-speakers. This worst case is in sharp contrast to the best case, where a polite German-speaking majority loves to speak French and makes French the official language of the discussions. Both of these examples do happen.

At the federal level, discussions in parliament are simultaneously translated into all three official languages. However, while the official record of Swiss laws and regulations is published in Italian, French and German, it happens that the documentation for parliamentarians is available only in one or two languages. The same is true of many government reports. Canada, for instance, goes much further, requiring every official document to be published in both English and French – probably because Canada has a more serious problem with the linguistic minority.

The Swiss are very conscious of the need for multilingualism: in all schools children are instructed in at least two languages. It is a myth, however, that these efforts lead to widespread bi- or tri-lingualism.[23] Most people rarely read newspapers or listen to news in a language other than their own, which means that they perceive politics by different media systems in the three linguistic regions. When face to face with a person speaking another language, it is normal, however, to try to communicate. Traditionally, German-speakers try to speak French to a Romand, even if their French is poor. Today young people, all of whom are taught English at school, are more and more using English as the *lingua franca* among themselves. Multilinguism seems to offer advantages in internationalised business, where it has become the *lingua franca*, too. The Swiss are actually rather proud of the multilingual aspect of their society and would find the question of whether German-, Italian-, French- or Romansh-speakers are better Swiss people rather silly.[24] Multilingualism requires public expenditure and fiscal redistribution in favour of the minority, both of which the Swiss are willing to bear. There are three complete public radio and television networks, one for each linguistic group. The smallest network, Radio Television della Svizzera Italiana, in 2007 received SFr 200 million, or 20 per cent of the whole budget of public radio and television, which is almost five times more than its proportional share would be.

These notions about language can be extended to cultural life in general. Cultural specificities exist also in life style.[25] There is a popular saying that German-speakers live to work, whereas French- and Italian-speakers, who are more sophisticated in their drinking and eating habits, work to live. These and other differences are an enriching element of Swiss life. They may sometimes create difficulties in communicating, but they are accepted as part of normal life. Thus, cultural and linguistic segmentation has disappeared less than that of religion. It has been kept – or rather has been reproduced – within the protecting boundaries of the cantons. Differences appear also in political behaviour, for instance with respect to federal votations. French-speakers are more open to government foreign policy proposals, while in issues concerning the armed forces they reject government proposals more often than German-speaking voters. With one exception, discussed below, sub-cultural segmentation has not, however, been a major political problem for Swiss society as a whole. The virtues of pluralism may lie partly in the fact that the different cultures are separated from each other by the political autonomy of their cantons. It may be true that internationalised economy makes many societal differences between the cantons diminish or even disappear, while those with some groups of foreigners become more salient. But still, federalism provides a kind of horizontal segmentation which allows the three main regions of German-, French- and Italian-speakers to live apart without bothering each other too much.[26]

1.4.3   The Jura – The exception to integration

Compared with the many multicultural societies which have difficulty in coping with their cleavages, one could ask why Swiss society has integrated so successfully. As we shall see, the Swiss are not more peaceful by nature than others, and the elite is not brighter than in other countries. However, the literature of comparative politics suggests that there are institutional factors which generally favour processes of multi-cultural integration, such as the non-ethnic concept of the state, federalism, proportional representation and other mechanisms of political power-sharing. Moreover, pressure from the outside may help national unity if it does not lead to armed intervention by a foreign power. All these factors helped in the Swiss case, and we shall come back to this topic in the conclusions of the chapter. Here, I would like to focus on one particular condition which can be decisive for success or failure of political integration. Geographically, cleavages of religion, language and economy can be overlapping or cross-cutting. Overlapping cleavages can mean that a linguistic minority is also a religious minority, belonging to the poor social strata of a society. If cleavages are cross cutting, minorities are split into different groups, for instance linguistic minorities belonging to the religious majority and eventually to the wealthy social strata. From a theoretical point of view, it is evident that in the latter case, integration has better chances: a linguistic minority, for instance, feels less discriminated against and may even be compensated for if it profits from economic wealth or of being part of the religious majority. In situations of overlapping cleavages, however, the same group may suffer from multiple discrimination, which creates a much higher potential of conflict.[27]

The Swiss case is characterised by cross-cutting cleavages. Among French-speakers, for example, there are both Catholic and Protestant cantons. Among socioeconomically poor cantons, there are both German- and French-speaking states. Thus, religious, linguistic and socio-economic cleavages do not coincide with geographical boundaries of the cantons, rather they cross-cut each other. The cumulation of different issues into one two-sided political conflict – for instance with poor Catholic French-speakers on one side and rich Protestant German-speakers on the other – could never develop. In practice, political majorities differ and vary from issue to issue. Most of the cultural groups have at the same time experienced being part of a minority, and this has been very important for the development of a culture of tolerance and pluralism.

There is an important case in modern Swiss history, however, where integration failed. It concerns the Jura region, once the northern part of Switzerland's second largest canton, Bern. In a struggle of more than 40 years which included riots and violence, the Jura minority, who felt discriminated against by Bern, fought for separation from the old canton and for autonomy. The creation of the new canton in 1978 will be described in Chapter 2, but the case is worth mentioning here because of the factors of integration discussed above. First, the

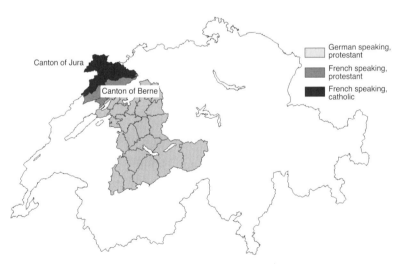

Figure 1.1   Bern canton up to 1978 showing the former boundaries of the canton, including the part of the Jura region which in 1978 became an independent canton

Jura region had a double minority – French-speakers practising the Catholic religion in a Protestant canton populated by German-speakers (Figure 1.1). Moreover, there were socioeconomic differences. The Jura region, located on the periphery of the canton next to the border with France, claimed to be economically neglected. In the Jura region, therefore, we find the rare case of overlapping socioeconomic, language and religious differences. This overlap, however, was not equal throughout the region. The southern part was economically better off and had a Protestant majority. Thus, the population was divided into pro and anti-separatist movements. After a series of votations the new canton of Jura was created, but the southern districts had voted to stay with the old canton and therefore the small ethnic Jurassian population, because of its internal fragmentation, has not been integrated into a single political unit.

Whereas the creation of the new canton was widely praised as the solution that corresponded most to the principle of self-determination by the people concerned, some separatist groups claimed that the southern districts should be reunited with the Jura canton. In other words, the potential for ethnic conflict was not removed by the 1978 solution. Catholics and French-speakers in the southern districts still complain about being a minority, cut off from the ethnic body to which they feel they belong. However, if the southern districts were to be integrated into the Jura there would be a new problem for the Protestant minority, which feels more akin to the Bern canton. The lesson to be drawn is evident; the ideal of ethnic and political unity, which is very common and popular in today's movements for nationalism, is a pipe dream. In most cases, while it does eliminate some minority problems, it cannot be realised without the creation of new problems.

1.5   The challenges of socio-economic inequality

1.5.1   A working class without a homeland

Compared with other European countries the industrialisation of Switzerland took place early, but it was somewhat different. Instead of concentrating in urban areas, important industries such as watch-making, textiles and embroidery settled in rural areas. This decentralised industrialisation prevented the sudden concentration of a mass proletariat in the cities. But, as in every capitalist country, industrialisation led to growing inequalities and the impoverishment of a new social class of workers whose jobs were insecure and whose earnings were low. As in other countries, democracy did not prevent the economic exploitation of workers nor inhuman working conditions.[28] In the 1870s, Friedrich Bernet, a radical politician, wrote: 'The Swiss constitution of 1848 has put much political and economic power into the hands of a few. This has allowed the rich to grow richer, whereas other groups such as farmers, craftsmen and industrial workers are downgraded to an indistinguishable proletariat'.[29]

At that time neither a socialist party nor a strong union organisation for workers yet existed. So it was a faction of the Radical Party which sought to defend the interests of the working class by a policy of 'entrepreneur-socialism'. They were concerned about growing social inequalities, which in their eyes were unacceptable in a democracy worth the name. The faction was the driving force behind the first regulations to protect workers and to make the use of child labour unlawful. This policy was strongly opposed by the liberal wing which, in the fashion of 'Manchester liberalism', wanted to avoid government intervention in the free market. This marks the emergence of two new economic issues slowly superseding the older cultural schisms in Swiss politics: To which extent should the government protect Swiss industries against international competition and intervene in the free market? And what role should be given to the government in order to compensate for growing social inequalities created by market competition?

Unlike in other countries, such as Austria and Norway, business itself was divided on the question of the free market. Whereas some export industries pushed for unconditional liberalisation, farmers wanted to be protected from international markets by levying duties on foreign products. Small trades and crafts enterprises were organised into corporations and they also sought protectionist state regulations for things that were beyond their own capacity to deal with. The first vocational schools, for instance, were run by trades and crafts corporations, but the state gave subsidies and declared professional schools mandatory for apprentices. This eliminated the problem of free riders: enterprises that abstained from investing in professional education but would hire employees from other enterprises that had invested in it. Thus, from the very beginning Switzerland's economy tended to develop organised relations with the state. In a kind of highly fragmented corporatism, a great number of professional and business organisations cooperated with the state. They sought particular advantages through state regulations or subsidies, which eliminated the risks of free competition. In return they offered to help in the implementation of government activities. Farmers' organisations, for instance, furnished the statistical data used in drafting agricultural policies, which helped to keep down the number of public administration staff. Despite their high praise of economic liberalism, and despite their tradition of anti-government ideology, organised professions and businesses have strong and influential relations with government up to today.[30]

In the race for the organisational build-up of economic interests, the workers were late starters and did not enter until the end of the nineteenth century. Workers had a common interest to defend: the betterment of their economic conditions, which was promised by emerging socialism in other European countries at that time. But this common interest proved difficult to organise in Switzerland. Workers were spread all over the country and were to a large degree isolated in smaller towns and villages, where the ties of traditional society and patterns of paternalism may have dampened the effects of economic inequality but also hampered collective identity and the organisation of the new working class. When the Social democratic party eventually became organised it achieved rapid electoral success. Social democrats and unions were among the first to use the instrument of the popular initiative as an instrument at the federal level. In 1894 they demanded the right to work and a programme of public industrial policy – 40 years before Keynes. But the hope that direct democracy would be the lever of social reform was dashed. In a popular vote the proposed constitutional amendment was rejected by a ratio of four to one. Later, cultural ties often proved stronger than economic cleavages. The Catholic conservative party, its social organisations and unions successfully united Catholic-only workers. Thus, the working class was divided. This did not prevent the social democrats from becoming one of the largest parties, but they never managed to form a coalition of equal strength to the bourgeois forces. Neither did unions succeed in influencing industrial politics as much as business did. This minority position of labour in politics and industrial relations is a Swiss characteristic.[31] It differs from other small European countries, such as the Netherlands, Austria, Norway and Sweden, where more of an equilibrium between labour and capital, and between the political left and right, can be observed. Cultural segmentation was a greater obstacle to the organisation of the political left in Switzerland, and labour forces were never able to make up the organisational lead of business or farmers.

1.5.2 From class struggle to economic partnership

In the first decades of the twentieth century the conditions of the Swiss working class worsened. For the period before the First World

War, historians note the development of a conservative, nationalist, sometimes reactionary and anti-democratic political right which resorted to a 'class struggle from above'.[32] Politically marginalised by the cooperation of bourgeois forces, the social democrats and the unions could not prevent the working class from bearing most of the burden of economic setback during and after the First World War. The worldwide economic crisis of the 1930s brought mass unemployment to Switzerland. Several strikes by angry workers were suppressed by federal troops, more than once ending in bloodshed. The political left was denied what Catholics and farmers had achieved: recognition, political influence, and participation in the Federal Council. Principles of proportional rule and participation were used to integrate cultural minorities, but not to resolve the problems of a growing socioeconomic cleavage in Swiss society.

The socialist movement split. A communist faction claimed that bourgeois democracy was a fake, an instrument of the capitalist class, and that the betterment of the working class could come only through political and economic revolution. In their view it was inevitable that a policy of class warfare would overcome the market and profit systems and install the working class in power. Social democrats, on the other hand, insisted on proportional participation in all democratic institutions and trusted in limited reforms, even if the state was in the hands of a bourgeois majority. They also aspired to a mixed economy, with a strong public sector and state intervention on behalf of social equality. This would not only improve the situation of the workers, but also protect the Swiss economy from the deep, worldwide market crisis that then seemed inevitable.

For almost four decades, until the Second World War, workers' movements, politically discriminated against, hesitated between polarising a class struggle and cooperation in the hope of achieving integration. Outside events in the end gave the latter the upper hand. Faced with the threats of fascism from Hitler's Nazi Germany, the social democrats gave up their opposition to militarise and voted for the modernisation of the army. An important treaty between employers' organisations and the trade unions of the mechanical-engineering industry was signed in 1937: the so called 'Labour Peace Convention' (*Friedensabkommen*) accepted unions as representative organisations of the workers, proposed to resolve all conflicts in their relations by negotiation, and promised to end strikes and lock-outs.

Economic and social inequalities – the predominant political issues in the twentieth century – thus finally began to be addressed through cooperation and integration. The social democrats obtained their first seat in the Federal Council during the Second World War and they were given proportional representation in the federal government in 1959. The unifying experiences of the generation that had defended Swiss independence and neutrality from 1939–45 had their effects. Ideological differences between the political left and right shrank. A large consensus amongst all political forces allowed the building up of a social security system, a health care and insurance service and a higher educational system, which reduced many areas of social and economic inequality. Economic growth led employers' and workers' organisations toward cooperation and away from confrontation. Collective contracts, similar to the 1937 Labour Peace Convention, became the rule. Despite the fact that the labour force was less unionised than in other European countries, Swiss workers and employees had a fair share in the growth prosperity.[33]

By the early 1970s the highest degree of integration of different social classes in Switzerland had been reached. Employers and workers had become used to partnership, and the political left had been integrated into the once purely bourgeois state. Political parties and economic organisations were able to reach consensus by compromise and power-sharing was effective. However, since then the social integration of Swiss society has somewhat declined. When economic growth turned into recession in 1974, the political left learnt that proportional participation did not mean proportional influence. In 1984, a minority of the Social Democratic party wanted to quit the Federal Council because political power-sharing was not shifting influence from the haves to the have-nots. Unions, which were willing to share the burden of recession by accepting pay cuts, were losing members and political influence. In the last decades, while achieving less from employers by way of contracts, unions have tried to promote social policy by way of legislation instead. This led to a shift from a liberal to a post-liberal welfare regime, in which social partnership plays a somewhat lesser role.[34] In the last decades, globalisation and liberalisation led to new conflicts between capital and labour, and between urban and rural areas as well. Despite polarisation between the right and the left, political power-sharing has persisted, but partnership between employers and unions has become more difficult to maintain, as we shall see in Chapter 4.

1.6 Proportional representation: The universal key to power-sharing

In the preceding sections we saw how linguistic and religious minorities became integrated, and then how conflicts arising from the social

Table 1.3   Use of the proportional rule: Institutions and criteria

	Language	Party	Gender
Federal council	x	x	x
Federal (vice) councillors	x	x	x
Supreme court	x	x	x
Election of the national council	(x)	x	(x)
Parliamentary committees	x	x	(x)
Federal commissions of experts	x	(x)	(x)
Nomination of high government officials	x	(x)	x

x = criteria normally used.
(x) = criteria sometimes important.

cleavages of modern industrial society were resolved. Conflict-solution in Switzerland relies on power-sharing rather than on competition for power. In the following, I will take a closer look at the proportionality rule. It is a universal key to power-sharing in a double sense: it opens many doors to political participation, and it can be used by new groups arising from new cleavages.

Let us first discuss the 'doors to power'. The proportional rule today is the key that unlocks the door to almost all political institutions. As can be seen from Table 1.3, the proportional rule is used for different criteria – or groups – in the same body. In the 'magic formula' of the seven-member Federal Council, for example, party affiliation is not the only criterion of proportionality. As already mentioned, the Federal Assembly follows the rule of linguistic proportionality, normally granting French- and Italian-speakers two seats. For long times, a provision in the constitution stated that there may not be more than one representative from the same canton. This criterion has been abandoned in favour of a new, informal gender rule. The latter is not yet consolidated but in 2008 has led to three women representatives in the Federal Council. Not only candidates for the Federal Council, but also high officials of the federal government must fulfil one or more criteria of proportionality to be eligible for a position. There is some criticism that this system means that the real job requirements are too often neglected (Box 1.9).

There is flexibility in the system, however, in that over- or under-representation is allowed but is compensated for over time. Moreover, we cannot speak of formal 'group rights' because in most cases they are mere political claims which cannot be enforced by law (but are respected in most cases, though). The great majority of Swiss are opposed to rigid legal quota but like the idea that all groups of

Box 1.9 Proportional rule and quotas

'American readers may wonder whether Swiss power-sharing amounts to a quota system, which would be unconstitutional in the United States. In the context of affirmative action programs, American courts do allow the setting of goals but not of quotas. Switzerland, however, does indeed operate to a large extent by a quota system, and the courts do not intervene. According to Swiss political thinking, not only individuals but also groups have rights. French-speakers, for example, should have the right to be represented among the top army officers. When a French-speaking three-star general retires, the search for his replacement is practically limited to French-speakers. But what about a German-speaker who may be more qualified than the top French-speaking candidate? The former is indeed discriminated against on the basis of his language affiliation. This is the price that the Swiss are willing to pay for their system of power-sharing. This price, however, should not be exaggerated. In the foregoing example, the highly qualified German-speaker simply has to wait until a three-star general of his own language retires. Sometimes, of course, bad luck may strike; no opening may occur when someone is the "ideal" age for a particular position. For example, a German-speaking Free Democrat of Catholic faith, regarded as a top candidate, may never make it to the Federal Council, because during his prime political years, his particular combination of attributes may never be demanded'.

Excerpt from Jürg Steiner, 'Power-Sharing: Another Swiss "Export-Product"?', in Joseph V. Montville, *Conflict and Peacemaking in Multiethnic Societies* (Massachusetts and Toronto: Lexington Books, 1990).

society should be fairly represented in public bodies. Proportionality, therefore, is a political rather than a legal practice. Finally, this element of political culture applies beyond politics and positions in government. It is practised in many cultural organisations and even in sport. This is true at least for the linguistic proportional rule. It would be unimaginable, for instance, that the executive committee of the Swiss Soccer Association would consist of German-speakers only.

1.7   The limits of Swiss pluralism – New challenges for integration

We may speak of true political pluralism if no societal group is discriminated against and if every group has a fair chance of exercising influence through political institutions. This does not require a value-free state, but a state that refrains from privileges for or discriminations against specific groups and whose laws enforce values common to all its inhabitants: human rights, basic rights and democracy, with all its implications of equality. Switzerland's multicultural society, thanks to the way it has been integrated, has achieved a remarkable standard of political pluralism. Peaceful conflict-resolution is not only a pattern of political but also of social life.

There are limits, however, to peace and pluralism in Swiss society. In sharp contrast to the mutual respect among the larger groups, there has sometimes been heavy discrimination against smaller religious and ethnic groups in the past. Children of gypsies, a group at odds with the rather rigid Swiss sense of order, have been taken away from their parents and raised in 'proper' homes. During the Second World War Jewish refugees were sent back to the German border in order to avoid additional difficulties with the Nazi regime. For a long time, the rights of patients in psychiatric clinics and of sentenced and remand prisoners, did not meet the standards of other European countries.[35] During the Cold War and after, the federal intelligence service not only spied on extreme left-wing militants, but on several hundred-thousand citizens who had done nothing more than support unorthodox political opinions or actions.

Another problem is gender. For a long time Swiss women had to live in a society which only reluctantly began to abandon traditional male-female roles. Until 1971 Switzerland was a comparatively incomplete democracy because it denied women the right to vote, let alone be given a political mandate. As we shall see in Chapter 2, federalism and direct democracy made womens' suffrage a difficult task. When, in 1981, a constitutional amendment introduced legal, social and economic equality for women, the Swiss became aware that despite political pluralism much discrimination had persisted. Since then legal discrimination against women – in the areas of family law and social security for instance – has been eliminated from all legislation. Today, the representation of women in the parliaments and executives of the cantons and the federation is on the level of other European countries. In the last decade the proportion of gainfully employed women has increased more than in most highly industrialised countries. On the other hand, women in Switzerland are still concentrated in less qualified jobs, are sometimes far from getting equal pay and are under-represented in the higher ranks of private management or universities. Whereas highly industrialised countries such as the US and Sweden have practised policies of affirmative action or equal pay for decades, Switzerland had to catch up in many fields of equal opportunity for women.[36]

Recently, rising violence has attracted much media attention. Frequent violent fights between groups of young Swiss and Kosovars, for instance, indicate that the social integration of immigrants is far from being perfect. Burning-downs of homes for asylum seekers or violence exercised by right-wing extremists are rare but are indicators of growing social tensions due to unresolved problems of immigration. However, some forms of violence are of indigenous nature, such as Hooliganism, assault, robbery and rape at schools, which make more headlines than politically motivated violence which is the rare exception. Even so, violence and crime run at quite low levels. In the yearly statistics of the European Council, Switzerland, with a rate of about 75 prisoners per 100,000 inhabitants in 2008, ranks in a middle position among the European countries,[37] while the number of victims of serious crime is particularly low (see Table 1.4).

Table 1.4 Victims of crime in European countries (per 100 000 inhabitants, 2003)

	Homicides	Assault	Robbery	Rape
Switzerland	2.5	91	59	7
Denmark	4.1	202	59	9
Belgium	8.4	624	248	26
Germany	3.4	546	73	11
Finland	9.2	555	39	11
France	3.9	224	208	17
Ireland	1.3	100	80	12
Italy	3.9	53	122	5
Luxembourg	12.9	298	95	8
Netherlands	11.4	330	127	10
Austria	1.8	412	54	15
Spain	3.2	61	222	4
England and Wales	3.3	1348	192	25

Source: Statistisches Jahrbuch der Schweiz 2007

Finally, there is the question of foreign residents. From the 1960s onward the rapidly fast growing economy needed additional labour. Workers from Italy, Germany, France and Austria, and later from Spain, Portugal, Yugoslavia and Turkey, found jobs in Switzerland. In 2007, foreigners accounted for more than 1.6 million or 21.1 per cent of the total population, and a great part of them work in jobs that the Swiss avoid if they can. They pay taxes and contribute to social security systems, but they have no political rights. Obtaining Swiss citizenship is difficult; until recently it was only possible after at least 12 years' residence. While Swiss enterprises actively seek foreign workers, Switzerland has become an attractor to refugees and migrants from Third World countries (Table 1.5). Social integration of this growing and heterogeneous foreign population was beyond the capacities

Table 1.5   Foreigners and asylum seekers in Switzerland

Origin of foreigners, 2006	Thousands	Per cent
Ex-Yugoslavia	345	20.6
Italy	299	17.9
Germany	201	12.0
Portugal	187	11.2
France	80	4.8
Turkey	71	4.6
Spain	70	4.2
America	66	3.9
Africa	65	3.9
Austria	35	2.1
Great Britain	30	1.8
Others	217	13.0
Total	1 674	100

Asylum seekers	Number	Quota of recognised refugees (per cent)
1975	1 324	91.5
1980	3 020	66.1
1985	9 703	14.2
1990	37 583	4.9
1995	17 021	14.9
2000	17 611	6.4
2005	10 061	13.6
2006	10 537	19.5

Source: Bundesamt für Statistik, *Ausländerinnen und Ausländer in der Schweiz, Bericht, Bern 2006*.

of political authorities, schools and civil society at many places. Severe political tensions have arisen. Xenophobic parties developed and brought pressure on the political authorities to restrict immigration and protect against the 'alienation' of Swiss society. Foreign workers, asylum seekers and immigration remain highly controversial issues.

To integrate foreigners in the same way as the native minority groups of the past will be much more difficult for Swiss society. It will take more effort than simple peaceful coexistence. Contrary to the past it will mean the integration of non-European cultural patterns, values, religious beliefs and mentalities. With more than 20 per cent, Switzerland has the highest proportion of foreigners of all European countries except Luxembourg. With a majority of foreign workforce or school children at many places, all 'melting-pot' theories may be wrong. For a long time immigration policy had followed the interest of industries that needed additional workforce with low qualifications but had systematically underestimated the cost of social integration of new immigrant groups. In addition, competition between domestic and foreign workforce creates social tensions when jobs are cut. No wonder that immigration policy has become one of the most controversial issues, and easy solutions are not at hand.

1.8 Conclusion

Until the middle of the nineteenth century Switzerland was neither a unified society nor a nation-state. It was composed of small societies with differing ethnic backgrounds, languages and religions that had become too limited to survive independently. In a bottom-up process, the cantonal peoples founded a united state. It was artificial, a product of historical circumstances, and could have failed. It lacked a coherent society. Surrounded by much more powerful neighbours, the Swiss state could still have been too small to survive. It could have been divided up or have fallen apart.

Yet, thanks to its political institutions, Switzerland became a nation willing to survive and has found its own identity as a modern society. The case of Switzerland is an example of the successful integration of different cultures and of dealing with social inequalities. In this long-time process of societal integration, at least four elements of the political institutions played a central role:

– *A non-ethnic concept of the central state:* The most important factor behind Switzerland's success may be that it never had the choice of building a state based on one religion, one culture or one language alone. Forming a nation-state on the basis of one culture or language does not resolve existing minority problems. Whether in merging smaller units with a larger one or in dividing up a larger unit into smaller ones, eliminating one minority problem merely creates others. In having no choice other than all minorities living together, Switzerland avoided mistakes of the mono-cultural nation-state. Instead, a non-ethnic concept of the central state allowed the different peoples of the cantons to recognise each other as having equal rights, regardless of religion, language or cultural heritage.

– *Federalism:* it was essential for the bottom-up process of nation-building, allowing for a compromise between the opponents and the advocates of a central state. Up to these days, federalism is giving utmost autonomy to the cantons and their different cultures but providing national unity.

– *Proportional representation:* it was, step by step, introduced at all institutions of the central state: in parliament and its committees, in the executive, at the Supreme Court and the federal administration. Proportional representation is applied not only for party affiliation but also for language, and lately for gender, thus giving all societal groups recognition and voice.

– *Political power-sharing:* Swiss democracy developed differently from the majoritarian model of the Anglo-Saxon world. Instead of competition between government and opposition, where the winner takes all, we find a grand coalition of government, and instead of majority politics, decision-making in Swiss politics is characterised by negotiation and compromise. The development, the characteristics and the functioning of this 'power-sharing democracy' will be explained later in depth. Here, I concentrate on the essential point: political power-sharing has facilitated peaceful conflict-resolution among culturally different groups. Affiliation to an ethnic group, to a language or a religion bears proscriptive characteristics and fixed attitudes or interests that cannot change their majority or minority positions in a competitive democracy. Power-sharing, as an alternative model, avoided the alienation arising from perpetual winner or loser positions and thus contributed to the peaceful solution of political conflict.

Looking at the process of national integration, we note that the effect of political institutions is neither immediate nor perfect. It took time to overcome the deep conflicts between Catholic and Protestant cantons, or between capital and labour. While the religious or the linguistic cleavages have cooled out, others like the social cleavage might catch fire again if the market economy produces new risks or inequalities. Moreover, while integration was successful for the main linguistic and religious groups of civil society, some small minorities were discriminated against. Women got political rights later than in other countries, and immigration is a new, big challenge for integration. Immigration, finally, has become a controversial and important political issue because it has created problems of integration that have not been solved.

Finally, we mention the external factors that helped national unity. Pressure from the outside was one of the basic motivations for the creation of the federation in 1848: the Swiss cantons, surrounded by much bigger nation-states, wanted to keep their autonomy and independence. Pressure from the outside has been relevant ever since, but did never materialise in armed intervention. Armed neutrality has allowed to keep Switzerland out of the belligerent conflicts between the Germans and the French in 1871 and World War I, and to resist plans of the Nazi regime to invade Switzerland during World War II. With the end of the Cold War in 1989, armed neutrality lost much of its importance in foreign policy but still is a commonly shared value of the Swiss: citizens feel that the government of a small state should not expose in international conflict. Yet in the present challenges, the Swiss seem to be less united. On the question of European integration they are divided between protagonists of membership and those who prefer bilateral treaties with the EU. Globalisation led to new social tensions between winners and losers, heavy immigration is followed by problems of integration. In times of pressure from the outside, as during the financial crisis of 2009 when the Swiss government was forced to renounce on the traditional 'banking secret' and to adapt OECD standards for cooperation in fiscal affairs, the Swiss are still undecided on their future identity. This is different from the past, when pressure from the outside had been a constant factor that brought the Swiss together in the idea of protecting and maintaining their national independence. In the end, however, this past is still present. To this day, the Swiss are strong patriots and feel as a 'nation of political will', and as 'being different from others'. While lacking common language or religion, and despite conflict, the Swiss are proud of what they all share as citizens: their political institutions. Their most important elements – federalism, direct democracy and power-sharing – will be described in the following chapters.

2
Federalism

2.1 Institutions

2.1.1 The Swiss interpretation of federalism

Until the time of the French Revolution, Switzerland was not a nation but an ensemble of cantons bound together by a number of treaties. In modern terms we could define this as a system of small independent states united by an international treaty. Since all the cantons claimed to be autonomous or sovereign states, common decisions in this loose confederation had to be unanimous and therefore all the decisions proposed by the assembly of cantonal delegates, the *Tagsatzung,* had to be ratified by the cantons. The question was how to create a single political unit out of this multi-state system in order to guarantee political autonomy while neighbours were forming modern nations and to provide a common market for its growing industry.

An obvious answer could have been to fuse the cantons into a single, larger territorial state in the way that European monarchies – such as Italy and Germany – had in the middle of the nineteenth century. This solution, however, was impossible for two reasons. First, the Swiss people had already had experience of a unitary state in the period between 1798 and 1803, when all power had been in the hands of a central government. This model, which had been imposed by France, was at odds with every tradition of the Swiss people who were – and mostly still are – rooted in their cantons. The idea of such a system was therefore not feasible – it was inconceivable that the Swiss people, who had successfully decentralised in 1803, would reestablish a unitary system 50 years later of their own free will. The second reason why the solution would be impossible to achieve was probably even more important. As described in Chapter 1, the creation of a common government for Switzerland was highly controversial between conservative Catholic and radical Protestant cantons, and the latter's struggle for political unification succeeded only after the short civil war of 1847. A peaceful solution for successful nation-building, however, had to take into account the interests of the cantons of the Catholic minority.[1]

Thus the creation of the Swiss federation was destined to follow a middle path between the *status quo* of an unsatisfactory confederation and an unwelcome unitary system. But it was also an institutional compromise between the conservatives, who were hostile to centralisation, and the radicals, who favoured a federal government strong enough to make the necessary decisions in the common interest.[2] The constitution of 1848 proposed the creation of a central authority by the cantons, who were to renounce part of their sovereignty as individual states. Nowadays we would probably not accept the logic of such a divided sovereignty. Logically there can not be two supreme powers. Politically, however, it was the common understanding of the fathers of the federal constitution that the cantons had not lost their sovereignty, merely part of their responsibilities – and their right to divide power between the federation and the cantons in the future. In their determination to maintain a large degree of political autonomy, the cantons retained most of their powers as well as participating in the future decision-making of the new federation. This solution rested on three factors:

- The Swiss people had already experienced a federal system in 1803, when the Mediation Act imposed by Napoleon restored cantonal powers in the former unitary Helvetic state.
- Between 1831 and 1848 some of the cantons had not only established revolutionary forms of direct and representative democracy, but had also developed and realised the idea of 'constitutionalism'.[3] This meant the establishment of a basic political order voted on by the people, granting limitations and separation of legislative, executive and judicial powers, personal rights and freedoms, and procedures for amending the constitution. The cantons maintained their own constitutions, which form the basis of their political autonomy and statehood.
- The American constitution successfully combined federalism with democracy, a crucial issue at the time. Doing so required an adequate integration of two different, or even contradictory, principles of decision-making: democracy follows the idea of 'one person, one

vote' whereas federalism seeks to grant equal influence to the members of a federation, regardless of the size of their populations.

After the victory of the protagonists of a Swiss federation in the civil war, the drafting of the federal constitution in 1848 and its ratification by a majority of the people and the cantons were achieved within a few months. Thus Switzerland became not only the first continuously functioning democracy, but also the first modern federation in Europe. In many ways the Swiss constitution resembles that of the US.

Since 1848 the Swiss federal system[4] has consisted of three levels: federation, the cantons and the communes. Each of them has a certain degree of autonomy, legal powers and responsibilities, the right to levy their own taxes, and the cantons have their own constitutions. Under the terms of the federal constitution, communes, cantons and the federation cooperate with each other and they are all bound to guarantee democratic election of their authorities and decision-taking. Furthermore they must respect the principle of separation of legislative, executive and judicial power. The Swiss are citizens of their commune, their canton and the federation. They elect authorities and vote on all three levels, exercise their rights and fulfil duties based on federal, cantonal and communal law.[5]

2.1.2   The division of powers between the federation and the cantons

The cultural diversity of the Swiss cantons, their political power and their claims for autonomy set narrow limits to central authority. In 1848 the powers of the federation were limited to a few essential areas. Its most important powers were to maintain all foreign relations and protect Swiss independence by maintaining an army and to ensure peaceful relations among the cantons. Moreover the federation was authorised to conduct a federal postal service, provide a common currency and coinage, and abolish cantonal customs duties. If we look at the information in Box 2.1 which shows the actual distribution of responsibilities between the federation, the cantons and the communes, we find that the responsibilities of the central Swiss government have considerably increased with the passage of time.

2.1.3   Non-centralisation – Not decentralisation

Even on the abstract constitutional level the distribution of powers between central government and the cantons cannot be defined once and for all. A federal state must provide rules on how to deal with

Box 2.1 The main powers of the federation, the cantons and the communes

<table>
<tr><td colspan="5">A. *Distribution of responsibilities between the federation and the cantons*</td></tr>
<tr><td>Issue</td><td>Exclusive legislative power by federation</td><td>Legislation by federation/ implementation by cantons</td><td>Legislation shared by federation/ cantons</td><td>Exclusive legislative power by cantons</td></tr>
<tr><td>Foreign Relations</td><td>X</td><td></td><td></td><td></td></tr>
<tr><td>National defence</td><td>X</td><td></td><td></td><td></td></tr>
<tr><td>Tariff law, currency and monetary system</td><td>X</td><td></td><td></td><td></td></tr>
<tr><td>Postal services, telecommunications mass media</td><td>X</td><td></td><td></td><td></td></tr>
<tr><td>Railways, aviation, nuclear energy</td><td>X</td><td></td><td></td><td></td></tr>
<tr><td>Utilisation of water power</td><td></td><td></td><td>X</td><td></td></tr>
<tr><td>Roads</td><td></td><td></td><td>X</td><td></td></tr>
<tr><td>Trade, industry, labour legislation</td><td></td><td></td><td>X</td><td></td></tr>
<tr><td>Agriculture</td><td></td><td></td><td>X</td><td></td></tr>
<tr><td>Civil and criminal law</td><td>X</td><td></td><td></td><td></td></tr>
<tr><td>Police</td><td></td><td></td><td></td><td>X</td></tr>
<tr><td>Churches</td><td></td><td></td><td></td><td>X</td></tr>
<tr><td>Public Schools, Education</td><td></td><td></td><td>X</td><td></td></tr>
<tr><td>Taxes</td><td></td><td></td><td>X</td><td></td></tr>
<tr><td>Social security, insurances</td><td></td><td>X</td><td></td><td></td></tr>
<tr><td>Protection of environment</td><td></td><td>X</td><td></td><td></td></tr>
</table>

B. *Responsibilities of the communes*
- Building and surveillance of local roads
- Local public transport systems
- Gas, electricity and water supply, removal services
- Local land use planning
- Election of teachers/building of schools
- Budget responsibility, imposition of taxes
- Public welfare

changes in the distribution of central and decentralised power, and it must decide whom to entrust with new responsibilities that have come about because of changes in the economy and society.

The question of what rules should apply with the redistribution of future responsibilities between central government and member states is crucial for federal systems because it implies shifts in power. In Switzerland, as in other federal states, centralisation or decentralisation is a constant political issue that prompts ideological, social and economic conflict. Centralisation is often urged by protagonists of a strong state, economic intervention and modernisation, and extensive social programmes. Decentralisation, on the other hand, is preferred by interests which fear big government, by protagonists of decentralised autonomy or a 'minimal state', and by minorities. In the nineteenth century, the principle of division of powers among the three political levels prevailed. Since then, the relations between the different levels of government have become by far more complex. For most responsibilities, we find some form of cooperation between the federation, the cantons and the communes.

The Swiss solution exhibits a marked preference for extensive cantonal and local autonomy, thus preventing any uncontrolled growth in the power of the federation. The constitutional rule in Article 3 says that all (future) powers shall be invested in the cantons, unless the Swiss people and the cantons decide, by constitutional amendment, that they shall be attributed to the federation. Here again we find similarities to the US constitution, which says, in its 10th amendment, that all powers not delegated to the United States by the constitution, nor prohibited by the constitution to the states, are reserved to the states respectively, or to the people. Both federations therefore, share the same idea: any major centralisation of powers should be decided by constitutional amendment, whereas in unitary systems, for example those of France and Britain, a governmental decision can create or eliminate local powers or even authorities. Moreover, we could say that the US and Switzerland share a common institutional arrangement which characterises federalism as a system of non-centralisation rather than one of decentralisation.

We note, however, that the same institutional arrangement is interpreted in fundamentally different ways. In the US, the 10th amendment proved to be a difficult way to shift powers from the states to the central government. Thus, US authorities developed the practice of 'implied powers' or the 'interstate clause' which allowed the federal government to assume new powers by mere interpretation of the existing constitution.

Not so in Switzerland. From the very beginning, the Swiss parliament was reluctant to provide the federation with new powers and has interpreted Article 3 of the constitution in a strict sense. Not only the establishment of a national bank, any form of federal taxes, the creation of a social security system, the construction of federal highways, subsidies to the cantonal universities, and the introduction of environmental policies, but also 'small' issues like subsidies for hiking trails all needed formal constitutional amendment and ratification. This is one of the reasons why constitutional amendments in Switzerland are proposed practically in every year while in the US they are rare events.[6]

The proposition to confer any new power on the federation needs not only a majority in both chambers of parliament, but also a majority of the cantons and of the people at a popular vote. Many proposed amendments fail several times before being accepted. The procedure has thus had a braking effect on centralisation, and this partly explains why many controversial policies – like the introduction of a national pension system – took a long time to be realised, and that is why central-government expenditure as part of the total public budget in Switzerland is far lower than in other countries (Table 2.1).

2.1.4 Relations between the federation and the cantons[7]

Although the role of the federation is in many ways restricted, within the bounds of its authority it exercises substantial legal control over

Table 2.1 Central government tax share and expenditure as part of total tax receipts and public expenditure (in per cent, 1995–2005)

	Tax Share	Expenditure
Federal States		
Switzerland	31.9	32.7
Germany	30	31.5
United States	43.9	58.4
Unitary States		
Denmark	64	65.1
United Kingdom	76.9	92
France	43.3	45.2
Netherlands	57.7	58.5
Spain	44.5	49.1

Tax share: Mean of the years 1997/2000/2005; Expenditures: Mean of the years 1995/2000/2005

Source: OECD (2008) National Accounts of OECD Countries: General Government Account. vol. IV, 1995–2006

the cantons and communes. The juridical foundation of this control is an important rule: federal law is superior to cantonal law. Some key issues of federal control are the following:

- Cantonal political institutions have to be 'democratic' in accordance with the principal rules governing the separation of legislative, executive and judicial power. The Federal Assembly, by approving amendments to cantonal constitutions, ensures that cantonal institutions conform with standards of federal law.
- The cantons must grant to their inhabitants all the rights provided for in the federal constitution. For example they must guarantee basic human and civil rights, equal protection by the law, due process of the law, and so on. These rights can be claimed by everyone through different legal channels and brought to the Federal Court.
- The cantons are bound to respect and implement federal law. However the principle that 'federal law breaks cantonal law' does not mean that 'federal policy breaks cantonal policy'. The implementation of federal law through the cantons, therefore, depends heavily on the political will of the cantons (see Section 2.3).

2.2 Federalist elements in the decision-making process

2.2.1 A bicameral legislature

2.2.1.1 *Election to the National Council and the Council of States*

The Swiss parliament consists of two chambers, the National Council and the Council of States. The mode of election reflects different ideas of representation.

The National Council represents the people and its 200 members are elected on the democratic principle of 'one person one vote'. Thus the 200 National Council seats are divided among the cantons according to population. The fact that the National Council is elected in 26 electoral districts corresponding to the 26 cantons has two consequences. First, the choice given to the electorate differs between small and large cantons. The citizens of the canton of Zurich can elect 34 candidates, since its population of more than one million represents about one-sixth of the Swiss people, whereas a citizen of the canton of Uri (35,000 inhabitants) will elect just one candidate. Second, the different size of cantons as constituencies is a relevant factor to the proportional mode of election. The proportionality rule, which replaced the winner-take-all majority system in 1918, should give smaller parties in the segmented party system of Switzerland a better chance. This objective is fully realised in large cantons such as Zurich, where a small party can win one of the 34 seats with less than 3 per cent of the votes. But in a small canton with say, two seats, the same party would need 34 per cent of the votes to be sure of winning one seat. For this reason the effects of proportional representation are weakened in small cantons, where small parties risk being left with nothing. Overall, the proportional rule favours the relative electoral strength of the larger, historical parties, and it can leave small parties underrepresented (Table 2.2).

The Council of States, following the federal role of equal representation of all cantons, is composed of two members from every full canton, and one member from each of the half-cantons. The election of the Council of States differs in two ways from that of the National Council. First, the cantons themselves determine the modes of election for the 46 members. Before direct election by the people became the rule, many cantons allowed their parliaments to nominate their representatives.

Table 2.2   Distribution of seats in the National Council and the Council of States (1995 and 2007)

Party	Votes (per cent)		Seats in National Council		Seats in Council of States	
	1995	2007	1995	2007	1995	2007
Governmental parties						
Radicals	20.2	15.8	45	31	17	12
Social Democrats	21.8	19.5	54	43	5	9
Christian Democrats	16.8	14.5	34	31	16	15
People's Party	14.9	28.9	29	62	5	7
Total	73.7	78.7	162	167	43	43
Non-Governmental parties						
Green Party	5.0	9.6	8	20	–	2
Green Liberals	–	1.4	–	3	–	1
Alternative Left	1.5	1.1	3	1	–	–
Liberals	2.7	1.9	7	4	2	–
Swiss Democrats	3.1	0.5	3	–	–	–
Protestant Party	1.8	2.4	2	2	–	–
Others	12.2	4.7	15	3	1	–
Total	26.3	21.3	38	33	3	3
Grand Total	100	100	200	200	46	46

Sources: *Année politique suisse 1995 and 2007* (Bern: Institute of Political Science, University of Bern). Data for the People's Party 2007 include electoral strength and members of parliament of the Bourgeois Democratic Party which in 2008 split from the People's Party.

Second, the members of most cantons are elected by majority rule. This means that a candidate must gain at least 50 per cent of the votes cast to be elected. Therefore it is rare for a candidate of a small party, even if she or he has a strong personality, to win an election. On the other hand, if a party enjoys the support of a good 50 per cent of the electorate it can secure both seats, as was the case in those small rural Catholic cantons that were strongholds of the conservatives (today the Christian Democratic Party) for decades. Today, however, none of the parties gets more than about 40 per cent of the votes in a canton. A joint list of two parties, making a ticket of the two candidates to be elected, has best chances for success. The most natural alliance, today, is between the two centrist parties of the Radicals and the Christian Democrats, while the left Social Democrats and the national-conservative People's Party have more difficulties to find strong partners and would never go together. The result can be seen from Table 2.2. In 2007, the two centre parties, thanks to their tickets, won a majority of 27 out of the 46 seats with only about 30 per cent nationwide electoral strength. Social Democrats and especially the People's Party, despite higher electoral power, were the clear losers because they were less able to form strong alliances.

2.2.1.2   Bicameral lawmaking[8]

Lawmaking in the Swiss parliament reflects equal importance of democratic and federal influence on all decision-making (see Box 2.2). Both chambers may initiate constitutional amendments, new bills and regulations, as well as propose the revision of existing laws and regulations. All bills must be passed by the committees and floors of both chambers, a common bureau deciding which chamber should consider the bill first. Every proposition or bill destined to become federal law has to be approved by a relative majority in both chambers.

What happens if a bill or some of its propositions fails to gain a majority in one of the chambers? In such events the two chambers try to eliminate their differences through a procedure which can comprise different steps. If the second chamber proposes changes, the bill is sent back to the first chamber before being returned to the second. If differences still remain, the chambers appoint an equal number of delegates to a joint committee, which then tries to find a common solution. Should the committee's solution fail to be approved by one of the chambers, the bill does not go through.

This procedure reflects the rule of absolute equality of the two chambers in all matters of legislation. The desire of the founders of the Swiss

Box 2.2   The powers of the Swiss parliament

A. Elections

The Federal Assembly of the two chambers – where the Council of States has one fifth of the votes – designates the seven members of the Federal Council, the Federal Chancellor (administrative function), the members of the Federal Court, the Commander-in-Chief of the army in times of war and other major federal bodies.

B. Legislation, budget, finance and controlling

Parliament is responsible for all political decisions of general importance. For parliamentary legislation, three main categories are distinguishable: constitutional, legislative and regulatory acts. In addition, the two chambers decide on budgets and finance and approve international treaties of major importance. The pre-parliamentary decision-making process settles many issues of a bill before it goes to parliament. Nevertheless, parliament is the key actor of legislation: it sets the political agenda through parliamentary initiatives, motions and propositions, and thoroughly examines and modifies proposed legislations. A parliamentary reform in the 1990s introduced permanent committees, each having responsibilities in a defined field of legislation or in finance, auditing or the supervision of the federal government and its agencies. The reform considerably strengthened the political influence of parliament.[9]

---

constitution for strong federalism went further than in other European nations. In Germany, for instance, the *Bundesrat,* which represents the subnation states of the republic, is composed of members of the governments of the *Laender.* The number of members of each *Land,* however, varies according to population size, and the *Bundesrat* is empowered to exercise its powers of veto only for constitutional revisions or in matters concerning relations between the republic and the *Laender.*

How does bicameralism work out in lawmaking? In the nineteenth century, the English constitutionalist Walter Bagehot noted that hot tea, poured from a first cup into a second, can be drunk cooler. Modern political science literature comes to the same conclusion: bicameralism produces decisions closer to the *status quo.*[10] In a federalist system, bicameralism can have further effects. In Switzerland, where the second chamber represents the cantons, we note several dimensions of over-representation. First, the 13 smallest cantons represent only about 20 per cent of the people but can, with 26 votes, block every decision in the 46-member Council of States. This is more than theory because the small cantons have affinities: they are more rural, more Catholic, more conservative and less tending towards the political left. Over time, these advantages of over-representation were used by different groups. In the early stages of the Swiss federation the main cleavage was between the victorious radicals, who favoured a strong central state, and the conservative Catholic minority from small cantons who were resistant to the idea of central power. The Catholics' deputation in the Council of States was therefore bound to prevent power shifting from the cantons to the federation. The rationale of these politics was evident: it allowed Catholics to maintain their conservative policies within the bounds of their majority influence. Later, in the first half of the twentieth century, the main division was between bourgeois forces (now often uniting Catholics and Protestants) on one hand side and socialists on the other, who were concentrated in industrial and urban cantons. The bourgeois majority, who enjoyed almost total control of the Council of States, were not opposed to new federal powers in general. However, they weakened or blocked measures aimed at improving the conditions of the working class that had been proposed in the National Council, where the socialists had much more influence. This slowly changed after World War II when the centre parties accepted the development of a modern welfare state. During all periods, however, the high representation of the rural regions in the Council of States led to privileged subsidies and regulations for agriculture. For a long time, the small chamber therefore had the reputation of being committed to eliminate inequalities between poor and rich regions and between urban and rural society, rather than those between upper and lower social classes.

One might conclude that the Council of States, despite its official mission and its reputation in the large public, does not primarily subscribe to the federal ideal of maintaining decentralisation and the prerogatives of the cantons. A more convincing perspective is that different political forces – the Catholics, then the bourgeois coalition and the rural cantons – used their over-representation in the Council of States to their own advantage. Thus the Council of States has often played a conservative role, protecting the *status quo* against innovations proposed by the government and the other chamber. Yet this is an effect of the specific political composition of its majority, and not of the system itself. If socialists or urban cantons had profited from over-representation, the role of the Council of States could have been different.

Therefore those who say that the Council of States does not represent a truly federalist point of view have strong empirical arguments. Moreover, this assertion is corroborated by a theoretical perspective: the members of the Council of States and those of the National Council are elected in the same electoral districts of the cantons, represent the same constituencies, and have the same interest of being re-elected. Thus one must expect that the members of the Council of States defend the same group interests as those who dominate the National Council, and that they have no specific incentive to promote the collective interests of the cantons. A systematic comparative analysis of the voting behaviour of both chambers 1995–1999 confirmed this hypothesis, but with a surprising point: with issues concerning the cantons, the Council of States was not more active than the National Council, but both chambers were highly committed and successful in defending the collective interests of the cantons.[11]

2.2.2 The people's and the cantons' vote

All constitutional amendments and some international treaties proposed by the Federal Assembly, and all popular initiatives proposing to change or amend the constitution, have to be approved by popular vote. With (mandatory) referenda and popular initiatives, we again find that democratic and federal principles are equal elements of the decision-making process. As in decisions taken by the Federal Assembly, there must be a double majority obtained: on the one hand a majority of all voters, on the other hand a majority of the cantons. The latter is calculated in a simple way: the yes or no majority of every of the 20 full cantons counts as one vote, the results of the six half cantons as a half vote, which makes a total of 23 votes. If the result is tied (11.5:11.5) the proposal is rejected. As in the Federal Assembly, there can be a collision between the principles of democracy and those of federalism. A particular constitutional amendment may obtain a majority from the people, but a majority of the cantons may reject it, and *vice versa*. The characteristics of the popular vote prohibit the application of a negotiation process; in the case of negative majority of one, the amendment fails.

The details of the mechanisms of direct democracy are explained in Chapter 3, but here we should note two points about the way in which the cantons participate in federal decision-making. First, every canton is entitled to hand in proposals for a federal bill. This is called the right of cantonal initiative. The proposal has to be approved by the Federal Assembly, and if it is rejected by one of the chambers it fails. In addition a collective of eight cantons has the right to demand a popular vote on every bill passed by the Federal Assembly. This provision was used for the first time in 2003 when cantonal governments were strongly opposed to a new federal tax bill. Second, the most usual and effective way of cantonal influence lies in pre-parliamentary consultation rather than in later decisions of parliament or popular vote. Given the importance of power-sharing in Switzerland, consultations preceding formal decision are a process of intensive negotiation, which we shall consider in Chapter 3. During such consultations the cantons are influential actors involved in agenda-setting as well as in the drafting of federal legislation whenever its subject concerns them.

2.2.3 Local government: The corner stone of the Swiss 'bottom-up' state

So far we have been mainly concerned with the federation and the cantons, but emphasis should also be given to the importance of local government.[12] Communes are a corner stone of the three-level federal system (see Box 2.3). Today, the federal constitution guarantees political autonomy to the communes. Despite variations in the degree of autonomy, which depends on cantonal law, we can identify a core of 'autonomy of the commune' that is characterised by the following rights:

1. *A (constitutional) right to exist, including the freedom to merge with other communes or to remain independent, which cannot be withdrawn by the cantons.* This means that the reform of local government 'from above', as was seen in Germany in the 1960s when the *Laender* forced small communes to merge, would be rather impossible in Switzerland. Indeed the number of communes, about 2600 today, had barely decreased until the 1990s. Since then, about 300 municipalities have merged into larger units, which is not astonishing at first sight because more than half of the Swiss communes count less than 500 inhabitants and have difficulties to fulfil their tasks. Even though reasons of efficiency are strong political arguments for merging, citizens sometimes prefer independence and autonomy. Mergers can fail because the majority of citizens must accept the project by a popular vote in every of the communes concerned.

Box 2.3   Communes: The corner stone of the Swiss 'bottom-up' state

Why and how the communes can be considered the foundation of the Swiss state can be illustrated by help of the following two topics.

Subsidiarity: The idea of subsidiarity is that a central authority should perform only those tasks which cannot be performed effectively at a more immediate or local level. It can be seen as a guiding principle for federalism. In the Swiss context, we find roots in Catholic social philosophy and liberal thinking which gave subsidiarity an additional meaning: the state should take responsibilities only in tasks which cannot be performed by other societal organisations. Both meanings can be considered to be a part of Swiss political culture long before subsidiarity became a constitutional guideline in 2000. In fact, surveys show that Swiss citizens expect less responsibilities to be taken by the state than do citizens from neighbouring countries, and that they prefer decentralised solutions whenever possible. This is exactly how the Swiss system reacts to new challenges. If state intervention is really necessary for new societal problems – for example drug prevention or e-government lately – solutions are first sought at the local level. Transfer of responsibilities to the cantons or to the federation happens only if and only to the degree in which local solutions turn out to be unsatisfactory or incomplete.

Swiss citizenship: As already mentioned, the Swiss are citizens of a commune, of a canton, and of the federation. If non-natives want to acquire Swiss citizenship, they have to start with local citizenship. The latter must be acquired before applicants can seek for cantonal and then for federal citizenship. The whole procedure is burdensome, and the highest hurdle is on the local level. Applicants must have lived in the same commune for a number of years; a local commission demands proof that the applicant speaks a Swiss language, has a basic knowledge of Swiss society and its institutions and is socially integrated. In smaller communes of some cantons, it is the full assembly of the citizens who finally decide on the applications. In the late 1990s, when discrimination happened against applicants from certain countries, the Supreme Court intervened, defining standards of fair procedure for the people's assembly. While the decision was welcomed by the liberal side, it was criticised by conservatives: In their eyes, the courts' instructions were an offence against the sovereignty of the local people. While the liberal side certainly reflects the modern concept of rule of law, the conservative position illustrates that several elements of traditional political culture are still highly valued: a bottom-up idea of the state, local autonomy, and a high degree of legitimacy of direct participation.

2. *The freedom to choose, within the boundaries of cantonal legislation, an adequate political structure and administration* (see Box 2.4). There are cantons with numerous small communes and others with fewer but larger ones, and the degree of autonomy of the communes varies greatly from canton to canton. Furthermore the traditions of direct and assembly democracy are stronger in communes in the German- and Romansh-speaking part of Switzerland, whereas communes in the French- and Italian-speaking regions favour indirect democracy with a legislative and executive body. However, the most important factor defining adequate political organisation is population size. In small communes, local government consists of a few elected part-time officials who are poorly remunerated. The larger cities have a parliamentary council and a full-time political executive heading professional services. This leads to somewhat strange proportions: the 20,000 local government officials in Zurich, the country's largest city with about 375,000 inhabitants, outnumber the total population of the smallest canton, Appenzell Innerrhoden, which has 15,500 inhabitants. Political parties are important at local level: they organise political life even in small communes.[13]

3. *The right to impose taxes for their own needs.* The right to impose taxes and to decide on local tax rates is certainly the most important element in assuring the autonomy of local government. Fiscal autonomy not only allows communes to decide on local infrastructure, services, land-use planning or other public utilities according to their own preferences. It also establishes responsibility on both sides of local government: Authorities are held responsible for using their resources according to the people's needs, and citizens have to contribute with their taxes to the services they demand. Thus, decentralised governance brings the state closer to the people. Whereas in Britain and the US local taxes are mostly determined by the value of real estate, the Swiss communes are entitled to impose an income tax. With more than 30 per cent on the long-year average, the proportion of the communes of total revenue and expenditure of the three federal levels is considerable.

4. *Freedom of action in matters that are not in the competence of the cantons or the federation.* The consequences of this principle are twofold. First, it defends local autonomy in situations of conflict. A corporation seeking a site, even it if claims to be offering something of public benefit, such as a nuclear power plant, normally cannot impose itself on a commune with the help of cantonal or federal authorities. Therefore, depending on the circumstances, the communes are also protected against

their canton. The Federal Supreme Court protects the autonomy of the communes in a similar way as it protects individual human rights. Second, the principle can encourage political innovation because the communes are in a first-hand position to spot the need for new public services. Some social services, schools for social workers, AIDS prevention or the recycling of waste are examples of new public activities that started in the communes. When those activities are further developed on the cantonal or federal level, we can speak of a trial-and-error process, which permits the use of small-scale experiences for large-scale policies.

2.2.4 Citizens' self-administration

In many sectors of Swiss administration, not all public tasks are fulfilled by employed civil servants or administrators. Instead ordinary people take part for a few hours or up to several days per week. In German this is called *Milizverwaltung,* a form of self-administration by people who have been nominated to work for a period of several years or to perform a specific task for the commune or the canton. This part-time work is sometimes remunerated, sometimes not, depending on the nature and the volume of the work. In some cantons the system dates back to the Middle Ages. In the canton of Valais, for instance, the water-supply system in the high valleys was realised in forms of *Gemeinwerk* (community work) in which every adult man was periodically drafted for several weeks to help with its construction.[14]

In its modern form, *Milizverwaltung* has three functions:

- The professional capabilities and talents of ordinary citizens are directly used for public administration. This allows non-centralised self-administration and political autonomy even for small societies. Small villages, for instance, cannot afford a professional local administration. By relying on the part-time involvement of their citizens, however, they are able to have not only their own community council and other political authorities but also their own community services.
- Self-administration, with a great number of persons being nominated for part-time tasks, posts and commissions, allows for more democratic participation. In their voluntary role, citizens are taking part in political decisions and cooperating in administrative work as well.
- Communitarian traditions in Switzerland have been able to survive. There are many private organisations working for the poor, the handicapped, for cultural affairs, for the protection of environment

Box 2.4 Local government: The institutions

The political structures vary considerably with the size of the communes. This is the reason why I distinguish between small and large communes in the following description.

	Small Communes	*Large Communes*
Legislative body	*Citizens assembly*: A type of 'assembly democracy'. All adult Swiss citizens living in the commune have the right to participate at the assembly.	*Communal parliament*: Elected by the people. A type of 'semi-direct democracy'.
	The plenary assembly decides on propositions submitted by the executive council of the commune and by ordinary citizens. All important communal questions can be the subject of discussion.	Important decisions must be approved by a vote (referendum). Other decisions can be challenged by an optional referendum. In the communes of most cantons citizens have the right to hand in an initiative leading to a popular vote.
Executive body	Collegiate council, elected directly by the citizens (exception: canton Neuchâtel, where the communal parliament appoints the executive council).	
	Part-time members as a rule, full professional office as an exception.	Professional full-time members as a rule; part-time office as an exception.
Administration	Relies partly or entirely on the non-professional services of volunteers.	Professional administration in combination with resources of non-professional volunteers.

Note: In some French-speaking cantons, the traditions of 'assembly democracy' as well as of the referendum and the popular initiative are less known. Even small communes therefore rely on types of representative democracy with an executive and a legislative council.

The main field of *Milizverwaltung* is local government.[15] In small communes of up to 1000 inhabitants there are often just two full-time professional posts: president and president's clerk. The other seats of the communal council, as well as positions in social services and the fire brigade, in commissions for land-use planning and school administration, are occupied by part-time volunteers or are part-time jobs. In larger communes and cities *Milizverwaltung* does not disappear, but is combined with professional administration.

or the promotion of other public goods. These non-profit organisations fulfil public tasks outside public administration, even though
many of them are subsidised by the federation, the canton or the
commune.

Milizverwaltung is found at the cantonal and federal level too, for
instance in the form of expert commissions. In the 1980s a first systematic inquiry found almost 400 federal expert commissions with
some 4000 persons involved.[16] A recent study, taking into account
only those commissions nominated directly by the Federal Council,
illustrates the importance of the federal *Milizverwaltung:* 40 per cent of
the 181 commissions have a consultative function, 43 per cent are
decision-making and appeal organs, while the rest fulfil leadership or
representative mandates.[17] Moreover many cantonal and district courts
work on the basis of *Milizverwaltung,* and all members of all parliaments – federal, cantonal and local – exercise the mandate on a part-
time basis. With the exception of executive members, most elected
politicians in Switzerland hold another job besides their mandate.

Advocates of *Milizverwaltung* claim that it is cheaper than professional administration, that politicians remain in contact with their
voters and that the system keeps the political elite from becoming an
isolated class. Opponents, on the other hand, consider it has led to too
much amateurism and not enough professionalism in Swiss politics, as
well as hidden transactions or even corruption if politicians do not
carefully distinguish between their private and the public interests.

2.3   Federalism at work

2.3.1   Cooperative federalism: How federal tasks are implemented by cantons and communes[18]

In the middle of the nineteenth century divisions between federalist
and anti-federalist factions led to a clear distinction and division of
power between the federation and the cantons. This concept, however,
has subsequently been overruled by the mechanisms of intensive cooperation between the three levels of the federal system. The complexities
of modern infrastructure, economic intervention and social programmes
stimulated the completion of federal legislation by the cantons, the implementation of federal programmes by cantonal and local authorities, and
extensive finance- and revenue-sharing.

The Swiss social security system provides a good example of this kind
of 'cooperative federalism'. Its main element, which gives a minimum

old-age pension to all retired persons as well as to widows and their children, was introduced in 1948 and has been regularly revised since then. The federation is responsible for the legislation which regulates insurance contributions, it supervises the implementation of the programme, finances part of the costs and, through the Federal Court, it guarantees equal application of the law.

Citizens may look to the national politics section of their newspaper to find the latest changes to social security payments, but it is the local and cantonal authorities or even private organisations with whom they have to deal. The monthly contributions of employees and employers are collected by regional agencies of the different industries, a reminder of the time when social security was based on private organisations. The same organisational scheme applies to other branches of social security, invalidity and unemployment insurance. The regional agencies and cantonal authorities are then responsible for most of the redistribution, along with the postman, who in earlier times took the money directly to pensioners. Indeed, the postal and telecommunication service, together with the federal railways (SBB), belong to the few federal services which deal directly with the public. Most federal programmes are implemented by the cantons and the communes, and there is no parallel federal administration, with its own regional services, agencies or even courts, like that in the United States. Where the social security system is concerned, the cooperation between the federation, the cantons and the communes goes even further. If a retired citizen is so poor that he or she cannot live on the federal pension, she or he may go to the local authority and apply for an additional benefit provided by the cantons. The fact that the federal government pays a substantial part of that grant is an incentive for the cantons to run complementary social security programmes (otherwise they would not obtain a share of this part of the central budget), but the cantons are in sole charge of the programmes. Implementation, then, is delegated to the communes, which are closer to the clients and therefore have better information based on which to evaluate the needs of claimants. At the local level, most of the other social services for which personal relations with clients are essential – social aid to the poor, social work, homes for elderly people, mobile-meal and health services – are organised by the communes, although sometimes they are delegated to private organisations and subsidised by the cantons.

This kind of cooperation again reflects the strong belief of the Swiss in the subsidiarity principle (see Box 2.3). Thus public intervention and public help should only occur in situations where private means would not suffice to achieve a goal. Furthermore, if a public programme is necessary, the Swiss look to the institution closest to its clients. As already mentioned, cantonal programmes are feasible only when local programmes do not suffice, and only if a task exceeds the capacities of the cantons do the cantons relinquish power to the federation. Consequently, even in federal matters not all responsibilities are centralised. Whereas the federation has become responsible for legislation on many issues that once were under cantonal rule, the implementation of federal programmes is delegated to the cantons and the communes whenever possible. This applies even to the fiscal state: it is the communes that collect all income taxes from the inhabitants – not only their own but also those of the canton and the federal government.

2.3.2   How a deadlock over a federal programme allows experiments: The energy-saving policies of the cantons

When the first oil crisis in 1973 shocked the industrialised world, the Swiss became aware of their extremely vulnerable energy supply. While water from the Alps can meet a good deal of the electricity demand, this constitutes the only major renewable energy resource in Switzerland. For about 80 per cent of its energy consumption it is dependent on international markets: oil from the Middle East and Africa, gas from northern Europe and Russia, and uranium from Canada and the US. In the view of the Swiss government, a national energy policy was then considered urgent and necessary. A commission of experts was appointed to provide long-term forecasts of energy supply and consumption. Its report for a national energy program to the government made three key recommendations: substitute for oil, research into alternative energy sources, and energy savings. In 1980 the Federal Council proposed a constitutional amendment which would have enabled a national energy policy to be developed. The two chambers of parliament eventually passed the bill. In a referendum in 1983 the constitutional amendment gained the people's vote but failed to win a majority amongst the cantons. It was not until 1990 that the federal authorities presented a new proposal for a national energy policy that survived the referendum process. This constitutional amendment presented only a few moderate suggestions. In the following decade, protagonists of effective energy saving polices handed in three popular initiatives proposing taxes for non-renewable energies and subsidies for alternative energies. None of them was successful, and two similar bills of parliament taking up the idea of subsidies for renewable energies were refused by popular vote in 2000. In 2001, the parliament accepted a law setting standards for the reduction of CO_2 emissions. Thus, it took the federation almost 30 years to acquire a mandate for a national energy policy whose limited ambitions are far from the original hopes of the government.

This long delay may be extraordinary. The example of energy policy however, is typical of one of the difficulties of the central government if it wants to acquire new competencies under the conditions of direct democracy. There have been other occasions when the people have rejected federal projects several times before finally accepting them in a different version. Even then it should be noted that the people may reject bills to implement a new policy when they have already approved its constitutional amendment. This was the fate, for instance, of a maternity allowance bill that was successfully challenged in popular referenda in 1987 and 1999, despite it having been approved in principle in 1945.

The combination of federalism with direct democracy, therefore, gives the cantons high veto power and means a considerable obstacle for any new federal policy. One of the most common arguments against innovations from Bern is mistrust of the federal government and defence of the cantons' autonomy. Anti-state, anti-centralist, as well as conservative and neo-liberal motives fit equally well into this pattern. They also played a role in the vote on the energy issue. It was argued that new federal initiatives to intervene in the market system were not necessary. Such activities by the federation would weaken the cantons' competences, and it was said that the cantons were already doing all that was necessary. Thus federal innovations are not guaranteed success, and they take time, because of the high consensus required in the double majority of the people and the cantons, and because of the double hurdle of two stages of legislation: constitutional base and regulatory enactment. Table 2.3 shows that more than one quarter of all constitutional amendments proposed by the Federal Assembly 1848–2007 were rejected.

Table 2.3 Constitutional amendments proposed by the Federal Assembly, 1848–2007, including counterproposals to popular initiatives

Went to a vote	221
Accepted	159
Rejected by the people only	3
Rejected by the cantons only	8
Rejected by the people and the cantons	54
Total rejected	62

The case of the national energy policy, however, needs further explanation. It involved that most controversial and polarising of issues: nuclear energy. In the 1970s the anti-nuclear movement successfully stopped the construction of a power plant after several months of occupation of the site. When first the greens and then the social democrats opposed the construction of new nuclear power plants, the issue divided parliament, political parties and the people. Nuclear power was controversial where technical risks and gains were concerned, but below this there lurked a fundamental conflict of values. Proponents of nuclear power considered that economic growth and technical progress were at stake; opponents were fundamentally engaged in the protection of nature and of future generations against the dangers of nuclear technology. A popular initiative against the construction of new power plants failed in 1979, but 49 per cent of the people voted for the initiative – the anti-nuclear movement had successfully reached the masses. On the other hand the protagonists of nuclear power were equally unable to win enough support for the continuation of the programme. When in 1985 the federal chambers authorised the resumption of construction of a nuclear power plant in Kaiseraugst, it encountered unanimous protests by the two neighbouring semi-cantons of Basel. Public opinion throughout Switzerland to a large degree disapproved of resumption of the work, and some federal authorities were convinced that completion would be impossible without police guards or even military protection.

The work was not resumed, and in 1989 the federal parliament dropped the project, paying Sfr 350 million in indemnities to the electrical company that had been licensed to undertake the work. This was two years after the nuclear accident at Chernobyl, whose radioactive fall-out reached large parts of Western Europe.

Thus neither the opponents nor the protagonists of nuclear power could win the argument. In this deadlock, a compromise was found. In 1990, the cantons and the people accepted a popular initiative for a ten-year moratorium on the authorisation and construction of new plants. Meanwhile, the moratorium has run out. Opponents of nuclear power launched two popular initiatives: one to renew the moratorium, the other to pull out from nuclear energy within ten years. Both initiatives failed by popular vote in 2003. A few years later, the industry launched plans for the replacement of two nuclear plants, which led the anti-nuclear movement to reorganise. Thus, as in other countries, the deadlock on nuclear energy may hold on.[19]

For a long time, the deep conflict on the question of nuclear power overshadowed and paralysed all issues in national energy policy. The deadlock of federal politics in the 1980s and 1990s, however, did not prevent important innovations in some cantons. In the canton of Baselland for instance, where opposition to two nuclear power plant projects was particularly strong, the authorities found a constructive way out of the dilemma: future energy shortfalls resulting from the rejection of nuclear power should be compensated for by effective energy-saving programmes. The authorities charged experts with analysing the potential for energy-saving in all household appliances, and in industry, public buildings and transport.

In the 1980s Baselland pioneered in energy saving, and the success of its policies were considerable. The new regulations for housing insulation, for instance, stimulated innovation in the construction industry. Within ten years energy consumption for heating in new houses dropped nearly 40 per cent because of better insulation and more efficient heating systems. Other cantons followed, and their laws gave incentives for energy saving technologies to be applied in industry and households. The decentralised energy policy was an early experiment. Cantons were a kind of laboratories where work was going on to solve the problem of how to live with less energy without giving up on comfort. Their experiments were realistic and allowed for the risk of failure and deadends. Decentralised experiment and cooperation allowed to keep the costs of failure low but let benefit all participants from successful innovation. Cantons became laboratories not only for technology but also for the federal authorities. When they finally passed national energy savings programmes, they could draw from the experience made in the cantons.

The success of these measures should not, however, be overestimated. Some cantons flatly rejected energy-saving programmes, others were reluctant or constrained by the national controversy about nuclear energy. Those who did participate had to realise that stabilising overall energy consumption was not an obtainable goal. Cantonal states are not authorised to raise gas or oil prices, which more than any other measure would stimulate a reduction in consumption. The cantons were able to stimulate the use of new technologies, such as solar energy, but cantonal markets are much too small to hope for economies of scale by mass production. There was no national policy helping the small innovative enterprises to become competitive on an international level. Meanwhile, other countries like Denmark or Germany have taken the lead in solar energy and other fields where Swiss innovative firms once were pioneers. Even so, the cantonal experience was not in vain. It was a substitute for the long times blocked federal policy, it contributed to overcome some of the deep conflicts on the energy issue, and it helped to develop ends and means of energy savings policies by a process of decentralised trial and error. Learning from decentralised or even competitive innovation processes may be one of the most important advantages of federal policies.[20]

2.3.3   How federalism copes with inequalities: The example of Swiss primary schools

While travelling in rural regions or hiking in the Alps, visitors to Switzerland are often astonished to see pretty and well-maintained school houses even in small and evidently poor villages. Indeed, having their own schools for their own children and a good schoolteacher is the pride of each commune. Another story, linked again to federalism, is how even small and poor villages are able to live up to this ideal.

In the middle of the last century education differed from canton to canton. In some cantons basic schools were run by the (Catholic) church, others were public. In mountain regions school lessons were given only in winter, when children were not needed to help in the fields. Curricula and the length of children's basic education varied considerably. The radical majority in 1848 wanted education to be a cantonal matter. This allowed for cultural diversity. Aware of the importance of education to a young nation and its democracy, however, the radicals stipulated that there should be some federal control. Thus a constitutional provision required that 'the cantons provide sufficient basic education'. This regulation was, above all, a plea for the state monopoly of schools and was directed against the Catholic church, which then controlled parts of the educational system. Second, the regulation obliged the cantons to offer a minimum standard of basic education, with a minimum number of years of schooling being free of charge but compulsory for everybody.

These requirements greatly influenced the evolution of the Swiss educational system. Providing equal-quality education and training became the common concern of the cantons. In earlier times there has been a 'brain drain' of the best teachers to rich communes offering better salaries. Although still nominated and paid by the communes, teachers today receive an almost equal salary throughout each canton. Curricula are coordinated by intercantonal bodies. Poor communes receive subsidies for the salaries of their teachers and the construction of their school buildings – but these have to follow construction standards that prohibit luxury buildings as well as insufficient class rooms. For long times, inadequately coordinated curricula created difficulties for schoolchildren when parents moved from one canton to another.

Whilst it makes sense, for example, for Bernese schools to concentrate on the cultural specificities and history of their own canton, the argument for federalism is less strong when there are 26 different cantonal teaching programmes in mathematics. Thus, many of the old particularities of cantonal curricula have been eliminated – not by dictate of the federal government but rather by means of inter-cantonal coordination.[21]

Fifty years ago, access to higher education was highly unequal. Students from rural regions, from lower social classes and women were underrepresented. This changed with federal programs – subsidies for the new, decentralised cantonal institutions, and for cantonal scholarships – that gave a big boost to higher education. Today, women as well as students from rural regions have equal chances. Social inequalities, however, are as big as they were 50 years ago, and they are a black spot in the Swiss welfare state. One has to consider, though, that social differences in access to higher education are more difficult to overcome than barriers set up by geographical distance or by gender.[22]

2.3.4   Swiss federalism means regional solidarity, not competition

The federal policy of minimum standards is not limited to schooling; other public services work in the same way. Public transport now reaches practically every commune, even those in high mountain valleys. A dense and decentralised network of public infrastructure has helped to maintain the private services of doctors, local banks or grocery stores even in small villages. If Swiss statistics define communes with 10,000 inhabitants as 'cities', there is some reason for doing so. In these small centres one can find lawyers and other professional specialists, computer and book shops, various other commodities and services, and even a local industry producing a particular product for export.

Instead of people flocking to where the money is, Swiss federalism has seen to it that the money is sent to where the people are, thus maintaining a decentralised economic and social structure. In the 1970s, when young people from mountain valleys found better jobs by moving to the cities, a large federal programme for public investment in the mountain regions was launched. Subsidies were given on the condition that different communes were willing to agree on a common regional-development plan. This plan had to demonstrate the intracommunal development potential of a larger region[23] and coordinate the federal investment in roads, schools, sports sites and other facilities. The programme helped to develop new tourist industries, and, together with other programmes, provided agriculture in mountain regions with a better chance of survival. In many regions the population drain was stopped. While evaluations of the programme were sometimes critical about its direct economic effects, its socio-political success was undeniable. The programme provided the communes with an incentive to get together to analyse their own situations from a wider horizon and find common perspectives of development. Encouraging a social experiment of 'endogenous development', some experts say, was even more important than money.[24]

With globalisation and the opening of the Swiss economy in the 1990s, this kind of regional policy became more difficult and less effective. It was cancelled. Even so, equalising policies for the different

Box 2.5   Mechanisms of financial compensation

Financial compensation serves to adjust differences in financial revenue and expenditure between rich and poor cantons or communes. There are two main reasons why Switzerland has such a policy. First, supposing that people in mountain cantons do not wish to leave, we are confronted with the problem that these cantons cannot compete economically with the urban cantons, where the starting position for individual economic development is much better. Besides different economic resources, the cantonal tax system can worsen the unequal starting position: tax revenues in the mountain cantons are very low whilst tax rates are rather high. Financial compensation seeks to strengthen 'poor' cantons and communes and to enable them to offer basic public goods of a quality similar to those of 'rich' communes. Second, there is what economists call the 'externality problem'. Some cantons or communes carry out tasks for others. They offer infrastructural services (for example universities or medical centres) which are used by residents of other cantons and communes. Instead of pricing these services for the individuals – which is not always reasonable – cantons or communes look for mutual compensation.

Thus, the federal system of financial compensation is based on two ideas:
- *Financial compensation of resources*: compensating for differences of resources between 'rich' and 'poor' cantons and communes.
- *Financial compensation of spillovers*: compensating externalities of public goods between the cantons and the communes, or between different levels of the federal system.

cantons and their regions are still at the core of Swiss 'cooperative federalism'.[25] The idea is that of a commonwealth of all regions, and of mutuality. At its core, we find a broad system of financial compensation between the federation, the cantons and the communes comprising revenue-sharing as well as financial compensation by block grants and subsidies[26] (see Box 2.5 and Figure 2.1).

The equalising policies of cooperative federalism are not uncontested. Some complain that shared responsibility makes actors less responsible, or that cooperative federalism encourages too much public spending. The critique was taken up in a major reform of Swiss federalism that started in the 1990s. Its most important element comprised a disentanglement of responsibilities between the federation and the cantons. It followed the principle of fiscal incidence: As much as possible, the geographical circle of payers for a public good should coincide with the circle of its beneficiaries. Better coincidence between payers and beneficiaries of public goods should strengthen political responsibilities in the federal system. It was the baseline for a reform of the system of financial compensation that was meant to become more transparent

Figure 2.1 Financial compensation between federation and cantons 2008, in million Sfr

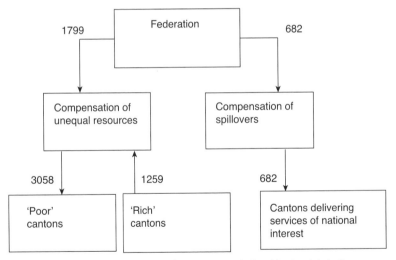

Note that this system functions in two dimensions, vertical and horizontal. As the federation financially participates in the compensation of unequal resources and spillovers of the cantons, we speak of vertical compensation. The horizontal compensation lies in the fact that 'rich' cantons participate in the financial transfers to the 'poor' cantons. Similar systems can be found in the cantons for compensations among the communes.

and subsidiary in its character. It was crucial, therefore, to clearly define objective criteria of relatively 'poor' or 'rich' cantons, which in the end are decisive if a canton ends up being a beneficiary or a net payer to the system of financial compensation. Even so, it was not easy to overcome the opposition of the rich cantons the more as the fiscal system is characterised by cantonal autonomy (see Box 2.6). We now see the political reason for the substantial financial participation of the federation: allowing that only a few cantons ended up as losers, it eased political conflict enough to guarantee success in parliament and by popular vote in 2004. Finally, federal subsidies, leading to overconsumption in the past, were mostly discontinued in favour of block grants.[27]

This concept of cooperative federalism is different from other ideas of federalism. Economic theory, for instance, relates federalism to competition. Some economists prefer many decentralised authorities to the monopoly of central government. According to this view, the ideal situation is where governments have to compete and where citizens have the option to vote for the government they prefer. One could say that US federalism is, and probably always was, influenced by this idea. The variety of US states is considered as something amongst which one chooses. Individuals migrating from east to west or from north to south are trying to make the best choice they can. US cities and communities are felt to be in competition with each other. Living in a wealthy residential area or a poor suburb can mean a difference between excellent or poor public services. People who find that the local public school is not good enough for their children send them to private schools or move to a better area. This can lead to vicious cycles where poor communities get poorer, and rich ones eventually become richer. 'Voting by feet', however, may be part of the American civic culture that favours free options, and it is a heritage of people who once took the 'exit option' to leave their former countries as emigrants.

The attitude of the Swiss is different. The Swiss passport does not mention 'place of birth', but the commune of family origin, dating back generations. In older times this kind of citizenship was of great importance. Before the creation of the modern social security system, the commune of origin was legally obliged to provide for its elderly, homeless and poor. Today most Swiss are still aware of their cultural roots, and feel emotionally attached to the communes and regions in which they live. Many feel that choosing to make a living in another canton means the loss of familiar surroundings and mentalities. One finds Swiss people of all professions who prefer to stay in their own

Box 2.6   The fiscal state: Paying taxes in Switzerland

Every year, each household gets a tax form from the local tax office. The responsible persons in the household are required to declare their revenue and fortune. On the basis of their own declaration and after control by the local authority, the taxpayers get their bill. The commune does not only collect its own taxes but is mandated to collect also those of the canton and of the federal government. This demands much trust in the taxpayer and the local authorities as well but is considered to be efficient for all parties involved.

The decentralised system allows cantons and communes to vary definitions of income and fortune, and to apply different tax rates. Households with the same revenue may thus pay different taxes for the same revenue. Thus Swiss federalism allows for competition, traditionally limited in its extent, which prevented a 'race to the bottom'. Even so, differences can be considerable. A family with two children, having an income of 150,000 francs, paid 24,000 francs in (poor) Délémont but only about 10,000 francs in (rich) Zug, which reflects how the different economic situation of two regions can affect also taxpayers. Tax competition has become a political issue when the Canton of Obwalden, in order to attract rich taxpayers, was the first to introduce a flat rate. This was considered unfair competition because the other cantons use progressive tax tariffs.

Two other points of tax competition have become controversial on the international stage: local 'tax treaties' and the national 'banking secret'. Both were legally defined offers to save taxes and to attract rich people and/or their wealth from the outside. While defenders of these privileges claimed legal and fiscal autonomy, the opponents, raising moral questions or inequality of treatment, were not much heard in the Swiss political discourse. Things changed when the biggest Swiss bank was accused in the US of systematically violating US tax legislation, and when in 2009 the OECD set Switzerland on a grey list in order to adapt its banking secret and to comply with its rules. While an international harmonisation of rules of tax competition seems to be logic and reasonable in times of globalisation, the Swiss government is worrying about who sets the rules, and what the future rules as well as their implementation are going about to be.

region rather than accept better job offers in other cantons or abroad. Moreover there are the language boundaries. Only a very small proportion of the population changes linguistic regions. Many of those who do so for professional reasons may later return to their region of origin. Things are changing, though. Under the pressure of globalisation, the Swiss economy is subject of rapid structural change, requiring workforce to become more mobile. University students, today, are offered mobility programs to get part of their education abroad. Nevertheless, living close to their native region is the first choice of most people. Under these conditions we can understand the great importance of regional solidarity in Swiss politics. Creating fairly equal living conditions in the different regions is vital if collective values of local cultures are to be maintained and if people continue to feel emotionally attached to their place of origin.[28] In contrast with the US, the Swiss culture of federalism is not based on competition, nor on voting with one's feet by migrating. By compensating for existing inequalities, Swiss federalism makes it possible for people to stay in their own region and thus favours the 'loyalty option'.[29]

2.3.5   Dealing with the separatist issue: The dolorous birth of a new canton

The problems of the Jura region have already been mentioned in Chapter 1 (Section 1.4.3). The Jura represents an exception to Swiss integration of cultural minorities. Historical factors and worsening language, religious, cultural and socioeconomic differences instead led to its separation from the canton of Bern.[30] The Jura region, which is mainly Catholic and French-speaking, was incorporated into Protestant, German-speaking Bern in 1815 at the Vienna Congress by arrangement with Prussia, England, Austria and Russia. As a minority located at the northern periphery of the canton, the people of Jura felt they were being discriminated against both politically and economically. An escalation of political clashes after the Second World War gave rise to a separatist movement, which triumphed in 1978 when the new Jura canton was created. Things were complicated by the fact that the population of Jura was itself divided: three southern districts had been Protestant since the sixteenth century, were economically better off and had traditionally better relations with the old canton. Thus the deepening conflict was not only between Jura and Bern, but also between 'separatists' and (Bernese) 'loyalists' within the population of Jura.

How were the authorities to deal with a region that wanted to separate from an existing canton and form a new one? The founders of the constitution had not anticipated this problem, so before the game could be played the rules had to be invented.

As far as the game was concerned it was clear that three actors would take part:

- the people of the Jura region, who had to decide whether they wanted to separate or to stay with the Bern canton;
- the people of the Bern canton, who had to decide under what conditions they would accept the separation, if that was the will of the majority of the people of the Jura region;
- the people and the cantons of the entire Swiss federation who would, following the amendment of the constitution, have to accept both the decision of the Bernese and Jurassian people to split up and the new canton as a member of the federation.

If Bern had long underestimated the importance of the Jura question, showing little regard for the cultural minority, it eventually was responsible for taking the most important initiatives to settle the conflict. In 1967 the Bern government presented the people of Jura with three options from which to choose: the *status quo*, a statute of autonomy, or separation from Bern by the creation of a new canton. In the following year a task force or 'federal advisory commission' was created: two former members of the Federal Council and two members of the Swiss parliament were appointed to investigate the implications of a statute of autonomy or of the separation of the Jura region from Bern. Institutionally this meant not the appointment of an intermediate third party, but also the unofficial involvement of a federal authority in a conflict that had become of nationwide importance.

In succeeding years the separatist forces continued to espouse independence, so the Bernese government proposed a cascade system of popular votes for Bern and the Jura region:

- In the first votation, all districts in Jura were asked: do you want to create a new canton?
- If the first votation produced a majority in any given district, one fifth of the electorate could demand a second poll to be held on the question: do you want to participate in the new canton or remain with the old one?
- After the second votation, the boundaries of the proposed canton having now been set, one fifth of the electorate of every commune lying on the border could demand a third poll on the question:

would you prefer to join the new canton or remain with the old one?

The purpose of this cascade system was clear. The first votation would establish whether the Jurassian people did indeed wish to create their own canton, but given the internal division of the Jura people between separatists and loyalists, no district or commune would be forced to stay with the old canton or go with the new one against its own will. Thus the second and third votation would protect regional and local minorities on either side of the debate.

In 1970 the Bernese people accepted the cascade system as a constitutional amendment by an impressive majority of six to one. In this particular votation the Bernese people did not vote on separation itself, but on the procedure relating to future separation which would permit the people of Jura to take an autonomous decision on whether or not to create their own canton. In other words, the Bernese majority had agreed to allow the Jura minority to separate from the canton if it so wished.

In 1974 and 1975 the people of Jura played the game according to the rules. In the first votation the inhabitants of all the Jura districts voted 37,000 for and 34,000 against independence. The cleavage between separatists and loyalists was clear: the northern districts voted for separation by three to one, whereas the three southern districts voted by almost two to one to stay with the old canton. Two of the three districts confirmed their preference to stay in the canton of Bern in the second votation in 1975, but in one of the southern districts the vote was split. Here a third votation was held: Moutier, the main city of the district, decided to stay with Bern whilst some northern communes in the district chose to join the new canton.

After these votations the boundaries of the new canton, Jura, were known, and in 1976 its people elected a constituent assembly which then drew up a draft constitution for the new canton. The constitution was accepted by the people of Jura in 1977, and one year later the Swiss people and the cantons accepted Jura as the 26th canton of the federation. The result of the national vote (1,310,000 for 280,000 against, with a large majority in all cantons) was interpreted as revealing the great respect and understanding of the Swiss people for its minority groups.

The creation of the new canton had split the Jura region, which was contrary to the political objectives of a good part of the separatist movement which, on grounds of ethnicity, culture and language, had embraced the idea of independence for the whole of Jura. They had proposed other procedural rules, for instance that the right to vote for the creation of the canton should be given to all persons originating from Jura, regardless of their present place of residence. Instead of the separatists' dream of uniting the entire ethnic group within a single boundary, three districts remained within the boundary of the Bern canton. Yet this solution was modern in the sense that it rejected the nationalist formula of 'one people, one language, one culture, one state', which always leads to insoluble minority problems. In fact migration and industrialisation have made single-cultural societies and their states more and more an exception. In this respect all boundaries become artificial. In Jura they were founded on the principle of territorial self-determination on the smallest possible scale: first the region as a whole, then its districts and finally its communes were allowed to choose. Because of its rationality the procedure may well be used again. There is nothing, in principal, to prohibit a future generation in the southern districts from demanding the reopening of the cascade procedure. In fact it has already been used by another district, the German-speaking but Catholic Laufenthal, which joined the Baselland canton in 1993. Sooner or later, the Jura question may come up again. While a popular initiative in the Jura in 2004 charges the cantonal parliament with working out a constitutional framework for a 'United Jura' that includes the southern districts, Bern authorities follow a different path: they propose a status of partial autonomy for the southern districts.

We could have witnessed a quite different outcome to the Jura question. Bern, instead of opening the way to separation, could have tried to continue a policy of oppression against the separatist movement. Further escalation of the conflict between the Bernese majority and the Jurassian minority without any realistic hope of solution could have made federal intervention inevitable. Instead the Jura minority, despite discrimination, profited from individual and political liberties that were broad enough to allow it to organise its successful separation. Federal intervention was limited to an informal task force that was able to gain the confidence of both sides, and the majority of the Bernese people, while anything but enthusiastic about the Jura minority, were willing to allow the Jurassians to separate from the 'grand old canton' if so wished.

2.4   The limits of Swiss federalism

2.4.1   Limits of implementation: Why some foreigners can buy real estate in Switzerland and others can not

People living abroad can acquire real estate in Switzerland only under certain legal restrictions. The history of this federal law goes back to the 1960s. Xenophobes then complained not only that the foreign-resident figure of 15 per cent was too high, but that there was reason to fear a sell-out of Swiss land to foreign capital. When the xenophobe movement announced the launch of a popular initiative to stop this development and the price of land soared, the government coalition had to react. It adopted a regulation limiting the acquisition of land and real estate by persons and firms with residence abroad. The issue was highly controversial. Liberal forces were against any state regulation of the real-estate market. The political left, on the other hand, wanted new regulations on land-use planning and on the protection of tenants, but not in the sense that the xenophobe forces meant. Yet the government coalition felt forced to do something to curb the political growth of the movement, which had begun to make demands which went much further than their original ones. Because of the highly controversial nature of the question the regulations were many times revised. The bill contains exceptions and it leaves room for complementary legislation by the cantons, which have to implement the programme.

After 20 years of implementation the success of the programme was hardly convincing. Whereas in some cantons the sale of land and houses to foreigners stabilised or even fell, it rose sharply in others. What had happened? A closer analysis[31] revealed that the cantons had made full use of their legislative and implementing powers, thus adapting the federal law to their own needs. In some cantons the objectives of the federal law coincided with their own strategies, as in Lucerne which aimed at the slow and gentle development of tourist sites. The federal programme and its cantonal complements were protective of the environment and were implemented in Lucerne without reservation. In the canton of Geneva the result was somewhat ambiguous. The city's most urgent need was to provide housing, especially for low-income residents. Thus the city said no to foreigners who wanted to buy existing villas. But it said yes to foreign investors willing to co-finance large apartment blocks on condition that some of the apartments were rented to families on low incomes. In a third canton, however, the objectives of the federal regulation were distorted in a contrary way. Ambitious development plans for new tourist sites in the canton of Valais were financed by foreign capital. At that time one could find advertisements in the business section of foreign newspapers saying: 'For foreigners, it's still possible to realise their dream of a Swiss Chalet'. Indeed it was, because Valais offered much more liberal conditions of authorisation than other cantons, thus attracting foreign capital to finance its development plans.

Whereas it is common for the cantons to adapt federal legislation to their own needs, it is rare for them to go as far as inverting its objectives. Yet, the Valais example shows what many other studies[32] have confirmed: The implementation of central government programmes in a federal system cannot be taken for granted. First, it depends on political will. If the political consensus is large, the cantons and the communes will make it a success, even if there are different technical problems in its implementation. Second, in a federal system consensus is required at different levels of government, but this condition may not be forthcoming. Programmes almost unanimously welcomed by the Federal Assembly may be controversial in particular cantons. An analysis of the federal housing programme, for instance, has shown that its subsidies were not used where housing was most needed, but in cantons where political forces willing to protect tenants were the strongest.[33] Third, lack of administrative resources can hinder a federal programme. Small cantons or small communes are often unable to implement environmental policies because the necessary resources and expertise to analyse, implement and control environmental standards are beyond their reach.[34]

2.4.2 The weakness of federal authorities, or how a canton can deny human rights to its citizens

In the nineteenth century Switzerland was one of the first countries to attain a democracy that was free of property and other restrictions on an adult male's right to vote. The realisation of women's equal rights in Switzerland, however, was a long and difficult process. The first attempts to introduce women's suffrage at the cantonal level failed in the 1920s in Neuchatel, Basel, Glarus, Zurich, Geneva and St. Gallen. In 1929 a petition demanding women's suffrage at the federal level was handed in with a quarter of a million signatures. The petition led to nothing. In 1959, in a popular vote, Swiss men voted two to one against women's suffrage. In 1971 Switzerland became one of the last countries to give women the right to vote, but it was a further ten years before women were given equal rights and constitutional protection against discrimination.

People often ask why recognition of women's political and civil rights took so long in Switzerland. One answer may be that women's organisations, after their early setbacks in the 1920s, had lost much of their courage to demand equal rights.[35] Another reason may be that Swiss society is generally more conservative than others. In fact the Swiss, who had had to defend their traditional values and autonomy during the First and Second World War and had never suffered a social revolution in the twentieth century, were particularly late in recognising the need for a change in women's societal position.[36] When in 1958 Iris von Roten published *Frauen im Laufgitter* – a very critical report on the economic, political, sociological and sexual situation of Swiss women – the author and her feminist work were destroyed by the media and were effectively silenced.[37] Only in 1991, when the almost forgotten book was re-edited, was *Frauen im Laufgitter* hailed as the Swiss equivalent of Simone de Beauvoir's *Le deuxième sexe* (1949) or Betty Friedan's *The Feminine Mystic* (1963). This clearly illustrates the late change of mind about the position of women in Swiss society.

From the perspective of a political scientist another factor should be recalled. The problem of the introduction of women's suffrage was that women were not able to participate in the decision. Men alone decided whether they were willing to abandon their historical privilege and share their political rights with women. In parliamentary democracies that situation is easier to deal with. A party that wishes to introduce women's suffrage can combine this proposition with other issues, for instance job security or minimal wages, in its election programme. Thus a worker fearing for his job would probably vote for that party, even if he was at odds with the idea of women's suffrage. Should that party win the election the introduction of women's suffrage would be likely, because once introduced the new voting power of women would most probably go to support the government that had enfranchised them. This procedure was not possible in Switzerland, where women's suffrage had to be introduced by popular vote – all men's vote.

Moreover, in order to prevent one issue from riding on the back of another, and to ensure that voters have the opportunity to express their preferences clearly, the constitution prohibits the combining of different questions in a single popular vote. Thus, when attempting to introduce women's suffrage in 1959, the federal authorities were not able to offer men some sort of incentive to share their electoral monopoly with women. All that the government was able to do was to convince men that women were equal or that human rights should be universal. The most helpful thing, however, was the example provided by the cantons and a number of communes which, during the 1959 votation and later, introduced women's suffrage at the lower level. In 1971 the federal government tried again. This time it was successful.[38]

A few bastions of all-male democracy withstood all attempts at persuasion, which they perceived as outside interference. The *Landsgemeinde* (popular assembly) of the canton of Appenzell Innerrhoden steadfastly refused to introduce women's suffrage until 1990. Finally, when deciding on an appeal brought by a number of Appenzell women, the Federal Court ruled that this situation was unconstitutional. Moreover the court intervened drastically: it redefined Appenzell Innerrhoden's constitution in such a way that it gave women the right to participate at the next *Landsgemeinde*.[39]

One may again ask why this process took so long. Was there no possibility of the federal government intervening earlier to end the unconstitutional situation in Appenzell Innerrhoden? Theoretically the answer is yes. The Swiss federation has several means of intervening if cantons fail to comply with federal law. In the event of public disorder it can send in troops. Under certain circumstances it can also withdraw subsidies. Both sanctions, however, would not have been of much help in this case. Moreover they are used very rarely. Federal authorities deal with the cantons with almost as much respect as they deal with foreign states. More common is intervention by the Federal Court. Since every cantonal decision is subject to the charge that it violates federal constitutional law, the court's role in implementing equal protection is most important. Indeed as the Federal Court deals with basic rights – freedom of the press, freedom of speech, the right to own property, freedom of association, equal protection by and due process of the law, and *habeas corpus* – it is probably the strongest authority of the central state. It says what can and can not be done under the flag of federalist autonomy. In setting common standards of constitutional law and equal protection, it acts as a counterbalance to the political variety of the cantons.

The case of women's suffrage, however, was rather special. When introduced at the federal level in 1971, the amendment provided for a certain delay on the part of the cantons to allow them to adapt their own regulations. This was done for two reasons. First, the delay clause was likely to improve the chances of a successful popular vote on the federal amendment. Second, it symbolised the hope that the male majority in those cantons that still refused women's suffrage would change their minds more quickly if the federal authorities refrained from exerting pressure. This hope was fulfilled in several cantons, but not in Appenzell Innerrhoden, where the Federal Court finally had to decide on this substantive issue and also to declare that the transitional period, after almost 20 years, had finally run out.[40]

The belief of Swiss political culture that it is better to refrain both from coercive power and from direct confrontation between cantonal and federal authorities seems to be indestructible, at least among the political elite. It is significant that the women's suffrage case was brought to the Federal Court by a few 'ordinary women' who had the guts to resist threats of harassment when doing so. The Swiss political élite, on the other hand, was not very creative in finding means of helping the Appenzell Innerrhoden women. They even renounced symbolic politics. When it was the turn of an Appenzell Innerrhoden member of the Federal Council to become president in 1989, parliament could have said: we do not wish a representative of this canton to be the head of our state as long as it denies women's essential human rights. Nobody did. When it comes to its member-states, the federation speaks softly and does not carry a big stick. The reason in the above case is simple: federal intervention in the realm of the cantons' autonomy would have been felt as an offence by the Appenzell (male) voters to decide 'independently'. It would probably not have helped women getting their voting right sooner.

In a more general way the question of how to enforce and implement human or civil rights poses problems in every federal state. Its central authorities have to guarantee equal rights, but they also have to protect minority rights and the historic particularities of local cultures. If equalisation is a question of money, it poses no problems. Money is divisible, and economic equalisation can therefore be negotiated through compromises. This is not always so with the equalisation of human or constitutional rights. Politically, problems of ethical values are often perceived as binary questions. In the view of many people, there is either the right to have an abortion or there is not, and the death penalty is either constitutional or it is not. Because of the fundamental nature of these questions parliaments or high courts sometimes decide them constitutionally for the whole of society.

Is there in sub-national units a right to difference in the name of federalism? Given the perspective that human rights are fundamental and universal, there can be no tolerance for federal particularities which deny them. Federal states should then be forced to comply with the solution decided for all. But such solutions can evoke fundamental conflicts. If the ethical question is highly controversial, the conflict can threaten other values – social peace for instance. In federal systems it may therefore be prudent to avoid single solutions when the issue is very controversial. Moreover, if human rights are perceived as an historical product of economic, social and cultural development and not as God-given, there may be an argument for different solutions in federal states. Autonomous solutions for particular member-states may not only prevent conflicts, but also allow the development of the endogenous cultural patterns that are necessary to make human rights effective in daily life. According to the constitutionalist Walter Kälin, the Swiss Federal Court seems to have followed both lines: after an initial 'unifying' period, it has later tried to valuate not only the federal, but also the cantonal tradition of constitutional rights, allowing regional and particular solutions.[41]

2.5   Challenges

2.5.1   Federalism vs democracy: Why one citizen from Uri outweighs 34 citizens from Zurich, or to what extent is federalism compatible with democracy?

Chapter 1 argued that federalism was an important institutional mechanism in Swiss democracy for protecting minorities and dealing with cultural divisions. However this institutional arrangement implies a conflict between two principles of decision-making. Democracy insists on the equal representation of every individual, that is, one person one vote, whereas federalism guarantees equal representation to the member-states of a federation, that is, an equal vote for every state. If the two modes of decision-making are used to decide the same question, they can lead to different results. There can be a collision between the principles of democracy and those of federalism.[42] In Switzerland such collisions may happen not only in a parliamentary decision when

Table 2.4   Popular votes with different majorities between the people and the cantons

Issue	Year	People (per cent for)	Cantons For	Cantons Against
Federal measures and weights	1866	50.5	9.5	12.5
Proportional representation	1910	47.5	12.0	10.0
Protection for tenants	1955	50.2	7.0	15.0
Civil defence	1957	48.1	14.0	8.0
Federal finances	1970	55.4	9.0	13.0
Federal education	1973	52.8	10.5	11.5
Federal economic policy	1975	52.8	11.0	11.0
Federal energy policy	1983	50.9	11.0	12.0[1]
Cultural policy	1994	51.0	11.0	12.0
Naturalisation of foreigners	1994	52.8	10.0	13.0
Abuse of asylum right	2004	49.9	12.5	10.5

[1]Beginning in 1978, the Jura brought the number of counting votes of the cantons to 23.
Sources: Germann 1991: 266 and Linder 2005: 185.

the Council of the States and the National Council disagree, but also in a popular vote, when the majority of the cantons and the majority of the people may not coincide. Table 2.4 shows instances of the latter.

Most of these collisions are recent. The number of referenda on constitutional matters has considerably increased. Before World War II, we count about ten referenda per decade. In the period after, this number quadrupled to more than 40. Constitutional amendments, once an exception, have become the norm for the introduction of all substantial new activities by central government. This leads to a greater risk of collision between the democratic and the federalist majority.

Moreover the differences in population size between cantons have increased because of migration from rural to urban regions. This has had an effect when popular votations require a double majority. It increases the importance of the federal principle, while the weight of the democratic principle is reduced. Whereas in 1848 one person from the small canton Uri cancelled out 17 persons from the largest canton, Zurich, when the majority of the cantons was counted, today it is 34 persons. When the 11.5 smallest cantons vote together, they constitute a blocking federalist majority representing a tiny democratic minority. Theoretically the smallest federalist veto power (51 per cent of the votes in the smallest cantons against all the other votes) represents just 9 per cent of the Swiss population. This means that 9 per cent of the population could theoretically block democratic majorities of 91 per cent in all popular votations on constitutional amendments. In reality it would be unlikely to find a 51 per cent against in the small cantons and 100 per cent for in the large cantons. We can determine, however, the practical 'minimal veto power' from the votes in Table 2.4, where in eight out of 11 cases the cantonal majority blocked a democratic majority. This is done for the seven votations in the twentieth century, calculating the no-votes from the 11.5 smallest cantons as a percentage of all votes cast. We see that the practical veto power of the small cantons represents a democratic minority of just 20–25 per cent (see Table 2.5).

The above cases were important and controversial, and the veto power of the small cantons has further consequences. Political analyses show that the voting behaviour of the cantons on specific issues is relatively stable. One of the issues where small rural cantons vote differently from large urban cantons is foreign policy. When voting on a trade agreement with the EC (1972), on the first project for membership in the UN (1986), and on the Bretton Woods institutions (1992), the small cantons maintained classical attitudes of neutrality or autonomy and preferred non-

Table 2.5 Federalist against democratic rule: Practical veto power of small cantons in seven referenda

Year/issue	No-votes from 11.5 smallest cantons as percentage of all votes
1955, Protection of tenants	25.3
1970, Federal finances	24.0
1973, Federal education	21.7
1975, Federal economic policy	20.5
1983, Federal energy policy	20.0
1994, Cultural policy	19.5
1994, Naturalisation of foreigners	22.5

Sources: Germann 1991: 266 and Linder 2005: 185.

engagement in foreign policy, whereas the large cantons were more open to Swiss participation in international affairs and organisations. As political scientists had predicted,[43] this pattern also held in the votation on Swiss membership of the European Economic Area, where 50.3 per cent of the people and 19 cantons rejected the treaty. But a mere 30 per cent of all votes, coming from the small cantons, were enough to block a federalist vote in favour. For a 'yes' to the treaty, on the other hand, a very strong majority of 59 per cent of the people would have been necessary to reach a minimum majority of 12 cantons. The same pattern – but this time with a positive result – was seen at the second referendum on UN membership in 2002: 54.6 per cent said yes to the UN, and this vote produced the smallest possible majority of 12 cantons. It is evident, therefore, that substantial decisions in foreign policy – as joining the EU for instance – will meet a particular difficulty when it comes to the popular vote. If such a decision is a constitutional matter, a simple majority of the people will not suffice. A rather strong preference of 55–60 per cent of the people will be necessary to achieve the compound democratic and federalist majority required.

To what extent is it justified that a small minority can overrule the democratic majority? 'Do not mix up two different things', would say protagonists from small cantons. To protect minorities against democratic majorities is the very aim and legitimacy of federalism. If you accept its principle of 'one state, one vote', you have to accept a federalist majority no matter how small a part it may be of the democratic electorate. 'Of course, minority rights are important', others might say. They might object, however, that a federalism weighing the votes of some persons 34 times more heavily than those of others is denying democracy and its principle of 'one person, one vote'.

Theoretically every federal democracy is faced with this problem. There is a contradiction, and a trade-off, between the principle of equal rights of the member states and that of 'one person, one vote'. It is not possible to find a general answer to the question of to what extent federalism may legitimately be allowed to outweigh democracy. Different solutions depend on a country's historical situation, and on the importance a federation gives to minority rights or to the autonomy of its member states. The collision between democratic and federalist majority rule may be settled more easily in bicameral parliamentary decisions, where there are ways of negotiating between the two chambers, than in popular votations which lack this possibility. Some countries may not be worried by and therefore not become aware of the problem of the collision between federalism and democracy. In the US the difference between the smallest and the largest states can reach a ratio of 1 to 50 or more. But small states such as Alaska, Wyoming, Vermont and Delaware do not often form themselves into a coalition in the way it is done in Switzerland.

There is, however, an important lesson to be drawn from the Swiss example. Because of migration among cantons the weight of the principle of federalism has increased in comparison with democratic majority rule. One could argue that this is against the logic of Swiss history, because the classical federal cleavages of religion and language have reduced during the past 100 years. Why not therefore reassess the relative importance of federalism and democracy? Why not go back to the equilibrium, for instance, of 1848?

Theoretically, many solutions are possible. One could redistribute the seats in the Council of States. Given the increasing difference in the population size of cantons, one could modify their equal representation, for instance, giving large cantons three seats, the middle-sized cantons two seats and the small cantons one seat. The majority of the cantons in a popular votation could be calculated in a similar way. Or one could imagine rules for a division of power that would allow the federation to undertake new activities without amending the constitution in every single case. Some such attempts have been made, but their failure was to be expected. Changing the rules of federalism is a game to be played under the existing rules of federalism, and there is no reason for minorities to renounce their long-held minority rights of over-representation when asked to do so.

Constitutional building of federalism has to be considered carefully. A simple democratic majority may grant over-representation to its small units. But the institutionalisation of such rights is a one-way street.

Federal minority rights, once introduced, cannot be revoked by the simple democratic majority.

2.5.2 Urban regions – The lost dimension in Swiss federalism

Urbanisation in Switzerland follows the same pattern as in other countries. It crystallises around historic centres, once complete microcosms where the same people were working, shopping, lodging and spending their leisure time. With the development of public transport and motoring, the 'complete' historic city has been torn apart, its centre attracts the service industry, and the more services concentrate in the centre, the more they can specialise and the more they attract people from far distances to use them. The service industry is able to pay higher rents than residents. Land prices rise. Residents are driven out. They may still work in the city, now a central business district, but they have to find an apartment in the suburbs. Old industrial plants, too, move out of the city into its surrounding areas. Consumers buy their commodities in shopping centres built close to motorways. Traffic grows faster than anything else. Urban people become commuters. Part of their growing income and leisure time has to be spent on longer daily travel between workplace, shopping and recreation areas and home. The old city is transformed into an urban region, or an agglomeration, as it is called in Switzerland, which overruns traditional communal boundaries and is composed of a central city with perhaps 30 or more peripherical communes.

Swiss urban areas, or agglomerations, may be smaller than those in other countries, but according to official statistics about 70 per cent of the Swiss population live in them. However, there is no political organisation for the common needs of their inhabitants. For military matters, there is the federation. For hospitals, there are cantons, and for sports facilities the communes are responsible. When it comes to the infrastructure of agglomerations however, there is no common authority. Other ways have to be found to finance and run public facilities of common interest. For public transport systems several organisations may work together: federal railways, private railways, buses run by the postal services and communal tramways or buses. In some agglomerations this kind of cooperation works well. In others it fails because every single suburban commune may exercise a kind of a veto on most issues.[44]

The balance between the quality of life in cities and suburbs has been disturbed. Central cities are worried about the concentration of pollution and noise, and about the runaway cost of public services such as theaters and schools, which are supported by city taxpayers alone even though the whole region uses them. Through social migration and segmentation the poor concentrate in the cities, whereas rich taxpayers – including firms – move out to suburban residential areas. In the last 30 years the idea that wealthy cities are the motors of their surrounding urban areas has changed considerably. Scholars differ in their assessments of the extent to which central cities are losing out economically to suburban communes. There is evidence, however, that in today's urbanisation process Swiss cities are living through a difficult period. They are hampered in their development and are running out of planning options that do not extend into surrounding communes. They risk being overrun by barely controllable commuter traffic. Some of them are becoming increasingly indebted, despite levying higher tax rates than apply in suburbia. No wonder political tensions between central cities and the surrounding communes are growing. Moreover, we see a revival of historical conflicts between the urban and the rural. Rural and urban societies seem to be faced with different problems. They develop different preferences in lifestyles and politics.

Should there be a kind of a metropolitan authority for all shared services and public goods in urban areas? There is a strong theoretical argument for it in the idea that electoral and fiscal responsibility for a public good should coincide with those who benefit from it. Yet metropolitan-area governments who decide on all public goods, from transport systems and area planning to health services, are rare in Europe. Instead of one political authority we find a multitude of special agencies, each dealing with one particular metropolitan service. In Switzerland the idea of a political statute for agglomerations runs counter to the tradition of local autonomy. One could argue that the country does not need a fourth tier in a federal system that is already too complex. But the problem remains. European urbanisation is transgressing national boundaries and pushing for larger dimensions. These pressures will probably help the Swiss to find their own solution.[45] So far, the inauguration of a 'Tripartite Agglomeration Conference' is an interesting innovation because it brings all three federal levels together in order to deliberate common problems. A stronger institution-building could follow two courses. Either the cantons and communes will see a revitalisation of historical districts,[46] with the advantage that the old geographical patterns of common political culture will be able to be utilised. Or consolidation of urban government will be achieved by the statutory creation of a special region. Urban regions can be designed to cover effectively the common geographic range of public goods. Yet people may consider them artificial because their boundaries do not represent patterns of common political culture or reflect a sense of political community. If both ways are unsatisfactory, a third option may be considered. It consists of a flexible organisation in which just those communes cooperate who are willing to share part of their facilities and public services. Prices for common public services are higher for non-members than for members. Thus the organisation helps to keep eventual benefits of cooperation among members and creates incentives for initial non-members to become members.[47]

2.5.3 The external challenge: Federalism in a period of globalisation

The last decades have been characterised by a rapid liberalisation and globalisation of national economies. Some Swiss industries – like agriculture or small trade – came under great pressure because the opening of the markets meant the end of national tariff and non-tariff boundaries that before had protected them from international competition. For the export industry, however, internationalisation was nothing new. Swiss banks, Nestlé, and the chemical and pharmaceutical products of Roche or Novartis are known on all continents. While political neutrality and stability have attracted investors and finance capital to Switzerland, the international firms have invested all over the world, and a great part of their working places are located at production sites and services centres abroad. To give the proportions: According to official statistics, in 2007 employment in Switzerland was numbered 4.8 million, among them 1.2 million foreign workers. In the same year, Swiss enterprises employed 2.3 million people abroad. Foreign trade amounted to 49 per cent of the national product, which is higher than in most other industrial nations. No wonder that Swiss export industries welcome globalisation which gives them wider options and new market chances.

Yet globalisation is more than an economic process. It has become profoundly political. For many problems the nation-state has become too small. International or supranational organisations are taking part in the political functions and responsibilities that once were the domain of the nation-state. The political dynamics of globalisation had deep consequences for Switzerland. First, it put into question the traditional foreign policy, which consisted of active participation in international economic affairs but saw neutrality as the guiding principle and refrained from engaging in international conflict. In the 1990s, the Swiss government redefined the idea of neutrality, allowing a more active foreign policy and engagement in international affairs.[48] This prepared the steps to become a member of NATO's Partnership for Peace and later of the UN. Second, the pronounced liberalisation policy of WTO made it impossible to continue Switzerland's double-faced economic policy: protecting the domestic branches of industry from international competition while fostering liberal world trade for its export industry. Third and most important: despite the fact that the Swiss people in 1992 had refused the proposed treaty with the EU, which would have offered comprehensive access to the single market, Switzerland is in a process of constant 'Europeanisation'. Because of their intense economic relations, Switzerland and the EU have concluded a series of bilateral treaties. Forced by circumstances, Switzerland adapts most of its economic regulations to EU standards. Thus, without being a member, Switzerland is in fact 'Europeanised' without being a member of the EU. The question is: How do globalisation and 'Europeanisation' affect federalism? Does Switzerland, in a process of international centralisation and harmonisation, have a chance to keep its national federalism and decentralised governance? To answer these questions, let us discuss some challenges resulting from pressure from the outside.[49]

A first challenge is a different rhythm of decision-making. One of the characteristics of the European integration process is its rapid evolution, and the great scope of many of Brussel's decisions. This is in contrast to Swiss policy-making, where federalism and direct democracy require time and allow for marginal innovation only. Moreover, as EU regulations and other international treaties can affect also cantonal responsibilities, cantonal governments have made much pressure for more participation in the federal government's foreign policy process. As a result, it is difficult for the Swiss government to formulate a foresighted and proactive policy. This makes Switzerland, as a lone standing and small country, more vulnerable, as can be illustrated by the example of the Swiss banking secret and fiscal law. For a long time, Swiss fiscal law gave authorities less instruments for investigating and prosecuting fiscal fraud than law in other countries. This was one of the points that made Swiss banks attractive for foreign assets, but in the past this was often criticised by other governments who feared tax evasion. In the G-20 London summit of 2009 where the global financial crisis was discussed, 20 strong countries were determined to tolerate tax havens not any longer. The perspective of losing a part of the banking secret was a big bang for the Swiss government and the banks as well. Both were not prepared to such an event. Ten years ago, the bourgeois majority in parliament had not listened to the warnings of the political left that proposed to look for alternatives to the banking secret, and they were astonished to lose part of national sovereignty in the matter of fiscal law.

A second challenge is the overruling of federalism. The majority of the Swiss people, for the moment, do not want to join the EU. But Switzerland cannot afford to cut itself off from the common market and have different economic regulations. Export industries and consumer organisations therefore push for the opening and the liberalisation of the Swiss market. The Swiss government therefore 'autonomously' adopts many EU regulations and looks for 'EU-compatibility' of new domestic regulations. Contrarily to proactive policy, in which we observe weaknesses, the Swiss government is quick and alert in reactive adaptation. Some say that the Swiss government is adopting more EU standards than many of the EU members. How is this possible? Political analyses see two reasons. Firstly, pressure from the outside can go hand in hand with part of the domestic interests. As already mentioned, many Swiss industries are interested in liberalisation and open markets. Pressure from the outside and from the EU is 'instrumentalised' by a strong coalition of government and part of the economy.[50] This coalition, secondly, legitimates shortcuts in the political process, in which the government is given more competencies to decide. This can be illustrated by traffic regulations. Before 1997, dimensions and weights allowed for lorries were regulated by a formal law. When in 1990 the government wanted to increase weights to European standards, opponents feared an invasion of lorries crossing the Alps and launched a referendum. In 1997 the parliament revised the law, delegating the competencies for the adaptation of weights and dimensions to the Federal Council. Soon after the government made use of this competency for the first time and 'harmonised' some regulations according to EU standards. Under this regime, referenda are not possible any longer. Thus, globalisation leads to a change of the internal power balances and strengthens the executive. This can go at the cost of the parliament, of the people's rights – and of federalism as is illustrated by the following example. In 1999, education ministers from 29 states signed the 'Bologna treaty' for the harmonisation of higher education in Europe. The Swiss minister also signed the treaty, but without much consultation of parliament or the cantons. This was remarkable, as most universities in Switzerland are cantonal, and as education matters are one of the key domains of the cantons. The overruled cantons, formerly eager to defend their autonomy in particularities in educational matters, did not protest, and the reform was implemented quickly. The example shows that federalism is ruled out not only in a formal but also in a substantial way. With the harmonisation of the Bologna reform Swiss universities cannot profile themselves any longer with their cantonal or national particularities and offer an internationally standardised curriculum instead. University students wonder if the promise of having a Europe-wide recognised master degree will give them better job chances on the domestic market.

This leads to a more general effect of globalisation. Many branches, agriculture or crafts, for instance, see no future because with higher production costs they cannot compete in an internationally liberalised regime. These losers of globalisation are located primarily in rural regions. Cantonal regulations and regional policies cannot help them any longer: globalisation not only makes national but also cantonal boundaries obsolete. The cleavages between the urban and rural segments of the population, and between rural and urban cantons widen. Swiss federalism is facing new conflicts.

2.5.4 The internal challenge or: Why the Swiss want to preserve federalism

Globalisation and especially 'Europeanisation' can put traditional Swiss federalism at risk. But there are more challenges. Some traditional cantonal particularities that have lost their significance, for instance judicial procedures in civil and criminal law which have been abandoned and unified by federal law. While such incremental steps for unification sometimes pass without opposition, we notice a fundamental critique. It pretends that the Swiss cantons have become too small to effectively exercise their responsibilities. Indeed, a canton with a population of 30,000 inhabitants may not be capable of running a high-tech lab for food control or run a specialised hospital. Critics say that instead of having 26 cantons of different population size, it would be better to have only seven cantons, each of them having a size of about one million inhabitants. These new federal units could benefit from economies of scale and be able to offer a higher quality of public goods at cheaper prices. One could object, however, that one million inhabitants is still small for a federal unit, go further and make a seven million unitary system without cantons. But even then, it would be much smaller than the Federal State Bavaria, a neighbouring federal unit of Germany. Is Switzerland then too small anyway? We would say no because the managerial argument of the advantages of big size overlooks one essential point: the smallness of political units is not necessarily a disadvantage but can offer advantages too: less bureaucracy, better political integration and identification with the authorities, and better responsiveness to the preferences to the citizens. Let us take up the last point, illustrating the example of the Swiss public health system. Partly regulated by the federation, its infrastructure and service is organised by the cantons, and therefore of a different level of specialisation. Naturally, small cantons are restricted in their possibilities, and most sophistication is to be found in the big urban cantons with university centres. In the latter, not only public health expenditure per capita is higher but also health insurance paid by the individuals. But while explaining differences, there is another dimension than urbanisation to be found: experts speak of an east-west difference of expenditure, with St. Gallen or Appenzell at the low, Waadt or Geneva at the high end. Some interpret this as a difference of mentality: People in the west have a higher appreciation of medical services and use them more intensely than people in the east. Thus, a centralised health system would give less satisfaction to both parts: people in the east pay more and get more than they want, people in the west less.

Maybe the time will come when some cantons merge with others. But this can happen only as a bottom-up process. If you ask Swiss people how they feel about their canton, you get different answers. Some identify strongly with their canton despite critique, or are attached to its history and its natural beauty, others like the emblem of their canton on the car plate, which in traffic distinguishes them visibly from drivers of another canton. But most of the people would say that the federal government of 'Bern' is far away and an anonymous bureaucracy, and that they feel more comfortable with the canton whose service they use every day. These may be traditional feelings or pure intuitions, yet not unfounded. The Swiss strongly prefer decentralised governance, which brings the state closer to the people. Thus long the Swiss are willing to pay for it. In today's welfare state, decentralised governance has modern meanings, as we have illustrated by the example of public health: it is more responsive to the different values and preferences of different peoples. This is the meaning of the saying: 'federalism makes happy'.

3
Direct Democracy

3.1   Introduction: The vote to abolish the Swiss army

On 27 November, 1989 the *New York Times* reported the following news from Switzerland:

Swiss Reject Plan to Scrap Army

Geneva. Switzerland today voted to keep its army as the best way of maintaining its neutrality. An initiative to abolish the army was turned down by a margin of almost two to one. 'A majority of the states rejected it', a Government spokesman said. Only in Geneva and Jura did the majority vote in favour of the proposal. The initiative, forced by a petition signed by 111,300 citizens, set off a fierce national debate on the usefulness of an army in a small neutral country.

Readers of the *New York Times* may well have been stunned:

- How is it that a handful of citizens are able to challenge a federal government to such an extent as to propose such a revolutionary idea as the abolition of the army? And if the Swiss people can revolutionise their country at the ballot box, why is Switzerland's government a symbol of stability and its policy so conservative?
- Does direct democracy really have an impact on policy, as the message of the vote on the army implies, or is it just a kind of theatre while the political elite is holding the real power backstage?
- If – as described in Chapter 1 – direct democracy is part of an ancient cultural tradition, has it not become obsolete? Can demo-

cracy in a modern industrial society keep up with growing complexity if the most important decisions can be made by ordinary people?
– And if so, how does direct democracy work? Who participates, who does not, and how do voters react when confronted with difficult questions? What are the effects of direct democracy's on the politics of government and parliament?

In this chapter I shall try to answer some of these questions.

3.2 Institutions, historical development and meanings of direct democracy

3.2.1 Obligatory and optional referenda

'Referendum' in this context concerns a popular vote on parliamentary decisions, with the citizens having the last word: they decide whether a parliamentary proposal becomes law or is rejected. In Switzerland there are two types of referendum. First, all proposals for constitutional amendments and important international treaties are subject to an obligatory referendum. This requires a double majority of the Swiss people and the cantons, thus offering a kind of federal participation (see Chapter 2). The obligatory referendum is relatively frequent. Since Article 3 of the constitution leaves all powers to the cantons unless specifically delegated to the federation, the authorities have to propose an amendment for every major new responsibility undertaken by the federation. Second, most parliamentary acts and regulations are subject to an optional referendum. In such cases a parliamentary decision becomes law unless 50,000 citizens, within 100 days, demand the holding of a popular vote. If enough signatures are collected within the stipulated period a popular vote must be held, and a simple majority of the people decides whether the bill is approved or rejected, the wishes of the cantons being irrelevant. Since the obligatory referendum refers to constitutional amendments and the optional referendum to ordinary legislation, the two instruments are often distinguished as the 'constitutional' referendum and the 'legislative' referendum.[1]

At cantonal and local levels referenda occasionally go further. Some cantons hold an obligatory referendum for most laws and important acts, and referenda may be held for some financial decisions about investments for large-scale government projects.[2] Semi-direct democracy is, on the whole, more widely used in the Swiss-German cantons and communes.[3] In the French- and Italian-speaking parts of Switzerland the opportunities for popular referenda are more restricted, especially at the local level.[4]

Table 3.1 Types of referendum and popular initiative (federal level)

Type, year of introduction and of eventual revisions	Requirements for application	Description
Constitutional referendum (1848), membership to supranational organisations (1921, 1977)	None (obligatory)	In cases of revision of the constitution, in cases of amendments and, since 1977, in decisions concerning membership to supranational organisations. All obligatory referenda must win a double majority – more than 50 per cent of the votes nationwide and a majority of votes in a majority of cantons.
Legislative referendum (1874), referendum on international treaties (1921, 1977, 2003)	Optional: (50,000 signatures or proposition of 8 cantons)	Any law of the Federal Assembly and any important international treaty may be challenged. If a popular majority votes no, the law is nullified.
Abrogative referendum I (1949)	Optional: 50,000 signatures	'Urgent' laws become immediately valid but may be challenged by way of an optional referendum during the first year after enactment.
Abrogative referendum II (1949)	None (obligatory)	'Urgent' laws without constitutional base become immediately valid but have to be submitted to an obligatory vote within a year. They are abrogated if the law is not accepted by the double majority of the people and the cantons.
Popular initiative for constitutional amendments (1891)	100,000 signatures	Citizens' proposal for a constitutional amendment. Government and parliament propose to reject or endorse the popular initiative. It is accepted if it gets the majority of the people and the cantons.
Popular initiative for the total revision of the constitution (1848)	100,000	The proposal is submitted first to the people. If a popular majority agree, parliament is dissolved and an assembly is elected to draft a new constitution. The resulting document will then be submitted to a referendum, in which it must gain a double majority. This has only happened once, in 1935, by the so-called Frontist Movement and was rejected.

3.2.2 The popular initiative

One hundred thousand citizens can, by signing a formal proposition, demand a constitutional amendment as well as propose the alteration or removal of an existing provision. The proposition can be expressed in a precise amendment, or in general terms upon which the Federal Assembly can make a formal proposition. After deposition the initiative is discussed by the Federal Council and parliament, which then adopt formal positions on the proposed changes. This can involve drawing up an alternative proposition or, if the popular initiative is couched in general terms, formulating precise propositions. Initiatives and their eventual counterpropositions are then presented simultaneously to the popular vote. As with all constitutional changes, acceptance requires majorities of both the individual voters and the cantons.

Whereas at the federal level the popular initiative is restricted to constitutional matters, it can be used to propose ordinary laws and acts at the cantonal or local level. The cantons dispose of additional instruments of direct democracy. The process leading to popular votes, for instance the percentage of signatures required and the time allowed for their collection, varies markedly from canton to canton. One would imagine that the height of this hurdle would influence the use of the referendum and the popular initiative. However this is not the case. There is no statistical evidence to suggest that in cantons with high hurdles referenda or initiatives are used less than in cantons with low hurdles.[5]

3.2.3 Direct and semi-direct democracy: Historical origins and development

Swiss popular rights have resulted from cultural patterns and history, political struggles and coincidences. There are some myths about direct democracy. Its protagonists in the nineteenth century claimed that it was a revival of old democratic freedoms. In reality the Swiss confederation in medieval times had its landlords and familial oligarchies just as their neighbours had their nobility. The French Revolution ended the *ancien régime* and the privileges of old cantons over subject regions in Switzerland. Democracy was imposed by Napoleon, not invented in old Switzerland. Alfred Kölz, in his book on the history of the Swiss constitution, proves that democratic institutions were directly influenced by theorists of the French Revolution, but official history in the nineteenth century declared them to be of Swiss origin.[6] When in 1831 the progressive cantons began to establish democracy, it was under the slogan 'sovereignty of the people', and the constitutional framework provided for the division of power and the free election of representatives. But the representative system reminded the protagonists of democratisation too much of the old regime and its power elites. Thus democratic forces called for full democracy, lawmaking by the people and self-government. Whereas the holding of referenda would give the people direct control of parliament by ensuring they would have the last word on its decisions, the initiative would bring in the citizens' own ideas on lawmaking. The democratic forces were successful. The referendum and the initiative were introduced first in the cantons, and later in the federation, whose original 1848 constitution more resembled a parliamentary democracy. When the legislative referendum and the initiative for partial revision of the constitution were introduced at the federal level in 1874 and 1891, there was a second motive behind the calls for direct democracy: to prevent political and economic power being concentrated in the same hands. Karl Bürkli, a fervent democrat and union leader, wrote in 1869:

> Our law-makers, elected by the people, are incapable of making good laws for the working class, even if they make excellent laws for the bourgeois class. Why? Because the representative bodies, in their majority, consists of capitalists and their servants who are hostile to social progress. As slave-holders are incapable of making laws in the interests of slaves, capitalist-representatives are incapable of making laws in the interest of the workers. Representative democracy is not the form of government able to improve the living conditions of the working class and to resolve social problems.[7]

But unlike Karl Marx, who 20 years previously had demanded a revolutionary class struggle against the 'bourgeois' and their state, Bürkli put all his hopes in direct democracy as lawmaking by the people. If direct democracy is realised, he wrote, 'the people will find the right way to social freedom, because they feel themselves its daily sorrows and the need for change'.

From the very beginning this expansion of the people's right not only to elect its authorities but also to vote on certain issues led to another understanding of democracy. The model of representative democracy – as realised in the USA at that time – promotes the idea of an elected government and parliament who decide for the people. They are entitled to do so because they represent the people or its majority. Representative democracy, however, requires trust in the parliamentary elite, and trust that the will of parliament is consistent with the preferences of the majority of the people. Karl Bürkli, cited above, was not the only political leader distrusting the political elites. In the cantons, many bourgeois politicians, too, were unsatisfied with the politics of the cantonal governments and the parliaments. *Distrust in 'government for the people'* led to the different idea of *'government through the people'*, or 'self rule' in the name of the 'sovereignty of the people'.

The Swiss were aware that government through the people was not possible for every decision. However they wanted the people to participate in the most important ones. Democrats demanded both that the people should not be excluded from participation in the most important decisions, and that there should be agreement between the authorities and the people on all important issues. The constitutional system can be seen as a concept involving three types of procedure (see Table 3.2):

- The most important questions are constitutional. Here the people always participate through initiatives (proposing constitutional amendments to be voted upon) or through obligatory referenda (voting on all amendments proposed by parliament).
- Questions of secondary importance are those of ordinary laws and regulations, decided by parliament. Here citizens can intervene if they so wish: the optional referendum permits a challenge to be made to parliamentary decisions. But on the federal level it is not possible to propose an ordinary law by means of the initiative.
- Questions of less importance are those of simple regulations or government ordinances. They are left to the government, or sometimes to parliament.

Table 3.2 Conceptual scheme: Constitutional selection of direct democracy issues at the federal level

Issue	Legal form	Deliberating authority	Participation by the people
Most important	Constitutional amendment	Parliament	Initiative, referendum (obligatory)
Important	Ordinary legislation	Parliament	Referendum (optional)
Of less importance	Ordinance	Parliament executive	No participation

This constitutional order has three functions:

1. *Control of most important decisions by the people*: The above given constitutional order provides a selection system. As already mentioned, not
   all decisions are open to the people but the people always have the
   last word on the most important issues of constitutional policies, and
   they have an option to control the legislation on important issues.
   The underlying logic of this order is obvious. In the ideology of the
   'sovereignty of the people', the people's own decisions are seen as the
   'purest' form of democracy. 'Authentic' decisions by the people enjoy
   the highest legitimacy because they constitute 'self rule'.
2. *Semi-direct democracy*: Only part of all laws are challenged by the
   referendum, and ordinances of the government are not open to direct
   participation. Indeed, most decisions in Swiss politics are taken by the
   parliament and the executive as in any other representative system.
   That is why the Swiss system is referred to as a 'semi-direct democracy',[8] which means that the decision-making system is composed of
   elements of representative and direct democracy as well. The constitutional order tells us how this shall be done, indicating who has the
   last word on a political decision. To put it simply, we may say that for
   the most important issues it is always the people, for important issues
   it may be the people, and for all decisions of lesser importance it is the
   parliament or the executive who have the last word.
3. *Constitutional protection of the people's right to direct participation*: In
   countries which have 'plebiscites', it is the parliament or the president who call a referendum. France's General de Gaulle, for
   instance, endorsed his project to give independence to Algeria by a
   plebiscite in order to have more political support and legitimacy to
   this historical decision. The Swiss referendum is different. It is not
   the competency of the politicians to decide if the referendum is
   called but it is the constitution which says that all constitutional
   amendments have to be voted upon, and that every law must be
   open to an optional referendum. Sometimes, constitutional lawyers
   have different opinions if an issue must be regulated by a constitutional amendment or an ordinary law, but this discretionary power
   is marginal. Thus, the constitutional order provides an effective
   guarantee of the people's right to direct participation.

In the last hundred years much of the great enthusiasm for direct
democracy has disappeared. Many of the hopes put on the effects of
'people's lawmaking', as expressed by Bürkli in 1869, have been dashed
by the experiences of semi-direct democracy. The political left had

to learn that the people did not want political revolutions. But the same people refused many projects of the bourgeois majority. Direct democracy did not replace, rather complement parliamentary politics, but in a specific way: both the referendum and the popular initiative developed to become the most powerful instruments of the opposition and allow for protest against the political elite. This partly explains why popular rights have become so popular: in surveys they regularly show up as the most precious elements of Swiss democracy, even by those who may not take advantage of them.

3.3   A closer look at the referendum and the initiative

3.3.1   The issues

We remember the call of democratic forces for 'sovereignty of the people' when fighting for popular rights. They believed that no decision of great importance should be excluded from the influence of the people. This

Table 3.3   Some issues from federal votations, 1985–2005

Issue	Type	Year
UN-membership	CR	1986, 2002
Motherhood insurance	LR	1987, 1999
Protection of moor landscapes	I	1987
Forty-hour work week	I	1988
Raise motorway speed limit to 130 km/h	I	1989
Abolition of the army	I	1989
Moratorium to build new nuclear power plants	I	1990
Voting age 18	CR	1991
International Treaty of the European Economic Area (EEA)	CR	1992
Naturalisation for foreigners	CR	1994, 2004
New railways (transit trough the Alps)	LR	1992
Remuneration for members of parliament	LR	1992
Restrictions for persons living abroad to acquire real estate	LR	1995
Cuts in the unemployment insurance	LR	1996
New federal constitution	CR	1999
Dispensing of heroin to drug addicts	LR	1999
Bilateral treaties with the European Union	LR	2000, 2005
Abortion to go unpunished	LR	2002
Regulation on asylum abuse	I	2002
Lifelong detention of violent criminals	I	2004
Law about the research on embryonic stem cells	LR	2004
Statutory regulations for homosexual couples	LR	2005

I = Popular initiative
CR = Obligatory (constitutional) referendum
LR = Optional (legislative) referendum

historical expectation was probably too optimistic. But when looking at the list of federal votations in Table 3.3 we can say that there is practically no kind of issue that is not subject to referendum or initiative.

3.3.2 Direct democracy's role in political agenda-setting

Table 3.3 shows a wide variety of issues that have been put to popular vote, ranging from minor subsidies to the abolition of the army. We could certainly ask whether these should both be removed from a future list of votations – the first because it is of too little importance to rate a popular vote and the second because it is of too great importance. Yet this possibility would not be in accord with Swiss thinking. With the optional referendum and the popular initiative, it is left to the people, political parties and other organisations to decide what they consider to be a case worth putting to referendum or a popular initiative. Politicians complain about the overloading of direct democracy with minor issues, but they would not overtly deny the right of any group to place a 'bothersome' problem on the agenda if it successfully attracts the required number of signatures.

As regards popular initiatives, there is first a formal control by the Federal Chancellery and then by the Federal Council over whether or not the proposal is compatible with constitutional law, or with principles of international law. With the proposed abolition of the army, for example, some department officials claimed that the proposal was unconstitutional because it would make impossible the fundamental task of the Swiss federation to defend its independence and neutrality in times of war. The Federal Council, however, did not find it politically wise to follow this advice and preferred a democratic vote to be held on the issue – they were convinced that the people would vote the 'right' way.

A role of the Federal Assembly is to ensure that popular initiatives are in accordance with the principle of 'unity of matter'. This means that a popular initiative has to refrain from combining different questions in one proposal, so citizens can express their preference on a single issue at a time. If an initiative should contain more than one issue it has to be split up into separate initiatives that are voted upon individually. On the other hand the Federal Assembly is reluctant to exclude an initiative on the ground that it concerns questions that do not belong to the constitutional domain.[9] This has had two effects.

First, the Swiss constitution is much less a historical document to preserve the spirit of the founding generation than an open book to which every generation of people and parliament are authorised to propose amendments. The Swiss constitution, therefore, has become a rather unsystematic charter, a collection of important principles as well as of rather unimportant regulations. This was the reason why, in 1999, the constitution was totally revised, bringing in more coherence into the constitutional text. Even so, with new amendments, the constitution remains a living document, with new propositions brought in every year. It is the written evidence on the development of Swiss politics and policies – initiated mostly by the parliament but controlled by the people and the cantons.

Second, the fact that any question can be made into a political issue is an important feature of the popular initiative. The openness of the political agenda is an unresolved problem in theories of representative democracy because, by tacit arrangement, ruling political elites can agree to circumvent questions that would impair their re-election. Some scholars go as far as to say that the 'politics of non-issues' – that is, withholding 'bothersome' questions from the agenda – represents the core of a hidden power game. It limits democratic discussion to questions of conformity and suppresses issues disliked by the power élites.[10] Direct democracy may correct some of these imperfections. In fact, many issues – the abolition of the army, immigration policy, restrictions on genetic engineering, protection of the environment and so on – were brought forward by means of popular initiatives and sometimes against the firm convictions of almost all of the political elites. Though their direct success is limited, popular initiatives widen the horizon of what is politically conceivable. Government and parliament do not have complete control of political agenda-setting, and direct democracy enables decisions to be taken on questions which the political elite would prefer to remain 'non-issues'.

3.3.3 The use of referenda and initiatives

In the first decades of the Swiss federation, popular votes were rare. After World War II, which brought a constant expansion of the tasks and the expenditures of the federal state, the number of votations became much more frequent. Today, on four weekends per year, the Federal Council organises a ballot, and the people vote on up to about 12 issues. Table 3.4 shows the number of popular initiatives and referenda from 1848–2006.

The first section refers to constitutional amendments proposed by the Federal Assembly, subject of the obligatory referendum. About one quarter of the proposals were rejected, which reflects the rather sceptical attitude of the Swiss people towards giving the federal government new responsibilities.

Table 3.4 National referenda and popular initiatives, 1848–2006

Obligatory referenda	
Went to a vote	206
Accepted by the cantons and the people	153
Refused	53
Popular Initiative	
Proposals handed in	254
Withdrawn or lapsed	83
Pending in 2006	11
Initiatives proceeded to a vote	161
Initiatives accepted	15
Initiatives refused	146
Counterproposals proceeded to a vote	15
Counterproposals accepted	6
Counterproposals refused	9
Optional referenda	
Bills subject to referendum	2260
Challenges by referendum	184
Parliamentary bill successful	87
Challenge by referendum successful (Lawrefused)	73

Sources: Bundesamt für Statistik

The popular initiative is widely used, but it does not always lead to a votation. In a few cases the proposal had become invalid for practical or legal reasons. About one third of all popular initiatives are withdrawn, sometimes after successful negotiations with the authorities for a counterproposal. At less than 10 per cent, the success rate of popular initiatives in votations is rather low. Counter proposals by the Federal Assembly, mostly voted upon in direct confrontation with the initiative, have had a considerably higher success rate.

The optional referendum is the instrument challenging the 'ordinary' legislative activity of the Federal Assembly. Groups contesting a bill may fail to collect the required number of signatures within the 100-day limit, and from the statistics above, we see that only about 8 per cent of all bills passed by the Assembly are challenged by a referendum. If, however, the referendum threat turns into a real challenge, opponents of the bill have a 45 per cent chance of success.

From these statistics we can draw some preliminary conclusions. Constitutional policies of the Federal Assembly, which is mainly concerned with providing legal bases for new federal responsibilities, suffer frequent defeats, being rejected once in every four votations. On the other hand groups of citizens who wish to promote new federal activities by means of the popular initiative have even less chance. Their success rate is a mere 10 per cent. From a first glance at statistics on ordinary legislation we might think that the optional referendum is of comparatively low effect. In fact the reverse is true for two reasons. First, the 8 per cent of referenda cases typically represent important bills of a controversial nature and, if there is a vote, the chances of the opponents of the bill are high. Therefore the risk of the referendum is seen as important by federal authorities. Second, and as we shall discuss in the next chapter, the perceived omnipresent risk of a referendum being called leads the federal authorities to avoid the referendum trap by two means. An intensive preparliamentary consultation phase is undertaken to ascertain the degree of opposition by interest groups, and the legislative bill itself is considerably transformed by a compromise backed by a large coalition of interest groups and parties.

3.3.4 'Braking' referenda and 'innovating' initiatives – Two different devices of direct democracy

Our previous discussion shows that both initiatives and referenda in some ways 'correct' the policies of the government and parliament. Yet for the rest the two instruments of direct democracy have fundamentally different functions. The referendum, particularly the optional form, allows people to raise objections to proposals by the authorities. The popular initiative, however, is conceived as an active way of shaping constitutional legislation – in most cases against the explicit will of the government or parliament. From a citizen's point of view we could argue that the referendum has a 'braking' effect and the initiative an innovative one. Let us take a closer look at the distinction.

3.3.4.1   *The braking effect of the referendum*

Democrats – the faction of the radicals that fought for the introduction of the referendum in the nineteenth century – considered themselves 'progressive', and they saw the referendum as a tool to promote progressive politics with the help of the people. Yet things turned out differently. From the very start, in 1874, when the referendum was introduced, it was used by the Catholic conservative opposition to their own advantage and the projects of the radical liberal majority were shot down as if with a machine gun.[11]

The democratic forces had to learn a lesson important to many institution-builders: the consequences of institutional rearrangements are very hard to foresee. Decision-making devices are tools which can be used by other actors and for purposes other than those envisaged by their protagonists. In many cases only history can reveal the effects of institutional mechanisms.

If the referendum is used as a plebiscite to give the authorities' policy greater backing and legitimation, the government should have the power to define under what conditions and on which occasions it should be held. This happens to be the case with referenda in France. The president of the French republic organises a plebiscite when, confident that he has the backing of the popular majority on an important issue, the popular vote would help him to continue the general policy of his presidential mandate. Even then this procedure is not without risks, as De Gaulle learned in 1969, when the defeat of his proposal for regionalisation and reform of the senate forced him to resign.[12] Yet if plebiscites are unsuccessful, politicians find ways to do without them. When in 2005 the French and the Dutch people said No to the European Constitution, the EU authorities proposed similar steps to integration by way of the Lisbon Treaty, for which no plebiscites in the two countries mentioned above were held.[13]

Swiss politicians have the discretionary power neither to make an issue subject to a referendum nor to delete a votation from their list. As explained earlier, the constitution says which type of parliamentary decision is linked with which type of referendum. Parliament cannot circumvent referenda, even though for some decisions it may be particularly difficult to obtain a majority. New taxes, for example, are not very popular in any state. In parliamentary democracies political leaders impose them after elections in the hope that the people will have forgotten about such an unpopular decision by the next election. This is not possible in Swiss direct democracy, where the political authorities have to convince the people that higher taxes are necessary. Therefore, the obstacles for success are high, not only for amendments of the constitution where the double majority of the people and the cantons is required. In ordinary lawmaking, the parliament can never rule out that its decision will finally be challenged by a referendum launched by a political party, an interest group or by a spontaneous social movement able to collect 50,000 signatures. Parliament therefore is bound to be cautious in lawmaking. Finally it seems that negative majorities are easier to build up than coalitions of supportive majorities (Box 3.1).

For these reasons, the referendum is an instrument of the opposition and favours the *status quo*. For decades, the referendum was the favourite instrument of conservative-right forces fighting against new

Box 3.1 Difficulties of building up 'constructive majorities': The example of taxation in theory and practice

If the government needs more revenue it must theoretically encounter tax resistance from all citizens. However, it may propose a solution that gets a majority of rational voters, for instance reducing the tax burden for a majority of modest-income households by a small amount and raising taxes for the smaller group with higher incomes. By doing so the government may expect a political majority for its project of a net fiscal gain. These hopes may be dashed for two main reasons. Firstly, the proposed solution may have an impact on participation behaviour: higher-income classes, highly affected by and opposed to the bill, may mobilise and participate more in the vote than people with modest income. Moreover, the government cannot be sure that the class with a modest income will vote for the bill offering them only a small gain: voters of lower social or economic status sometimes do not vote according to their actual status, but according to the status to which they aspire. So they may vote no, as if they belonged to a higher-income class. Secondly, opponents may bring up the argument of 'federalism', stating that new taxes are much more important on the cantonal than on the federal level. The 'federalist' argument is strong because in many issues it is able to divide the entire electorate.

Thus the government will end up with a coalition of three groups voting against the bill, but for different reasons:

- higher income groups affected by higher taxes;
- lower-income groups voting as if they are of higher-income status;
- all income groups preferring cantonal taxes.

On the supporting side the government may expect one group only: lower-income groups preferring federal taxes. The supporting side thus may be smaller than expected and may therefore lose against a heterogeneous opposition.

In practice, the federal authorities were able to raise revenue in the past but seemed to be aware of theoretical difficulties as mentioned above. Consumer taxes, disliked by most households, are lower than in other countries, and federal revenue relies much more on income than on consumer taxes. Progression of income tax is high – a minority of people with high income contribute much more to federal revenue than all other households. The regime on federal income taxes is always limited in time – after a decade or so, the people vote again on it. Finally, a good part of federal revenue is paid back to the cantons in the form of transfers. All these reasons may have helped to build 'constructive majorities' on a difficult issue.

competencies of the federation and the development of the welfare state. In the last 20 years, however, it has been the political left which successfully used the referendum against conservative-right propositions to cut social security programs or to liberalise working regulations. This illustrates that the *status quo* bias of the referendum is of a systemic nature and can be used against any innovation from any side. The referendum appears to be a versatile vessel, comparable to a sailing ship propelled by the wind of popularity, no matter from which direction that wind blows. But there is no doubt about the rock the opposing crews on referenda ships are heading for: the defeat of a bill. And this means the maintenance of the *status quo*.

We now see the direct effect of the referendum on the political process. Its *status quo* bias makes 'big innovation' unlikely. Political elites must anticipate the risk of defeat in a future referendum and are therefore bound to incremental progress. For every political project they have to look for an oversized coalition that overcomes the veto power of the eventual opposition in the popular vote.

This leads us to a second, indirect effect. The referendum has profoundly changed the Swiss way of political decision-making. When, at the end of the nineteenth century, the radical majority realised it could be overcome by a 'destructive' conservative minority via the referendum, it changed its policy of pure majority rule in government, allocating one of the seven seats of the Federal Council to a Catholic conservative. The majority thus began to seek political compromise with the minority, solutions that do not threaten the *status quo* of groups capable of challenging the bill. This is the integrative pressure of the referendum that transformed majoritarian politics to power-sharing – an institutional effect of direct democracy I will discuss in the next chapter.

Finally, the referendum and its *status quo* bias had important long-term effects on the development of the federal state. In comparison with other industrialised Western democracies, we note:

1. *The historically late development of the activities of Swiss central government,* especially in social policy. As every new federal responsibility must get the double majority of the people and the cantons, the obstacle is high. In fact, many proposals for amendments to the constitution were rejected by a first step and accepted only by a second attempt;
2. *The low (30) percentage of total public expenditure accounted for by central government and the small public sector,* which accounts for less than 40 per cent of Switzerland's GNP;

3. *The unique fact that amongst industrialised democracies Switzerland's central government is the only one which can rely on income tax only on a provisional and temporary legal basis;*
4. *A small bureaucracy.* Only one third of all Swiss administration and public service employees are working for the federation, most of them in the postal and rail services; public administration and public service employees in Switzerland count for only about 13 per cent of total employment;
5. Compared with other neutral states, a rather *discreet position in international affairs.* In 1992, the Swiss people and the cantons rejected to join the Treaty of the European Economic Area and is not likely to become a member of the EU in the next future. Switzerland was one of the last countries to join the UN – the first to do by a popular vote in 2002, however. One important reason for the sceptical attitude of Swiss voters in foreign affairs is neutrality. Neutrality is more than an elite's preference in foreign policy. It is part of the national identity, even a myth of the majority of the people that Switzerland should always stay neutral and not be committed too much on the international stage.

3.3.4.2 The innovating effect of the popular initiative

In contrast to the referendum, the popular initiative is a promoter of political innovation. Moreover: it promotes innovation against the will of the political elite. We have already discussed one such innovating effect: the initiative widens the political agenda and gives voice to problems that remain non-issues as far as the elites' policy is concerned. Yet agenda-setting does not mean gaining majority approval of a proposal. Statistics show that hopes of political change by means of the initiative are dashed in 90 per cent of cases that come to a vote. If the people are so sceptical towards grass-roots innovation, we have to ask why so many initiatives are handed in. Practice shows that the popular initiative may serve different objectives.

1. *Direct success against the authorities in the popular vote*: In parliament, the permanent coalition of the governmental parties may constantly pass the claims of the opposition parties. Thus, the popular initiative can be an instrument for the minority groups in parliament. They hope that their issue will be popular enough to find the majority in the votation – even against the mainstream of the political elite. For a long time, it was primarily the social democrats and trade unions

who used the initiative to compensate for the lack of support for social reform in parliament. They made the experience, however, that an initiative is a good instrument for political protest but less suited to realise their claims. For all initiatives seeking direct success, the degree of innovation must be modest. Typical examples were the introduction of a national holiday on 1st of August in 1993, or the protection of moor landscapes in 1987.

2. *Indirect success through negotiation with the authorities*: As already mentioned, direct success with the popular vote is rare. But defeat does not always leave proponents with nothing. Sometimes the federal authorities pick up ideas from the initiatives by drafting a counterproposal or simply by fitting them into a current legislative bill. This way the long shots of popular initiatives are transformed into proposals that are more in line with conventional wisdom and therefore stand a better chance of being accepted. At the heart of many important federal policies – from social security to the environment, or equal rights – we can find a popular initiative. In this way, ideas too innovative in the first step can sometimes be transformed into proposals that are acceptable to the majority. In the long run, these indirect effects of the initiative may be even more important than rare direct success.[14]

3. *Mobilisation of new issues and political tendencies*: The choice of radical groups may be different. They prefer agenda-setting and discussion of political taboos and non-issues, which is provided by the arena of a popular vote. They refuse to pay the price of negotiation and compromise. Therefore these groups draft 'long-shot' propositions, even if their chances in the vote seem to be minimal or even zero. The initiative on the abolition of the Swiss army is a good example. From the very beginning, its proponents were aware that they would not win a majority of the vote but used the four years' discussion to change political attitudes on the formerly taboo subject of Swiss military and peace politics, and with considerable success.

4. *Self-staging and mobilisation for electoral success*: Political parties and social movements use the popular initiative as a platform for electoral success. Popular initiatives not only create issues but also help to establish new political parties. This is typical of the way in which parts of the grass-roots movement of the 1970s put environmental issues onto the national agenda and finally established a new, national Green Party. The xenophobe movement regularly launched popular initiatives asking for restrictions on immigration. This served the small anti-immigration parties not only to

keep their pet issue on the political agenda but to survive for a long time.[15]

3.4 Participation in direct democracy

3.4.1 The deciding majority, or who are the people?

On the evening after a popular vote, the news readers on television and radio often say: 'The Sovereign of Switzerland has accepted (or rejected) the following propositions ...' The allusion to the 'Sovereign' is an old expression for the highest democratic organ or authority, but who or what is that? The expression 'direct democracy' implies that it is the people, or at least 51 per cent of them. We shall see that, in practice, it is far from this.

First, the number of people who are qualified to vote in Switzerland is about only 65 per cent of the total population. Those under the age of 18 and foreign residents, who make up more than 20 per cent of the population, are not allowed to vote. Then again not all those who do qualify take part in a vote – participation averages about 40 per cent. If voters are split roughly 50:50, the deciding majority may become rather small. Using the above figures, 100 per cent × 0.65 × 0.4 × 0.5 equals 13 per cent of the entire population. Figure 3.1 shows the deciding majority in federal votations as a percentage of the total Swiss population since 1880.

Figure 3.1 shows that during the long decades of male-only democracy, before women's suffrage was introduced in 1971, the deciding

Figure 3.1 Deciding majorities as a percentage of the total Swiss population in federal votations since 1880–2006

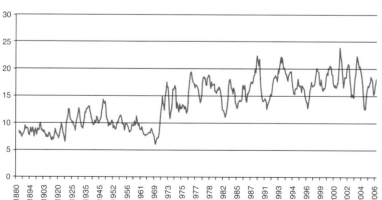

Sources: Bundesamt für Statistik (effective turnout), own calculations

majority of the 'Sovereign' was as low as 5–14 per cent. Since then, the deciding majority has varied between 11 and 24 per cent. Even so: the democratic majority never represents the majority of the population, and the 'will of the Sovereign' is the real vote of a minority. And, as we shall see, the participation of the different strata of citizens is far from being equal. One could argue, therefore, that a serious survey of 30,000 people would cost less and give even more accurate information on the true preferences of the people. This argument, however, misses the point. The sense of a votation is not the most precise reproduction of demoscopic opinions but the participation of active citizens in a collectively binding decision. This process of direct participation gives high democratic legitimation to the decision at stake, and this for several reasons. Firstly, the legitimating effect lies in the fact that all citizens are offered the chance to participate, and in that those who do so put time and effort into making up their minds and casting their votes. Secondly, a popular vote is regularly accompanied by intensive campaigns for and against the proposal, including controversial public meetings, party recommendations, lobbies slogans and extensive coverage in newspapers and other media. This process of public deliberation and decision-making may lead to changes in public opinion and individual preferences. It is a collective learning process. Thirdly, the collective decision is authentic: people are binding themselves with the consequences of their own decision, it is their own decisions, not the decisions of political elites imposed on them. Direct participation corresponds to the idea of 'self rule'. This all creates double legitimacy – for the concrete decision at stake and for the democratic institutions in general.

From a normative point of view one could still argue about two imperfections of direct democracy. First, what about the foreigners living in Switzerland who, despite paying taxes, are excluded from participation? Indeed, while a large part of the Swiss citizens would not be willing to change this rule, others call it an imperfect state of democracy. This reminds us that the concept of democracy continues to change. The entitlement to vote has evolved over time: once it was restricted to adult married men with some degree of wealth. This restriction was later abolished. While Switzerland may have been late in granting political rights to women, there is one canton that introduced political rights for foreigners as long ago as the nineteenth century: in the communes of the canton of Neuchatel, foreigners have participated in elections and votations since 1850.[16] The canton of Jura followed in 1977, but in other cantons many popular initiatives to introduce political rights to foreigners failed. Since

1992 Swiss citizens living abroad, counting for more than half a million, have the possibility to vote if they register. This illustrates that the historical process of the 'inclusion' of political rights is long but certainly not at its end yet. The second question is: does low participation not discredit direct democracy despite its procedural values? Should not a turnout of, say, 40 or 50 per cent be required, the result being invalidated if participation falls below that level – an idea that is applied in Italy for example? In order to answer this question, let us have a closer look at popular participation.

3.4.2   Regular voters, occasional participants and abstentionists

As shown in Figure 3.2, the level of participation in federal votations varies above and below an average of 45 per cent, depending on the attractiveness of the issue to be voted on. Controversial subjects of great importance to everybody attract the most voters, such as those to abolish the army, limit immigration, or amend the constitution in order to join the UN.

From Vox-Analyses, the regular surveys on Swiss votations, we can conclude that Swiss voters fall into three groups which differ in behaviour and general attitude towards voting.

- The first group, comprising about 30 per cent of citizens, virtually always votes. These 'duty-conscious citizens' interpret their political right to vote as being a citizen's duty as well.
- The second group of about 20 per cent, the 'abstainers', never parti-cipates at all. Different reasons can be found for such behaviour.

Figure 3.2   The participation of qualified voters in the ballots 1980–2004

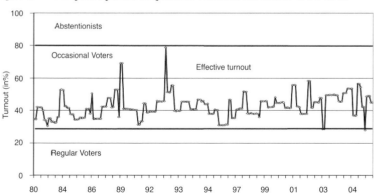

Source: Bundesamt für Statistik (effective turnout), VOX analyses, own calculations

Some are disillusioned; some feel incapable of dealing with the issues involved; others are simply not interested in politics.
– The third and largest group, some 50 per cent of the electorate, consists of occasional voters, participating *à la carte*. Their selective interest in politics according to the issues involved leads to the fluctuating participation rate of between 30 and 70 per cent. Occasional voters participate when they feel they are personally involved or when concrete advantages or disadvantages for them may be at stake.

The criticism is often made that the low level of participation, which occasionally can go down to 25 per cent, discredits direct democracy. However, proposals to introduce a minimum participation rate for the vote to be valid have been widely rejected by politicians and the public. Indeed such a measure would probably be more likely to punish and disappoint active voters than incite the inactive majority to take part in the vote. The strongest argument against minimal participation rate, however, is that it destroys the deliberative nature of a votation: While proponents have to argue with substantive arguments for the project, opponents can renounce on any argument by a simple call to boycott the vote. The opposition not only has better cards in the game but destroys it: if non-participation pays better than participation, the legitimation of direct democracy will be suffering.

We also have to recognise that participation in direct democracy is very demanding. Voters in Swiss democracy are supposed to vote on issues that are sometimes very complicated. To read the official documentation on four or five proposals can take several hours. Together with votations on cantonal and local affairs, a voter is supposed to give his or her preference on up to 20 or 30 issues a year. In none of these can he or she expect to have more than an infinitesimal chance of being the one who makes the outcome decisive. The cost of participation therefore outweighs the expected individual benefit, and following the logics of economic rational choice, the voter would stay at home. So if many deplore the low participation rates, it could be argued that a turnout of 30 or 40 per cent is surprisingly high. Thus there is no satisfactory criteria to judge whether 40 per cent participation is low or high. And we cannot say whether this participation rate is a bad or good sign for sound democracy and a mature civic culture.

However there are other reasons for worrying about low participation. As mentioned above, many of the abstainers are disappointed or feel unable to participate. Direct democracy does not provide guarantees against political frustration or alienation. More importantly, international research into participation reveals two common findings:

– the lower the overall participation, the greater the difference in voter turnout between higher and lower socioeconomic groups.
– the more demanding the form of participation, the greater the difference in voter turnout between higher and lower socioeconomic groups.

In Switzerland both factors come together. First, especially if participation is low, as in the example of the ballot in Table 3.5, the choir of Swiss direct democracy sings in upper or middle-class tones.[17] VOX analyses reveal that in such cases workers and lower-grade employees participate less than high-grade employees or independent professionals by a factor of up to three. As in other countries, well-educated people with higher income are more likely to vote than their less-educated or working-class counterparts. Second, direct democracy is demanding. One should not underestimate the general capacity of ordinary citizens to understand the questions they are voting upon. But besides their personal motivation and political interest, also their capacity to understand the issue at stake varies. If the issues of the vote are complex, part of the citizens feel unable to cope with it. In sort of a self-censure, they refrain from voting. The second issue in Table 3.5, the referendum against a new law on enterprise taxes, for instance, was difficult to understand, because it involved many technicalities. And we notice that people with lower revenue and education participated considerably less, even though the first issue of the ballot was considered to be easy to decide.

Besides education and income, there are other socio-demographic characteristics that influence political participation: younger citizens, women, and non-married or divorced people participate less than their counterparts. Moreover, some political characteristics make a difference: people with no party affinity, with no confidence in the authorities participate less, and the most important single factor that determines participation is political interest.

From a normative perspective, however, the most important defect of direct democracy lies in the unequal participation of the social classes. Direct democracy, if its procedures and issues become too complex, turns out to be what I like to call 'middle-class democracy'. To avoid this, the conclusion is clear: Direct democracy must be simple in its procedures and in the formulation of issues proposed to the vote.

Table 3.5   Typical profile of a popular vote

Issues: a) Popular Initiative 'Against noise of military airplanes in tourist
          regions'
        b) Revision of Enterprise Tax Law
Overall voter turnout: 38.2 per cent
Turnout, depending on the following political and sociological characteristics:

Characteristics/Categories	Difference from average turnout (per cent)
Political Interest	
Very interested	+30
Quite Interested	+9
Not really interested	−21
Not at all interested	−31
Age	
18–29	−21
30–39	−9
40–49	+3
50–59	+7
60–69	+14
70+	+23
Education	
Compulsory School	−7
Vocational/Technical school	−8
High school	−1
Vocational school	+11
University	+14
Social Structure (household income in CHF)	
below 3000	−11
3000–5000	−2
5000–7000	+5
7000–9000	+5
more than 9000	+6
*Sex**	
Male	+3
Female	−3
Region	
German	−1
French	+9

*Gender is not significant, all other categories are highly significant at the 1% or
  0.1%-level.
Source: VOX-Analysis No. 95, Hans Hirter and Wolf Linder, 2008.

3.5   The people between knowledge, trust and propaganda

This section will address some key questions about direct democracy: Do citizens understand the issues they vote upon? What are their motives when saying yes or no to a proposal? What is the role of the political elites and their campaigns? And is it true that, given enough money and propaganda, any votation can be won? When discussing these questions, we can draw upon a fast growing number of scholarly studies of voting behaviour in Switzerland.[18]

3.5.1   Example of a vote: Should there be tougher restrictions on refugees seeking asylum in Switzerland?

In the 1980s, the number of refugees seeking asylum in Switzerland grew drastically from about 3000 per annum (1980) to more than 37,000 (1990), and federal and cantonal resources became overstrained. Many refugees had to wait for several years for a decision on whether they would be awarded refugee status. A negative decision meant expulsion, which was considered to be inhuman by many Swiss, who even tried to hide or protect refugees who faced expulsion. On the other hand there was a growing reluctance among a section of the population to allow the refugees to stay in Switzerland, in addition to the more than one million other foreigners. In 1985 the federal parliament passed a revised asylum law. It sought to process more rapidly the growing number of demands for asylum and to effect expulsions more efficiently.

The revision of the law was a compromise: right-wing and xeno-phobe forces were against encouraging a 'growing mass of refugees', who according to their view were mostly 'false asylum seekers' coming for economic reasons and not because of political persecution. These proposed severe measures to keep refugees out of the country and a simplification of the legal procedure. Refugee organisations, the greens and the political left, on the other hand, were opposed to changes in the liberal existing law and its procedure, which offered refugees many ways (and the time) in which to appeal against negative decisions on asylum. Parliament finally chose a middle way, restraining the pro-cedure for asylum, but leaving doors open to refugees according to the standards of international law and the humanitarian tradition of Swit-zerland. The revised law was not to the taste of Swiss refugee organ-isations, which, together with the greens and parts of the left, successfully launched a referendum challenge that was voted on 5 April, 1987. The challenge failed: 1,180,082 voted for the revised law and 572,339 voted against it, giving a majority of 67.4 per cent (see Box 3.2). It was not

Box 3.2   Tougher restrictions on refugees: Cleavages, motives, interests and voting behaviour

---

A. *Cleavages*

According to the VOX survey data,[19] voting behaviour first mirrored the strong divide between the right and the left, which was mobilised by the slogans of the political parties: voters with affinity to the People's Party (90 per cent), the radicals and liberals (88 per cent) and Christian democrats (70 per cent) massively supported the law. On the other hand, voters with affinity to the social democrats (41 per cent) the greens (37 per cent) and small left-wing parties (9 per cent) were clearly opposed to the policy of asylum restrictions. The ratio between voters of the political right and left was about 2:1. Note, however, that voters with no party affinity constitute a good majority of all voters. In the vote of April 1987, they supported the project by 72 per cent. In questions, such as the above where the traditional division between the right and left is decisive, the left has a chance to win only if it can sway voters with no party affinity.

Besides the right-left divide, the VOX survey revealed a social divide. There was higher support for tougher restrictions from lower social strata. Education, particularly, had a strong effect: the higher the level of education, the more liberal the attitude toward hosting refugees. Citizens with basic education massively supported the law (88 per cent), whereas voters with university education rejected restrictions (41 per cent).

B. *Motives and Interests*

From 1970 to 2008 the Swiss have voted almost 30 times on questions of immigration and asylum seekers. With a proportion of 23 per cent of foreigners among the resident population today, problems of integration and social conflict have persisted as one of the most salient and controversial political issues.[20] In the votes on immigration and refugees one can observe a similar pattern, which reflects the social tensions around the issue. In general, one can distinguish three main groups, all with different motives and interests:

– *Categorical opponents of growing immigration:* protagonists of restrictions on immigration and asylum seekers share a variety of motives that range from feeling the necessity to set limits on the proportion of the foreign population, wishing to protect

Box 3.2 Tougher restrictions on refugees: Cleavages, motives, interests and voting behaviour – *continued*

> traditional Swiss values, to overpopulation or the loss of Swiss identity. Unskilled Swiss workers feel disadvantaged by growing immigration of unqualified workforce, taxpayers are reluctant to accept refugees who cannot be integrated into the labour market.
> – *Categorical defenders of liberal immigration*: protagonists of free access of asylum seekers are mainly acting according to humanitarian and egalitarian beliefs, but they may have had different reasons: congruence with political ideologies of the left and the greens, or the fact that higher educated people had been less exposed to the negative effects of a high immigration flow.
> – *Pragmatists*: whereas the attitudes of categorical opponents and defenders rarely change and lead to a stable voting behaviour, pragmatists are more flexible. More than defending social values, the voting behaviour of the pragmatists depends on utilitarian considerations. In the vote on workforce immigration, pragmatists therefore can take the option of the liberals because as professionals they take advantage of foreign workers or new consumers. In questions of refugees, as in the referendum of 1987, however, they vote with the opponents of immigration because asylum seekers imply public expenditure with no immediate benefit. Pragmatic attitude is to be expected especially among occasional voters with no party affinity.

the first of several referenda on the refugee-problem, and others followed, which illustrates the salience of the problem up to our days.

The referendum case of restrictions on asylum seekers gives us some first insights on voters' behaviour. Firstly, we notice that the rationality of voting has different roots: social background and corresponding experience, ethic values or political beliefs can be important for some groups of voters, while others behave in more pragmatic ways. Political scientists, for a long time, had a controversy on the question if political behaviour depends on individually defined self-interest or on shared social values. Evidence from other studies on direct democracy confirms what is illustrated in our case: both models of behaviour, self-interest and shared social values up to solidarity, do exist. Secondly, the voters' behaviour is influenced by the voting campaign: to a certain degree they follow the recommendations and slogans of political parties or other actors, and they may change their mind. This brings us to the next point, the voting campaign.

3.5.2 Shaping opinions in a voting campaign: The actors

Citizens cast their votes individually and secretly, but they make up their minds during public discussions on the issue. Votations are preceded by intense political campaigns. Different actors provide information, try to convince, praise or denounce, to mobilise and attempt to lead the voter to say yes or no. Even the most complex issues must in the end result in a simple yes or no. Therefore, especially at the end of a campaign, the issue has to be treated as a simple message. Let us first consider the actors involved in a voting campaign, and then, in Section 3.5.3, evaluate their impact on voting behaviour.

Citizens and their predispositions: In the political asylum case many people would have had first-hand experience of the problem under discussion. They might have had a job where their colleagues or customers were foreigners. Many may have liked foreigners and refugees because they were good customers or were willing and cheap workers doing jobs the Swiss had refused. But, even if people liked foreigners for these reasons, they may have said that there were already too many of them in Switzerland. They may have felt like strangers themselves because their colleagues at work all come from the Balkans, Turkey or Algeria. They may have feared that their children would learn less in school because the majority of their classmates were foreigners speaking perhaps seven different languages but only rudimentary German, French or Italian. In this case, people have firm attitudes based on first-hand experience. If a popular vote on the issue comes up, they feel able to decide the question on the basis of their personal experience. The voting campaign may mobilise voters and confirm their own preference for a yes or no but does not change their minds because they are *predispositioned*. Yet there are other issues difficult to decide. Tax reforms, for instance, may be complex issues. In some cases even specialists are not able to predict their consequences. Voters cannot appreciate from their first-hand experience if the proposed reform will improve or worsen their own situation. They must rely on the information and recommendations of campaign actors they trust. In this case, the campaign becomes very important because the issue is *not predispositioned*. Arguments, recommendations by political parties, clues and slogans of propaganda are able to influence voters in the shaping of their opinion. The campaign, in such cases, may have a decisive effect on the outcome of the vote.

The Federal Council: The executive plays an important role. It decides the date and the issues of the ballots. The Federal Council provides the official information on the issues at stake. In a booklet sent to every voter, it describes each proposition, gives an account on the arguments of parliament and states its own recommendation for the vote. Part of the booklet is reserved to the position of the opponents. This, and the sober account on the issue may be two reasons why voters pay much attention to the Federal Council's booklet; it is one of the prime sources of information they consult when voting. Later, the Federal Council takes part in the campaign, promoting the position of the majority of parliament.

The political parties: Political parties strongly engage in the campaign. Popular votations are the opportunity to profile themselves, valuating the concrete issue against the background of their basic ideologies and programmes, the presumed interests of their voters and their affinity to interest groups. Thus, in their slogans and recommendations for the vote they often emphasise the basic cleavages such as left vs. right, urban vs. rural, ecology vs. economy in which they are permanently positioned to attract their clientele. The ways political parties engage in the campaign have fundamentally changed. In earlier times, local and cantonal party assemblies were at the centre of their opinion shaping and mobilisation. Today, political parties mostly rely on the media: Their politicians take part in media debates, try to have their positions published in the print media, use the internet, seek face-to-face communication in shopping areas, without forgetting about some of the old instruments of political propaganda: posters and newspaper ads.

Pressure groups: Vested interests of industry, employers organisations and labour unions, social movements and other non-governmental organisations have a direct interest in the outcome of the vote if one of their issues is at stake. Their means of campaigning vary to a great deal. Some of them, like labour unions or social movements, try primarily to mobilise their own members through their social networks. Others, like industries, launch public propaganda campaigns, sometimes with big money.

The media: Radio, television and print media strongly engage in the campaign. They explain and comment the issue, provide platforms to politicians and political parties and give background information. Not only do they investigate the people's opinions and air the views of government and its opponents, they also present their own view of the issue. There is a public service of radio and television in each linguistic region, and it is bound to observe a balance between pro and con. In earlier times a great number of newspapers were affiliated to specific parties and therefore represented their views. These newspapers have disappeared. Today the press has become as commercial as almost any other product, yet its positions are not 'neutral', rather they reflect the preference of editors or what is presumed to be the preferences of their readers. Since the beginning of the millennium, permanent internet homepages, websites, blogs and e-mail networks have become a new element of voting campaigns.

Producers of propaganda: Marketing agencies and public relations agencies are not independent actors in the process but offer their service to any actor willing to pay. This may be the organisation of an entire campaign for one side, or simple voting propaganda, which I define as information whose only objective is to forge the majority desired by those who pay for it. By its very nature, propaganda need not tell the whole truth, and sometimes it has little to do with the issue or nothing to do with the truth. Political advertisement in newspapers and on posters, propaganda flyers and pamphlets are dominated by slogans, photographs, graphics or cartoons. Their message is aimed at mobilising good or bad feelings, emotions and cues about the controversial issue. Campaigning has become highly professional, and short-term propaganda is not its only means. Today, actors with big interest and big money sometimes hire marketing agencies to launch long-term public relations campaigns. The first example dates back to the 1970s when, following a major scandal, the social democrats launched a popular initiative for tougher restrictions on banks. To counter this proposition, one of the big Swiss banks began a public relations campaign, regularly taking an entire page in many newspapers to describe banks activities and their importance to Switzerland's economy. Just occasionally there was a mention of the popular initiative. Four years later the banks had succeeded in positively changing their image. In the last months of the campaign on the initiative the banks deemed it unnecessary to run a propaganda campaign as the public relation campaign had achieved its objective. The initiative failed.

3.5.3 Are voters capable to decide on high policy? Theory and the Swiss experience

Democratic theory is profoundly divided on the question if ordinary citizens are capable of reasonably deciding on political issues. On one hand, adherents of elitist or representative models of democracy argue that the mass of the citizens are not qualified to decide about high politics. Therefore their influence should be restricted to elect those who decide for them. And Sartori, the Italian theorist, goes as far as to say that direct democracy 'would quickly and disastrously founder on the reefs of cognitive incompetence'.[21] Adherents of the model of participatory democracy, on the other hand, argue that direct democratic choice is not only desirable from a normative point of view but also feasible. It is not necessary that all citizens decide all questions fully informed and on a systematic appreciation of all arguments. If capacities and motivation are lacking to do so, they can resort to *simplifying strategies*. Using shortcuts and cues, they can delegate the search for information to others and take recommendations from authorities they trust to be competent.[22]

This notion of *simplifying strategies* is important and needs some explanation. Just as in daily life, when we are at the limits of our knowledge we begin to rely on trust. To drive a car safely we need some instructions on how to handle it, but we do not need to know how the engine works. Nobody knows precisely how all the complex components of a nuclear power plant work. It is designed, built and run by specialists who each trust in the professional knowledge of others. In politics, we can make similar observations. Parliamentary members specialise in some preferred fields, and an expert on social policy, for example, may rely on the advice of colleagues when it comes to a vote on fiscal policy. He then decides on cues or heuristics. And finally, the same mechanism, substituting trust for knowledge, works with voters. They rely on recommendations from other people who are supposed to know more about the tax or nuclear issues at stake. So we should not blame voters for knowing little about the subject of the vote; substituting trust in heuristics and cues from others for one's own knowledge is behaviour not specific to direct democracy.

As Swiss direct democracy, after more than a century, has not 'disastrously foundered on the reefs of cognitive incompetence', we may reject Sartori's proposition and concentrate on the question: to which degree do voters rely on a systematic appreciation of arguments or on cues, or use simplifying strategies?

Kriesi's extensive study on direct democracy,[23] using VOX-survey data from 148 votes between 1981 and 1999, provides interesting empirical evidence and insights. First of all, the voters' capacity should not be underestimated. In their majority, voters decide on a systematic evaluation of arguments. As expected, these are mainly the well informed, motivated voters. Moreover, voters decide on arguments if they have strong preferences for an issue, based on personal knowledge. In contrast, heuristic voting is prevalent among voters with weak opinions, ambivalent or ignorant of the issue at stake. The study shows that differences between systematic and heuristic voting are not absolute: Argument voting strongly relies on arguments provided by the political elites, and many arguments of the political elites do not differ very much from heuristics and cues. Yet voters seem to make intelligent use of heuristics; they do not take them mechanically but look at the context of the actors who provide them. In all, the study comes to the conclusion that voters do not correspond to the model of 'rational ignorance' provided by elitist theory, and that heuristic voting in general does not lead to irrational choices. These findings, though, depend on an essential other factor: the campaign and the quality of arguments offered by the political elites.

3.5.4   The role of the political parties and their campaign

Political parties play a crucial role for the outcome of the vote. In the ideal referendum case, when all of them support the project unanimously, success with the popular vote is practically guaranteed, and this is not surprising. The compromise proposed anticipates possible opposition, presents a *pareto optimal* solution in which nobody is losing compared to the *status quo* ante. Interest groups also back the proposition. Therefore, opposition in the campaign is weak and cannot propose a more attractive solution. This ideal situation, however, is relatively rare. More frequently, the political elites are split: one or more of the political parties defect and play the game of an *issue-specific opposition*. This may happen already during parliamentary proceedings, or later by decision of the political parties, which not always back the position of their own parliamentary faction. In all these cases the risk of defeat for the government increases considerably. In earlier times the center-right coalition, as a natural majority after all, was able to win two out of three votations against left-wing opposition.[24] With the People's Party seeking a stronger right-wing profile by way of issue-specific opposition, the center-right coalition is often split, which puts the government project at risk. If two parties leave the grand coalition, defeat of the governmental project is predictable with a high probability.

A great part of votations, however, are placed in between these highly predictable extremes of government's success or failure. In all these cases, two factors play an important role for the outcome of the vote: the composition of the party coalitions of government and opposition and, to a lesser degree, their campaigning.[25] The latter is astonishing, as campaign money comes largely from interest groups. Yet to make propaganda trustworthy, it must be embedded in the campaign strategies of the political parties. Moreover, the intensity of campaigns

– and the amount of money spent for propaganda – varies to a great degree, depending on the closeness of the vote expected by the elites.

In all these cases, the outcome of a popular vote is characterised by high uncertainty. The outcome of campaigns, as tennis matches between two equally strong players, cannot be predicted from the past. Models of scientific research are able to analyse outcomes *ex post* but cannot predict the outcome of upcoming votations, and this may even be beneficial for direct democracy. The main conclusions, however, are the following: Political elites, their coalition and campaign strategies play an important role for the outcome of a popular vote. Even so, they do not control direct democracy. The government coalition sometimes loses, and opposition success sometimes is a big surprise. Government and political parties have learned to live with it.

3.5.5   Can money and propaganda buy votes?

After a votation, the losing side often complain that the other side has won because it had more money to spend on propaganda. And indeed, it happens that the antipodes in a votation have different resources at hand: propaganda budgets of one side may exceed that of its opponents by a factor of 20. The question if money and propaganda can buy votes is therefore of practical importance. In an early study on the subject, Hertig found a strong statistical correlation between success and propaganda in all 41 federal votations between 1977 and 1981.[26] An even stronger correlation was found in 20 cases where the propaganda effort was very lopsided; that is, when the propaganda of one side dominated the other by a ratio of at least three to one. Predominant 'Yes'-propaganda won 12 out of 13 cases, whereas predominant 'No'-propaganda was successful in all of its seven cases. These statistical correlations, however, do not provide absolute proof that votes can be bought. It is possible that some votations could have been won without money being spent on propaganda, or that one-sided propaganda results from existing one-sided preferences. The study gave rise to a public debate. How much money should be allowed to be spent by a single actor on a campaign, and to which degree is it tolerable that one side may spend more than the other? Swiss law guarantees voters a constitutional right for fair conditions to express their undistorted preferences. Critics have argued that fair conditions of voting have become an illusion because of the influence of powerful private actors and unequal campaign budgets. Bourgeois parties, the main beneficiaries of campaign money, however, were hostile to any idea of regulating political propaganda as it exists in US states such as California and Colorado.[27]

The Hertig study was not the last word on the question. Further studies showed that the effect of propaganda was not the same for all issues: it was weaker with dispositioned issues, when voters were confronted with 'simple' questions such as abortion or speed limits which they can evaluate against the background of their own experience. Non-dispositioned issues,[28] containing complex questions, however, are like empty labels, on which propaganda can inscribe its clues because voters cannot decide on the basis of their personal experience.

In his study of 2009, Kriesi demonstrates that there is no simple equation between propaganda and success.[29] As already mentioned, the amount of propaganda money spent will depend on the expectations of the outcome. If a tight outcome is expected, more money is spent on the campaign, and in these cases money may indeed be the deciding factor. In other situations, propaganda is of less influence. Moreover, campaign money does not play the same role for the government and the opposition camps. In the hands of the latter, it is worth more. In the end, according to Kriesi, truth is in the middle: money buys votes neither ever nor never, but sometimes it can.

3.6   Conclusions

3.6.1   Semi-direct democracy – An exceptional system

The Swiss system is at odds with mainstream of political thought. It contradicts theories of representative democracy that consider the people's capacity too limited for reasonable direct choice. The Swiss case provides evidence that intensive political participation beyond the occasional election of a political elite is possible and, as a complement to the parliamentary process, can play an important role. It shows that a substantial proportion of the population are willing to discuss and express their preferences, even regarding the most complex political issues. And if there are shortcomings in the system of semi-direct democracy, Switzerland has neither suffered anarchy, as some have feared from the nineteenth century up to our days, nor has it experienced the political revolutions others dreamed of. Direct democracy and the complexity of modern society are not mutually exclusive. On the contrary, direct democracy is an important device for social learning processes which make people politically aware and able to deal with political complexity. The federation, the cantons and the communes fulfil their responsibilities and functions just as well as political authorities in other countries.

Moreover direct democracy has changed the political system. Use of the referendum was an important factor that has led to the institutional system of *Konkordanz* or consensus democracy. In the next chapter I will describe this historical process in which the referendum became an institutional constraint that induced cooperation among all major political parties and led to negotiated legislation and mutual adjustment among interest groups. In other words, power-sharing is an institutional arrangement to reduce the risks of defeat of government policies by the popular vote. These indirect effects of the referendum on the legislation process have become as important as those of direct votes.

3.6.2   Direct democracy between integration and polarisation

Does direct democracy polarise or integrate the people? There are good arguments for both views. On the one hand, direct choice is the final word in a political conflict. For a certain time all quarrels are ended. As a verdict, the popular vote is respected by the authorities. The Federal Council, if defeated in its proposition, would never say that the people's decision was wrong. On the other hand, the campaign before the vote heats up conflict. The articulation of social and economic antagonisms, sometimes in polemic and populist ways, are a reliable means of mobilising the voters.

An empirical study on direct democracy from 1874–2006 gives evidence if the political parties tried to mobilise or to attenuate the basic cleavages in Switzerland in every one of the 537 votations,[30] and how the cleavages were perceived by the participating citizenry. It reveals that in a historical perspective two of the cleavages – dealing with religion or language – have cooled out during the twentieth century also amongst citizens. As an astonishing result, however, we observe a rising polarisation of the citizenry on the cleavages of urban-rural and of labour-capital conflicts for the last four decades. Is this a conclusive proof that power-sharing by the political élites is in vain? I do not think so. One must imagine that the evolution of the cleavages is basically dependent on the conflict-laden modernisation processes of economy and society. Institutional politics can only fuel or attenuate them. In Switzerland's semi-direct democracy, the political elites are forced to seek compromise and thus generally attenuate basic societal cleavages. Popular votations, however, are the arena of issue-specific opposition, and political parties use this arena not only for attenuation but also for fuelling basic cleavages. Thus parliamentary and direct democracy represent two different arenas. This does not mean the clear distinction of a parliamentary arena of integration and a direct democracy arena of polarisation. But, political parties, regularly bringing up cleavages in their campaigns, string up the underlying conflict rather than attenuate it.

Thus the role of direct democracy in societal conflict is ambiguous. On the one hand, we find integration. The vanishing of the religious and the linguistic cleavages is evident, and it corresponds with the facts that political parties are trying to bridge these divides not only at the occasion of popular votes. On the other hand, in Swiss society there is evidence of raising cleavages between rural and urban regions, and between capital and labour. In these issues, the salience of basic societal conflicts is regularly emphasised. In the last decade, the People's party launched or bolstered a series of popular initiatives on unresolved immigration problems. One of them, the prohibition of constructing Muslim minarets, in 2009 even had success against all odds. Uneasy feelings with Muslim practices or even fear of Islamic fundamentalism were part of its success. The 300,000 Muslim community, however, had reasons to feel discriminated against. As in other cases, it was controversial whether or not the popular initiative violated constitutional or international law. The risk of direct democracy is twofold. One, the popular initiative can be exploited for electoral purposes, which is not new. But it makes a difference if this is done by a marginal or by a governmental party. In the latter case, this can be detrimental for the functioning of the governmental coalition. Two, initiatives can be discriminating against minorities, especially if they become part of a permanent electoral campaign. Thus, in dealing with social conflict in direct democracy, the political elites have a great responsibility for the quality of campaigns, which corresponds with the findings of Kriesi mentioned above. Direct democracy, in the twentieth century, was able to deal with salient conflicts, thanks to political parties that renounced populism. The hope is that this will last in the twenty-first century.[31]

3.6.3   The political culture of direct democracy – Particularities and limits

Some Swiss may criticise their politicians, parliament and the federal courts, the Federal Council, federalism or power-sharing. There is one thing, however, which almost nobody would criticise: the political rights of the people and the institutions of direct democracy. In surveys, direct democracy regularly shows up as the most precious element of the political institutions, and only small parts of the interviewees agree with the idea of restricting the referendum in favour of more parliamentary power. The fear that something of the people's right to the referendum or initiative may be lost if Switzerland enters the European Community is one of the most important obstacles for those Swiss authorities and parties who are advocating membership. For many

Swiss 'democracy' means 'direct democracy', and some find it even difficult to accept decisions of parliament or the Federal Council as truly democratic. Against the background of the high esteem of 'self rule' one would expect the Swiss to be particularly participative in economic and social life. An unbiased outside observer, however, would probably be astonished that the values of direct democracy have not had more impact on Swiss society beyond politics. He would find no evidence that Swiss schools are more participative than those in the Netherlands or Italy. Moreover, our observer might be stunned to realise that workers and employees in Switzerland have fewer formal rights of codetermination at the workplace than their colleagues in Germany and Sweden, despite the fact that Swiss employers and unions have been practising social partnership for more than 70 years.

We may conclude, therefore, that direct participation has had little influence on Swiss economic and societal life. Rather it is conceived as the specific Swiss culture of institutional democracy. With such a perspective, we can better understand the popularity of people's political rights. They are valued as self rule of the citizens, and as a control of the political elite. At the same time, direct democracy is considered to be one of the most important particularities distinguishing Switzerland from other countries.

4
Consensus Democracy: The Swiss System of Power-Sharing

4.1   The development of Swiss consensus democracy

In the earlier chapters, we have already mentioned some elements of power-sharing, consociational or consensus democracy which the Swiss call 'system of concordance'. Its two main characteristics are the following: First, the executive is composed of a grand coalition with the objectives to let participate all important political forces in governmental politics, and to share political responsibilities with all these forces. Secondly, decision-making in a grand coalition implies permanent negotiation and striving for compromise. Power-sharing or consensus democracy is not unique; forms of power-sharing can be found in countries as different as Belgium, the Netherlands, India or South Africa. Power-sharing democracy is a contrasting type to the predominant, Anglo-Saxon model of majoritarian democracy, in which the government is composed of a simple majority, holds all power and imposes its decisions to the minority. I shall come back to this topic in the last chapter. Here, I want to describe the Swiss power-sharing institutions, their development, their functioning, their strong points and weak spots. If you ask the Swiss today why they like power-sharing, a typical answer is: 'I find it fair that all languages, all regions and political parties are represented in the government. This is better for our country because Switzerland needs political compromise rather than majority decision.' History tells us, however, that in 1848 the Swiss constitution was partly conceived as a majoritarian democracy. For several decades it was one single party, the radicals, that held power in a majoritarian regime. The development of power-sharing institutions and practice came later. We can distinguish three factors that favoured the institutional conversion of the majoritarian regime into a power-sharing system. The first one is federalism. The small, mostly Catholic cantons had a veto position in federal decision-making right from the beginning. This forced the ruling radicals to make political compromises. The second one is the introduction of a proportional electoral system in 1918, which was the success of a coalition of Catholic conservatives and social democrats fighting the radical predominance. As a consequence, the radicals lost their majority in parliament, and the party system became fragmented in the following elections. The third and most important element is direct democracy. We have already mentioned that the referendum is a strong incentive, or even a constraint to cooperate in an oversized coalition because otherwise the risk of defeat in the popular vote is too high. This indirect, institutional effect of the referendum is as important as the direct effects in the votes.

4.1.1 The impacts of the referendum on the composition of the government

The reader is reminded of the period following the introduction of the optional referendum in 1874 (see Section 3.3.4.1), when the Catholic conservative minority used the device like a machine gun to shoot down important projects of the radical majority.[1] The latter could see no other possibility than to come to an arrangement with the opposition. To integrate the Catholic minority the radicals offered them a seat in the previously one-party government. The conservatives accepted and from thereon they had a voice in the Federal Council. But this also meant sharing political responsibility for the solutions proposed by the collegiate council. So, behind this 'amicable agreement' there was a coercive pressure to cooperate. The radicals saw their large majority in parliament becoming useless if referendum challenges by the Catholic minority were not curbed. On the other hand, the Catholic minority, who were unlikely to obtain a parliamentary majority, could win more through partial cooperation with federal government projects than they could through systematic opposition.

Concern for similar integration of all other important political forces led to wider power-sharing in the Federal Council. The Catholic conservatives negotiated to increase their number of seats. In 1928, the farmers and burghers, who ten years before had split off from the liberal radicals, were reintegrated with a seat in the government. In 1935, the social-democrats became the largest political force in the National Council. Some cities had left-wing majorities. Social-democratic claims for participation in the federal government, however, were turned down by the bourgeois parties because of the prevailing class struggle. In 1943, however, during the Second World War when political integration and unity were most needed, the socialists were given their first seat. In 1959, following a short period with no social-democrat participation, the 'Magic formula' was born. Until 2003 the Federal Council comprised two radicals, two Christian-democrats (formerly Catholic conservatives), two social-democrats and one member of the People's Party (formerly the Farmers and Burghers Party). After the 2003 elections, when the People's Party doubled their voting power in three consecutive elections, the PP got a second seat at the cost of the Christian democrats, which corresponded to the logic of 'arithmetic' power-sharing in the government.[2]

4.1.2 Impacts on the legislative process

Integrating the main political parties into a governmental coalition was important; co-optation gave the newly represented parties in government a feeling of being recognised as equal. Co-optation, however, was not a free lunch but a deal. The new members of the government coalition were expected to cooperate in parliament, supporting legislative compromises strong enough to have success in a referendum. This was not always the case, and the lack of appropriate procedures for parliamentary compromise led even to a crisis of the Swiss political system. In the period of worldwide economic depression in the 1930s, the bourgeois coalition not only came under pressure from the political left but also from their 'own' interest groups who challenged bills put forward in the federal chambers. Moreover, extremist forces, impressed by nazi and fascist propaganda in Germany and Italy, tried to undermine trust in democracy and parliamentary institutions. Their so-called 'Frontist Initiative', which proposed a new political order, was overwhelmingly rejected in a popular vote, but the legislative process became blocked by referenda challenges from all sides. The Swiss political authorities had to learn that the referendum could also be successfully used by relatively small groups, and that it was difficult to obtain a sufficient majority even with the support of interest groups and parties. In the years before the Second World War the Federal Assembly began to implement the 'urgency clause' of Article 89 of the constitution which authorises parliament to pass laws without a referendum when rapid decisions are required. Bypassing ordinary legislative pro-cedure in this way helped to overcome the economic crisis of the 1930s. Democratic movements, however, criticised the utilisation of the clause (Box 4.1).

After the Second World War the legislative process was modified. A popular initiative in 1949 successfully restricted the rules of the 'urgency

Box 4.1 Direct democracy in situations of urgency and times of war

Decision-making in direct democracy takes time, and its results can remain uncertain. How can the Swiss government cope with these difficulties in times of economic crisis or war, when rapid decision-making is necessary?

We have to distinguish between two different mechanisms.

First, there is an 'urgency clause' in the federal constitution. It authorises parliament, if immediate action is necessary, to *adopt laws (Dringliche Bundesgesetze) without a referendum*. After excessive use in the 1930s the urgency clause was revised twice. A first amendment introduced in 1939 restricted the terms of 'urgency' and required the absolute majority of both chambers, while a second amendment in 1949 provided for time limits on urgency ordinances. Under these rules, all urgency ordinances of the Federal Council today are limited in time. If a law remains valid for more than one year, it becomes subject to an 'abrogative referendum'. This means that the law has immediate effect after its adoption, but in cases of successful (optional) referenda, the law is abrogated after one year. The Federal Assembly can even adopt laws that are not compatible with the constitution. If this kind of urgent law remains valid for more than one year, it becomes subject to an obligatory referendum which also has an abrogative effect after one year. Since 1949, therefore, direct democracy is no longer bypassed by the urgency clause, merely suspended for one year.

The last period of frequent use of the urgency clause was in the early 1970s, when the Federal Assembly used urgency law to cope with economic and ecological problems. Criticism was made that the actual regulations still provide too much power to the Federal Assembly.[3] On the other hand it cannot be denied that legislation in direct democracy needs too much time if parliamentary decisions have to be made in urgent situations such as natural catastrophes or – as lately – worldwide financial crises. Today, article 185 of the constitution of 2000 explicitly allows the Federal Council to edict temporary ordinances in situations of imminent threats to internal or external security.

In addition to the urgency clause used by the Federal Assembly, the Swiss parliament had delegated or recognised an *emergency power of the Federal Council* in times of World Wars I and II. These 'full powers' – not mentioned in the constitution of 1874 but given to

Box 4.1   Direct democracy in situations of urgency and times of war – *continued*

the Federal Council in 1914 and 1939 – comprised all measures necessary to ensure the survival of the population, notably the food supply.
Using its 'full powers' during the Second World War, the Federal
Council issued some 1800 emergency ordinances, whereas the Federal
Assembly, in the same period from 1939 to 1945 adopted some
220 laws and ordinances. The emergency ordinances of the Federal
Council were subject to some control by parliament, but were not
subject to referenda. There is no doubt that the Federal Assembly and
the Federal Council would rely on the same procedures as in the past.

Sources: Jean-François Aubert, *Traité de droit constitutionnel suisse* (Neuchâtel:
Ides et Calendes, 1967/1982) nos 1122 sq; supplementary information from
the author.

procedure' (now Article 165 of the constitution). Moreover, the authorities developed mechanisms for a better integration of political parties,
interest groups and the cantons into the lawmaking process. A consultation procedure allows the latter to be consulted in the shaping of
economic legislation that affects them. However it is the authorities
who decide who is affected by a particular project, and the informal
right of being consulted does not mean that the authorities have to
accept the views of the interest groups.

The pre-parliamentary process has two major elements. First, the Federal Council, when confronted with the need for new legislation, nom-
inates a study group or a committee of experts, which evaluates the
necessity of and the various options on a new bill. The composition of
these committees is worth mentioning. Some of the members may simply
be experts, but most of them combine knowledge and power. The Federal
Council is concerned to appoint members who represent the standpoints
of the different groups affected by proposed legislation. Individual members may have a reputation as experts on an issue, but the composition of
the committee is made as representative as possible in order to cover all
positions that could prove divisive during later discussions on the issue.
Second, there is a consultation procedure whereby the department in
charge of the project, following completion of the report by the committee of experts, circulates the first draft of the bill to the cantons, the political parties and the relevant interest groups. Only after evaluation of the
responses from this procedure does the Federal Council decide whether

to further the project. If the decision is made to go ahead, it is then handed over to the federal chambers.

Both elements of the pre-parliamentary procedure have the same objectives: to reduce the risk of a referendum challenge, and, in the case of the obligatory constitutional referendum, to reduce the chances of failure in the popular vote.[4]

4.2   The system of power-sharing: Actors and the political process[5]

4.2.1   The actors and their functions

While in parliamentary democracies decision-making is concentrated on the parliamentary majority and its executive, the Swiss system of power-sharing is somewhat more complex: more actors are engaged in the decision-making process, and, with different functions, have considerable influence. These actors have to cooperate, and we would not find one sole centre of power. Figure 4.1 shows the main actors and illustrates the process of legislation as a 'policy cycle' in the system of power-sharing. Let us start with the actors.

The parliament: According to the ideas of the fathers of the constitution of 1848, the two chambers of parliament were the 'highest authority' of the federation. Indeed, the parliament, up to now, still has much power. Besides its main function of lawmaking, it elects the members of the Federal Council and the courts, supervises the administration, and can intervene in many ways. As there is no vote of confidence to bring down the government, parliament is independent to criticise the projects of the Federal Council or to reject them. Even so, the parliament has lost its institutional 'supremacy'. Its freedom of action is restricted by direct democracy, by the interest groups who intervene in the pre-parliamentary process, and by the Federal Council which largely controls the agenda of foreign policy.

Direct democracy: Direct democracy began to play an important role when the people's rights, originally restricted to the constitutional referendum, were extended to the mandatory referendum (1874) and the popular initiative (1891). In the previous chapter we have discussed their influence at large.

Interest groups: Their prime arena of influence is the pre-parliamentary procedure, which was institutionally formalised after World War II. Note that participation in expert committees and in pre-parliamentary consultation is open not only to economic interest groups but also to social organisations and the cantons. We have shown why they have more

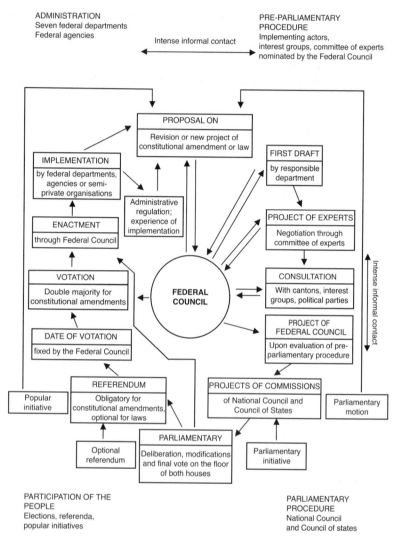

ADMINISTRATION
Seven federal departments
Federal agencies

Intense informal contact

PRE-PARLIAMENTARY
PROCEDURE
Implementing actors,
interest groups, committee of experts
nominated by the Federal Council

PROPOSAL ON

Revision or new project of
constitutional amendment or law

IMPLEMENTATION

by federal departments,
agencies or semi-
private organisations

FIRST DRAFT

by responsible
department

Administrative
regulation;
experience of
implementation

ENACTMENT

through Federal Council

PROJECT OF EXPERTS

Negotiation through
committee of experts

VOTATION

Double majority for
constitutional amendments

FEDERAL
COUNCIL

CONSULTATION

With cantons, interest
groups, political parties

DATE OF VOTATION

fixed by the Federal Council

PROJECT OF
FEDERAL COUNCIL

Upon evaluation of pre-
parliamentary procedure

Intense informal contact

REFERENDUM

Obligatory for
constitutional amendments,
optional for laws

Popular
initiative

PROJECTS OF COMMISSIONS

of National Council and
Council of States

Parliamentary
motion

Optional
referendum

PARLIAMENTARY

Deliberation, modifications
and final vote on the floor
of both houses

Parliamentary
initiative

PARTICIPATION OF THE
PEOPLE
Elections, referenda,
popular initiatives

PARLIAMENTARY
PROCEDURE
National Council
and Council of states

Figure 4.1 The legislation process: Actors and the policy cycle

influence than pre-parliamentary lobbying that can be found elsewhere:
the additional bargaining power of interest groups lies in the fact that
they can use the referendum threat as a pawn. Moreover, interest groups
play an important role in 'semi-private' or 'para-state' arrangements.
Social partnership between labour and capital, or public-private partnerships once played a predominant role with the design and the implemen-

tation of economic and social policies and are still important (see Box 4.2).

The federal administration: With the growth of the social and economic activities of the federation after the Second World War, the *Federal Administration* has acquired greater political influence for two reasons. First, it has its own experts, who often direct the pre-parliamentary process. Second, it has all the feedback knowledge of implementation, which often stimulates proposals for legislative reform and by this way can also define its own interests.

The Federal Council: The main function of the Federal Council is the steering of the entire political process. Giving the go-ahead for most formal steps of decision-making, setting priorities in substance and time, the Federal Council has a great influence on the political agenda. It disposes of all the professional resources of the administration, which allow it to prepare its own policy projects. Political leadership of the Federal Council is limited, however, for two main reasons: Consensus in an all-party government is limited, and parliament, not obliged to support the government because there is no vote of confidence, can always turn down the propositions of the Federal Council. In foreign policy, however, the formal leadership of the Federal Council is given for the institutional reason that it is in charge with all proceedings of international diplomacy.

4.2.2   The legislation process: The policy cycle

The policy cycle of Figure 4.1 shows all the phases of the legislation process. It is conceived as an ongoing process of political problem solving which starts with the first ideas for a new piece of legislation and provisionally ends with the implementation of the political program. At every stage of the process, negotiation and the appropriate decisions result in modifications, radical changes or even the abandonment of the project. If the new program enters the phase of implementation, this is not the end: sooner or later the experience of implementation will lead to propositions for a new reform, and a second round of the policy cycle begins.

The pre-parliamentary procedure: The cycle starts with propositions for a new law or a constitutional amendment. It can be handed in by ways of a popular initiative, a parliamentary motion, or by the administration which is the informal gateway for pressure groups seeking reform. If the Federal Council carries the proposition, it organises the pre-parliamentary stage of the process. According to the situation, it charges the administration or mandates an expert committee to draft a first project. As the committee experts are also representatives of interest groups, the committees give interest groups the first chance to announce their positions on the legislation in question. The actors declare under which conditions they would support or fight the bill. This leads to mutual adjustments, for instance between employers and trade unions on a social-security reform. The administration will defend its own views and interests but will also try to play a mediating role in conflicts not directly negotiable between antagonistic interests. The subsequent consultative process involves further organisations, who each try to formulate a position that represents the view of their members. When evaluating the results of the consultative procedure, the administration seeks to maintain only those reforms that have found sufficient support and to avoid leaving actors worse off than before. If the draft happens to fulfil these conditions the Federal Council has good reason to believe that the participating actors will support the constitutional amendment in the obligatory vote or refrain from an optional referendum in the much more frequent event of an ordinary legislative proposal. In the form of a 'Message of the Federal Council', the draft enters the parliamentary procedure.

The parliamentary procedure: Each project has to find the majority of both chambers. If proceedings in the Council of State and the National Council end up with a difference in substance, negotiation procedures between the chambers are organised to align on the same solution. If this is not possible, the project has failed. For a long time in the twentieth century, the Federal Chambers had the reputation of being a weak parliament, accepting too much the compromises found between the vested interests in the pre-parliamentary phase. Today, such an appreciation is certainly wrong. In the 1990s, Parliament has realised a substantial reform of its own organisation and procedures which led, among others, to a strengthening of its committees. These standing committees have become the centre of intense deliberation and negotiation. Empirical studies show that today parliament modifies the projects of the Federal Council much more than it did in earlier times.[6] Eventually, the Federal Chambers realise their own projects by means of a parliamentary initiative, which bypasses the pre-parliamentary process. As mentioned earlier, only about 8 per cent of law projects passed by parliament are challenged by an optional referendum. This means that the chambers seem to have a good flair for avoiding the referendum risk. This is due to several factors. The draft coming from the pre-parliamentary procedures has a story to tell: Parliament knows which issues were controversial and which were accepted unanimously, and they are familiar with the positions of the important interest groups and of the Federal Council. Part of the members of parliament have intense relations to interest groups whose points they support. The modifications of all phases of the procedure are documented for every article of the new bill. Thus, the members of parliament and the factions know all about the difficulties and fragilities of any compromise that has been reached, and about the robustness of a solution. Parliament's factions, too, try to avoid the risk of a referendum being called, and look for a compromise that is supported by as many parties as possible.

Direct participation of the people: Our description of referenda campaign in the previous chapter left one question open: how come that a seemingly well balanced law project gives rise to opposition, and that opponents take the chance of an optional referendum?[7] There are several answers to this question. First, the referendum may be called by a governmental party. As already mentioned, consensus amongst the four of them is not reached in all cases. One or in rare cases two parties articulate opposition in parliament, and the majority of parliament, not giving in to the claims of the opposition, takes the risk that its bill will be tested in a vote. Sometimes, the referendum is taken by a cantonal section of a political party despite the support of the governmental project by its faction in the federal parliament. This is because the political parties are as 'federal' as the political system, and deviant positions of cantonal sections cannot be impeded by the national party. In similar situations and ways the referendum is called by strong interest groups. Secondly, we observe that also small political parties or even grass-roots movements are able to launch a referendum, and in rare cases they may even be successful: In 1969, the students of the Swiss Federal Institute of Technology raised a referendum against a new law on their university – and won.[8] Even though success of a small party or of outsider groups is rare, the latter sometimes are able to mobilise a considerable part of the voters. This means that the compromise of the political elites is not always appreciated by the ordinary people. Thirdly, if the consensus of the political elites *is* fragile, a small outsider can initiate a chain reaction in which other actors or even a governmental party defect the compromise and join the referendum. This resembles the situation on a cargo ship, loaded with barrels barely fastened. If one of the barrels gets loose and rolls from one board side to the other, many barrels will follow, and the ship keels over. These cases are hard to predict. Even though the referendum cases make only 8 per cent of all legislation projects, sometimes they come as a surprise for the political elites.

The verdict of the people is binding and has immediate effect. In cases of referenda, the project is enacted or has failed. In cases of success of an amendment to the constitution, implementation may take more time if it needs implementation by means of a federal law, which has to pass a new policy cycle. This may be difficult, too, if the amendment is due to a popular initiative which was accepted against a majority of the political elite.

The Administration: Once a law project has passed the parliament's decision or got the majority in a popular vote, it comes into effect. The implementation is an important part of the policy cycle.[9] In many cases, policy programs for proper implementation have to be developed or revised. As most programs are implemented in cooperation with the cantons, negotiations with their administrations take place. It is one of the characteristics of federalism that the federal authorities have little means of coercion and thus have to respect the autonomy and the preferences of the cantonal authorities in the implementation process. Resistance from the cantons may impede implementation. Conversely, negotiation and compromises may lead to intense cooperation, which facilitates implementation of federal policies. Thus, we may speak of a form of vertical power-sharing.

Box 4.2   Social partnership and public-private partnerships – The second arenas of power-sharing

---

A. Social Partnership

In first decades of the twentieth century, industrial relations between labour and capital were characterised by class struggle, strikes and lock-outs. This ended on the eve of World War II, when the Federal Council urged leaders of employers and labour organisations of the mechanical-engineering industry to resolve their conflicts by ways of negotiation and cooperation, which would better help to overcome the economic crisis. This marked the beginning of a new era: The 'Labour Peace Convention' of 1937 proposed employers and unions to resolve all conflicts in their relations by negotiation and promised to renounce on strike and lock-outs. In the following decades, similar conventions were concluded in most other industries. Thus, industrial relations are characterised as 'Social partnership' (*Sozialpartnerschaft*), which led to a typical pattern of social policy. Social policy was developed on a contractual way by employers and unions and the circle of beneficiaries was restricted to the workforce in the industries. Both partners relied on the principle of 'subsidiarity': State intervention should be the exception, restricted to those problems which social partnership was unable to resolve. This pattern of a 'liberal welfare state' has gradually changed in the last decades. As elsewhere, globalisation reduced the bargaining power of the unions. As the contractual way became unfavourable for them, they changed their strategy and used the way of legislation. The passage from contract to the law transformed the Swiss state to a 'normal'

Box 4.2 Social partnership and public-private partnerships – The second arenas of power-sharing – *continued*

welfare state, more and more responsible for all sorts of social policy. The unions were successful because their strategy of legislation let all people, not only those working in the industries, benefit from welfare and defend its benefits also by popular votations.[10]

B. Public-Private Partnerships

Intensive cooperation between government and private actors is known in most highly industrialised democracies. It has a long tradition in Switzerland. As early as the end of the nineteenth century, private organisations, especially those in agriculture, fulfilled legal tasks for the federal government, which at the time lacked a professional administration of its own. It can be said that Swiss government at all levels sought to avoid building up a large professional administration. Whenever possible, government preferred to use private organisations or create semi-private (parastate) organisations to carry out public policies. The most important example was agriculture, which had dozens of parastate organisations that proposed and implemented production regulations and organised the pricing, distribution and marketing of most agricultural products.[11] The intensive cooperation between private organisations and the state is also known as 'neo-corporatism'. I doubt, however, if one can speak of neo-corporatism in the case of Switzerland. For other European countries the term denotes the tripartite arrangement of labour, capital and the state to regulate economic conflicts by concerted action. The Swiss case differs in many respects. First, there is no equilibrium of power between employers and unions. The latter are weaker. Second, concerted action does not happen because arrangements are decentralised and vary considerably from sector to sector. Third, arrangements between private actors and the state comprise also social, cultural or environmental policies and are not always tripartite. I would therefore prefer to speak of public-private partnership.

Lately, public-private partnerships have changed considerably. With liberalisation, former semi-public or parastate-organisations have disappeared or been privatised. This is particularly the case with agriculture, a domain where WTO-regulations forced Switzerland to abandon great parts of its traditional protectionism. While many public-private partnerships still exist or expand in new domains, liberalisation generally leads to a more restricted role of the public partner, and to the exposure of the partnership agency to market competition.[12]

4.3 The features of power-sharing

4.3.1 The main characteristics of political compromise:
No single winner takes all, everybody wins something

We have seen that the entire political process aims at the achievement of a political compromise. Instead of a majority that imposes its solution to a minority, we find mutual adjustment: No single winner takes all, everybody wins something. Some people attribute this behaviour to a specific preference of Swiss culture. Indeed, there are some studies that show such cultural differences: German economic elites, for instance, seek less compromise in conflict and use hierarchical power more than their Swiss counterparts.[13] From a political science perspective, however, the effect of institutions seems to be paramount. The referendum challenge, the strong influence of the cantons and the multiparty system are veto points that do not allow for majority decisions and compel political actors to cooperation and compromise. This means that every actor must renounce part of his expectations, which is not always easy (see Box 4.3).

Box 4.3 'No single winner takes all, everybody wins something': Conditions of good or poor compromise

Different politico-economic conjunctures
The idea that 'no single winner takes all, everybody wins something' has not always worked out. Mutual adjustments were most successful in the period leading up to the 1970s, when economic growth also allowed the distribution of more public goods. In the aftermath of the Second World War – an experience that unified the small country – many old antagonisms between party ideologies disappeared. Optional referenda were few and the success rate of obligatory referenda was high. Consensus became more difficult after the recession of the 1970s. With lower economic growth after the first oil crisis, there was less surplus to distribute. Political redistribution in social security and the health system became a zero-sum game, in which what one actor won the other lost. Ecological sustainability became a political issue and prompted new conflicts. The party system fragmented and new social movements arose. In conflicts over industrial and post-industrial values, and with the rise of neo-liberalism and neo-conservatism, part of the basic Swiss consensus melted away. At the

Box 4.3   'No single winner takes all, everybody wins something':
Conditions of good or poor compromise – *continued*

end of the 1980s, important legislation failed or remained incomplete. In the last two decades, globalisation functioned as pressure from the outside, leading to quicker and larger steps of political innovation, but also to higher polarisation, winners and losers of internationalisation, and the deepening of old cleavages.

Different issues
The feasibility of the idea 'no single winner takes all, everybody wins something', then, depends on the issue. As long as money is involved, and as long as there is money available, compromises can be easily reached. But conflicts can involve 'indivisable' topics. In 1977, the Federal Council proposed to introduce daylight saving as many Western European countries were doing at the time. Farmers refused to put their clocks one hour forward in the spring and then back again in the autumn, claiming that cows would give less milk. The typical Swiss compromise was not possible in this case: advancing the clock half an hour would have helped nobody. It was easy for the well-organised farmers to call for a referendum, and their challenge was successful. However, living on a 'time isle' in the centre of Europe did not prove to be very practical. Two years later, a new bill passed in parliament and the farmers gave in. Similarly, compromise can be most difficult, if an issue involves fundamental values such as abortion. Whether or not a woman should be given the right to have an abortion is considered by many people to be a question of principle. Contrary to the daylight saving issue, pragmatic experience would not change preferences because its interpretations can go both ways. In Switzerland reform of the abortion law led to several popular votations from both sides. Neither proponents of liberalisation nor opponents finding the *status quo* too liberal, however, could win a majority for their propositions. Even the federalist idea of letting the cantons decide was rejected: While liberals accepted that cantons would practice different solutions, the conservatives insisted that in no canton any liberalisation should be permitted. In other countries, such dead-locks are often solved when elections bring new majorities and a new government. Not so in Switzerland, where the government coalition rests the same. The deadlock lasted for more than 20 years before a solution was found. The example shows that mutual adjustment has its limits in Swiss politics too.

4.3.2 The technique of political compromise: Compensations that transform conflict from zero-sum to positive-sum games

Consensus, theoretically, requires a *pareto optimal* solution in which no actor is left with losses. As illustrated in Box 4.2, it can be difficult or even impossible to meet this condition. In times of general budget cuts, for instance, compromise must distribute losses, and one of the few possibilities to reach consensus is 'symmetry of sacrifices', in which each actor has the perception that the others agree to bear similar losses as he is willing to pay. But also under normal conditions, *pareto optimal* solutions are not always at hand. Similar to neighbours of airports or noisy main roads who sometimes are remunerated for their sacrifices in favour of others, actors in the political process receive compensation. Compensation is facilitated if the agenda of the issues to be negotiated is widened or the number of participants increased. The compromise reached under these circumstances may suffer from little effectiveness, though, if it violates the economist Tinbergen's rule, stating that one means allows to achieve just one end.

4.3.3 Cooperation, trust and deliberative learning processes

Game theory shows that in a single game self-interested actors defect from cooperation if this offers the chance of an extra profit. This risk is considerably reduced, however, if the same actors play many games. In this case, players may mutually sanction defection, which then is not attractive. This is exactly the case with a steady power-sharing arrangement, and it allows actors to develop mutual trust. An additional advantage for cooperation is found if politics involve different cleavages in which the opposed camps, for instance of the left-right or urban-rural cleavage, are not the same. This leads to coalitions different from issue to issue, leading to an important consequence in the ongoing process of power-sharing. Political actors, opposed today on a particular issue, may find themselves as coalition partners tomorrow on a different issue. This favours mutual respect. Indeed, studies on deliberation give empirical evidence that under conditions of power-sharing political opponents have more respect for each other and listen more to the arguments of the other side than in majoritarian settings.[14] Thus, power-sharing allows for deliberative learning processes. The weak spot is, however, that conditions for changing coalitions are not always given. In the 1980s, for instance, the three parties of the centre-right alliance regularly overruled the green-left coalition in the major issues of public finance, energy or environment. Behind the screen of power-sharing, informal majoritarian politics were practised. This is a bad constellation: Instead of combining advantages, informal major-itarian and formal power-sharing politics combine the disadvantages: the ruling majority refuses accommodation and compromise, and is not exposed to the risk of losing power through competitive elec-tions as in a majoritarian system. In such a position the 'eternal' majority can afford not to learn – in Deutsch's term a pathological use of power.[15]

4.3.4 Political elitism and its limits

Power-sharing produces strong formal and informal contacts amongst the entire political elite. Lijphart's early theory of 'consociationalism'[16] proposes that power-sharing also leads to the development of common values and attitudes. Elites must be able to develop a common way of understanding the problems which must be solved and to develop per-spectives that go beyond their specific group interests. This gives rise to criticism that power-sharing leads to a cartel of 'the political class' which neutralises electoral competition and democratic control. In the Swiss case it may be argued that indeed elections do not lead to a change of roles between government and opposition and therefore play a minor role for democratic control. Direct democracy, however, is a corrective to elitist consociationalism. Every political party and its leaders have to defend their compromises in the people's vote. This imposes limits to elitism.

4.4 The critics of Swiss consensus democracy

4.4.1 The referendum as an instrument of vested interests

I have shown that the referendum is a pawn in the hands of interest groups, giving the latter additional influence in all matters of legis-lation. Thus, direct democracy, instead of being the voice of the people, has partly become the instrument of vested interests. Indeed, this critique has some strong arguments, especially for the long period of time when the Swiss parliament was weak and often adopted the pre-parliamentary compromise between the interest groups without major modification. A famous constitutionalist went as far as to say that the law is no longer the result of the parliament but the result of nego-tiating non-democratic, vested interests.[17] Today, however, the image of a *Verbandsstaat*, a state of vested interests that dominate parliament, may correspond less to political realities for several reasons. Not only has parliament become stronger in shaping legislation but with the process of globalisation, some of the strongest interest groups of the domestic market, such as those of agriculture and industries, have significantly lost political influence, and many traditional coalitions, such as those of industries or between employers and unions, are split today, thereby neutralising each other.

4.4.2 Inequalities of influence

The weak spot of democratic pluralism is that it cannot guarantee fair competition in the sense that all interest groups and political parties have equal chances of influence. According to the theory of collective action, the negotiating power of a group depends on two factors: its organisational ability (for instance, to mobilise members) and its capacity to deny contributions that other actors need.[18] This leads to inequalities of political influence. In negotiations and law-making by mutual adjustment, the 'haves' are better off than the 'have-nots', whose refusals have no trade-in. Moreover, organisations which defend specific short-term benefits for their members are likely to be stronger than those promoting general and long-term interests. The agribusiness industry, for instance, can easily mobilise its lobby against restricting regulations on genetic engineering, and its argument of relocating its research activities out of Switzerland is a strong argument for parliament not to pass such a bill. Consumer organisations on the other hand are confronted with more difficulties. They constitute much larger groups, but probably less powerful ones. Their interests may conflict: part of the consumers would not see risks in genetic engineering and may favour genetic engineered products, so only part of them will mobilise against it. As their only means, the consumer boycott, is not efficient in the long run, they do not have a plausible threat and have therefore no trade-in in negotiations. Environmental groups, in particular, face the problem of having to fight for a long-term public good. They are popular and outnumber the biggest political parties in membership. Faced with vested industrial interests, however, they are not able to articulate comparable threats. On the whole, therefore, negotiations do not necessarily eliminate the twofold objections against political pluralism: the 'haves' retain their advantage over the 'have-nots', and negotiations amongst interest groups favour particular short-term benefits at the cost of general long-term interests.[19] One may object, however, that these inequalities are not a peculiarity of Swiss semi-direct democracy but are valid for all pluralist systems. Even more: negotiating in the shadow of direct democracy offers a chance for weak actors to take the challenge of a referendum as a last resort.

4.4.3   Lack of innovation?

Negotiation and compromise seem to have provided important advantages. In the absence of electoral change, there are no abrupt discontinuities in federal policy. The sobering effect of negotiation cools down ideological exaggeration and promotes pragmatic solutions. Cooperation in commissions, in government and in parliament leads to mutual adjustments where learning processes occur over the substantive issues of legislation. Reaching a satisfactory compromise may take more time than a majority decision, but once the agreement becomes law most actors are prepared for it. This context increases the chances of new laws and policy programmes being implemented.[20]

Yet, criticism of consensus democracy is as old as its praise. Political scientists have noted that consociationalism has made a strong opposition impossible. Elections do not provide the possibility of the government and the opposition changing places the way they do in parliamentary democracies. Therefore, the Swiss system also lacks the larger innovatory and social learning processes that are brought about by changes of power in parliamentary democracies.

Two scholars proposed radical changes in order to stimulate innovation. The first one was the political scientist Raimund Germann, who already in 1975 proposed scenarios for a comprehensive institutional change to a majoritarian parliamentary system.[21] He was concerned with the problem of incrementalism in domestic politics and later with European integration. In his view, the Swiss had to adapt to the much faster pace of decision-making in the EU.[22] The second one, the economist Silvio Borner, focused on the negative economic impact of negotiation practices in Swiss legislation.[23] In his view the strong position of interest groups in the legislative process led Swiss enterprises towards seeking state rents instead of taking their chance on the market. Industries, getting short-term benefits from protectionism, would in the long run lose their capacity to innovate and compete on the international markets. The proposition of both authors was clear: more competition is necessary not only for Swiss politics but for Swiss economy as well. The message was appreciated by neither politicians nor the public. The reason was simple: Germann and Borner were honest enough to tell the price of more political competition: Installing a bi-polar competitive system would require not only less direct democracy but also less federalism and less bicameralism. Direct democracy and federalism, however, are sacrosanct in the eyes of both citizens and politicians. So, the Swiss rest with their consensus democracy.

4.5   Consensus democracy under stress

4.5.1   Political polarisation and the 'Konkordanz' crisis 2008[24]

The last decades brought increasing volatility in elections. The People's Party more than doubled its electorate, became the biggest political party and was given a second seat in the Federal Council in 2003. This success was at the cost of the political centre, radicals and Christian democrats, while the left with social-democrats and the greens stagnated. Many of the small parties did not survive, disappeared from the political arena or merged with others, such as the liberals with the radicals. Higher electoral volatility is nothing extraordinary as such, but it was accompanied by increasing political polarisation. The People's Party, taking over the old xenophobe parties, moved to the right and in many issues attacked not only the left but also the centre parties. This considerably changed the Swiss party system. The bourgeois alliance is partly broken, leading to a tri-polar system of political forces: a strengthened political right, a stagnating left, and a weakened centre. The rise of the People's Party began in 1992 when its charismatic party leader mobilised successfully against the EEA Treaty. The People's Party became the party of Euroscepticists and later opposed the *Konkordanz* systematically also in issues of immigration, social policy, and institutional reform. Originally confined to an electorate in the German-speaking cantons, the People's Party won new voters all over Switzerland and from all social strata. The party is much more professionalised in organisation and has much more resources for costly campaigning. It fosters its nationalist-conservative profile in an aggressive, often populist style,[25] thus becoming the political agenda setter in the media. This was much more than usual issue-specific opposition, and the other parties accused the People's Party of betraying the spirit and the rules of the *Konkordanz*. This was a blame made particularly to the political leader, Christoph Blocher. Elected in 2003 as the second representative of his party in the Federal Council, Blocher continued to act as an informal leader of the People's Party. In 2007, a coalition of social-democrats, Christian democrats and greens successfully boycotted Blocher's re-election, bringing another member of the People's Party into office. The reaction of the party was vigorous. It declared that it felt no longer represented in the Federal Council, excluded the two elected federal councillors from the parliamentary faction and declared 'fundamental opposition' to the government. This developed to a real crisis of the *Konkordanz*: the two excluded members founded a new small party, and the People's Party now complained that it was no longer represented in the government. The 'fundamental opposition' of the people's party, however, lasted for only one year. Its leaders realised that one single party alone could not break up the system of power-sharing: the institutional constraint for cooperation amongst the rest of the governmental parties was stronger. Thus, when one of the former PP-members of the Federal Council resigned, the People's Party claimed for the seat. The result was a compromise: The People's Party did not succeed in getting Blocher into office again but got one seat back with another candidate of their own. Thus, the *Konkordanz* in its arithmetic formula of proportional distribution of the seats in the Federal Council is halfway restored, and the second step will certainly be made sooner or later. Even so, higher voter volatility and the newly installed practice of non re-election of councillors in office may lead to less stability of the power-sharing government and greater changes of the composition of the Federal Council as well.

4.5.2 Power-sharing in a polarised parliament

Growing political polarisation raises the question if parliamentary compromise is still possible. Indeed, until the end of the 1980s a relatively stable block of the three bourgeois factions did not have any difficulties to find a majority in cases of opposition from the left. With the partial disintegration of the bourgeois forces, this seems no longer to be the case. With the People's Party making issue-specific opposition as often as the social democrats, the government coalition is exposed to opposition from two sides. No wonder that the media today often blame parliament factions of being incapable to find consensus amongst each other. An exhaustive analysis of about 8000 decisions of the National Council from 1995–2004, however, reveals a different picture.[26] Blocked situations in which parliament cannot decide on a governmental proposition are, at least statistically, very rare, and parliament decisions are still characterised by manifold winning coalitions that vary from issue to issue. Particularly, Christian democrats sometimes vote with the social democrats and the greens, which means that the National Council is practising the game of power-sharing in a more open way than in the 1980s. In the long run, issue specific coalitions also change, an indication that political conjunctures are more important than stark ideologies. Finally, the study shows that the political centre – the Christian democrats and the radicals – is the most important policy shaping actor in the parliamentary arena. Their coalition is most successful in forging winning coalitions. It benefits from situations found in many controversial issues in which propositions from the left and from the conservative right cancel out. These findings contrast with public opinion, which perceives the People's Party as the strongest force and agenda setter. The People's Party has electorally benefitted from polarisation but in some way pays for its strategy of fierce and sometimes populist opposition with less influence in the parliamentary arena.

4.5.3   The pressure of globalisation

Globalisation opens national economies, reduces economic protectionism, and stimulates market competition, liberalisation and privatisation. Politically, international authorities and supranational organisations become important regulators; the sharp distinction between domestic and foreign policy fades away, and the national state loses autonomy and sees its own sphere of influence vanishing. Switzerland is exposed to all these general effects. In Chapter 2, I have presented the particular situation of Switzerland in the process of *Europeanisation*. Good relations of the country with the EU are primordial for the Swiss economy and, not being a member of the EU, the Swiss government tries to develop them by the way of bilateral treaties. It pays a high price for the bilateral way. Equal treatment of Switzerland with regard to its member states is a legitimate interest of the EU. This means that Brussels influences regulation much beyond the bilateral treaties, without the Swiss having influence on the development of the *acquis communautaire* of the EU. Therefore, Switzerland today is highly integrated into the European market and has little chance not to do so. Globalisation in Switzerland, to a high degree, means *Europeanisation,* and it has also changed the political structures and processes of power-sharing:[27]

- The dynamics of the EU's economic integration puts Swiss politics under permanent pressure. This may be one of the reasons why power-sharing, despite polarisation, is working.
- The agenda of Brussels is conceived in Swiss politics as an imperative for liberalisation, privatisation and economic reform. Europeanisation has changed the balance of powers. Export industries and part of the consumer interests use Brussels as their ally and have become stronger. In contrast, unions, farmers, artisan industries and other actors of the domestic market have lost a considerable part of their influence.
- Internationalised regulation in Switzerland, today, exceeds domestic law in volume and growth. It is government and diplomacy which control the agenda in international relations and are the actors of treaty making. Parliament is involved in early consultations

but in cases of a treaty can only reject or accept the government's proposition. Thus, it loses influence in many issues.

These developments have led to kind of a two-pace regime. Decision-making in globalised affairs has become different to the conventional patterns of power-sharing. In the 'globalised regime', the executive is much more in the centre of the process. Some of the classical veto positions are weakened: pre-parliamentary consultation is more selective, vested interests of domestic policies have little bargaining power, and the policy shaping role of parliament is reduced. Federalism, the strongest veto position besides the referendum, can be overruled, as I have illustrated in section 5.3 of Chapter 2. In contrast to the process still incremental in domestic issues, policy shaping and policy-making in Europeanised affairs are developing a different pattern:[28] innovation passes more quickly and makes bigger steps. The short-cuts of the process, which bypass or reduce the veto power of many actors, however have their price. *Europeanisation* and globalisation produce the salient issues fuelling polarisation amongst the political elites. More than that: today, we observe that the cleavages between urban and rural regions, and between the social strata have become stronger also in the perception of the citizens.[29]

4.6   Conclusions

4.6.1   Swiss Democracy – An exceptional system

So far, I have discussed three main features of Swiss democracy: federalism, direct democracy, and power-sharing. At first sight, these three elements are not an exclusive Swiss particularity: worldwide, we count about 30 federal systems. Direct democracy is practised also in the individual states of the US, and power-sharing can be found in the Netherlands and Belgium as well. Moreover, direct democracy can combine with majoritarian democracy, and consensus democracy with a representative system (see Table 4.1).

Table 4.1   Different types of democracy: Some examples

Type of democracy	Representative	Semi-direct
Majoritarian	Great Britain New Zealand	States of the US
Consensus	The Netherlands Belgium	Switzerland

It is the combination of the two elements of power-sharing and direct democracy, however, that puts the Swiss system at odds with much political theory and with the mainstream of political thought. The combination of these elements has important consequences. In contrast to other countries like the Netherlands, for instance, Swiss consensus democracy is not the result of negotiations amongst the political parties after elections but a permanent institutional constraint due to the referendum. In the United States, direct democracy is not practised at the national level as in Switzerland and has not led to power-sharing in the single states of the US. And while we see elections to parliament as the deciding element of competition for the change of roles between government and opposition, they do not have such an effect in Switzerland. Thus, the same institutional elements may function in different ways, and that is why these institutional elements interact and function together as a system.

Table 4.2   A system comparison between Great Britain and Switzerland

Great Britain: Representative, majoritarian democracy	Switzerland: Semi-direct, consensus democracy
Strong competition between parties. Winner takes all.	Weak party competition. Proportional representation.
Salient elections, lead to: Periodical alternation of power.	Low salient elections; power-sharing amongst political parties prevents alternation of power.
Enactment of the political and programme of the government, backed changing by the parliamentary majority.	Integration of cultural minorities of conflicting group interests; coalitions for different issues.
Big innovation possible.	Incremental innovation.
Political legitimation through changes in power or re-election of government satisfying the voters' expectations.	Institutional legitimation through different forms of participation: the most important decisions being taken by the people, important ones by parliament and the rest by government.
Underlying idea: politics for the people.	Underlying idea: politics through the people.
Participation as a form of general and programmatic influence: voters elect a government and its programme for the entire legislative period.	Direct participation as 'single-issue' influence: people vote on specific questions. No strategic government policy, no influence of voters on a specific government programme.

Let us compare the most different countries of our Table 4.2, the United Kingdom and Switzerland (see Table 4.2). In Great Britain, which provides an almost ideal example of a majoritarian and representative system, political power is concentrated in the hands of the political party that wins a majority. Intense election campaigning is linked with fierce interparty competition in which the winner takes all. The electoral system is designed to bring about changing parliamentary majorities, formed of one or two parties at most. The elected government sets out to implement the programme it had laid before the electorate, but if it fails to carry its programme through both houses of parliament, defeated in a vote of no confidence, it is possible to attempt to create another coalition or dissolving parliament and calling for a new election. Strong innovation is possible, also against the opposition. The influence of the voters can be regarded as programmatic since it is they who choose among the programmes of the major parties and thus set the political agenda for several years. Sometimes the programmes call for major policy changes, so elections provide political legitimation, innovation and change all at the same time.

In semi-direct consensus democracy, on the other hand, party competition is low because elections do not lead to a change of role between government and opposition. The system places its trust in final control of all the important issues on the political agenda. Institutional legitimation comes from the most important decisions being taken by the people. Proportional rule in elections and mutual adjustment in legislative decision-making favour the idea of 'no single winner takes all, everybody wins something'. In direct democracy, voting is on a single issue at a time, and each case produces different winning coalitions, which are barely foreseeable by the political elites. A popular vote, even when about a fundamental issue, involves just one clear decision independent from others. The Swiss government, which is free of the fear of not being re-elected will not spend much time on programmatic policies. The narrow limits of manoeuvre imposed by an all-party government and the risk of a referendum being called drastically curtail any efforts to design comprehensive governmental programmes and, at least in domestic policies, allow for incremental innovation only.

Both countries, in their particularities, are unique. But while Great Britain and its Westminster democracy have become a mainstream model for democracy all over the world, the Swiss polity with regard to its combination of direct participation of the people and power-sharing, is an exceptional case: Swiss democracy is at odds with the prevailing idea of democracy as a competition of élites.

4.6.2   Who has more influence on politics: The British or the Swiss Voter? – or: The trade-off between elections and direct participation

The comparison between Great Britain and Switzerland has shown fundamental differences of the way the idea of democracy is realised. These are not only differences of 'systems' but also differences of how citizens can influence politics. A British voter chooses, by means of his/her ballot, which political party, its leader and its program should be elected or voted out of office. The electoral choice of every British voter is of utmost importance. Victory and defeat of a party in elections decide on the political future of the country, and stock markets in London react, going up or down. Between two elections, however, the British voter has little to say, and the ruling government is not too much impressed by bad records of popularity in surveys. The Prime Minister, as long as his or her majority in parliament is not put at risk by a vote of no confidence, has little to fear from polls. In contrast, the Swiss voter knows that before and after elections there will be the same government. Electoral swing may lead to some changes of the relative influence of the factions in parliament and even in the composition of the government. But looking back at the last 50 years, the voter may be very sure that an all-party government, composed proportionally to the relative strength of the biggest parties, will be in power. The Swiss stock market is not impressed. Between two elections, however, the Swiss voter exercises his/her rights of direct participation: saying 'yes' or 'no', he or she has the last word on the important decisions of parliament. Obviously, British citizens have a maximal voting influence, but no say by direct democratic choice. For the Swiss citizen it is the reverse. This raises two questions.

The first is: Can British and Swiss voters have it both ways, that is: having a maximum of influence by elections as well as by direct participation? My answer is no. While the idea of more democratic influence by both elections and direct democracy is tempting, it cannot be realised institutionally within the same political system. I have already shown for the Swiss system that an institutional change to more electoral competition is possible only by reducing direct democracy, notably the referendum which requires power-sharing. Similarly, regular referenda in Great Britain would destroy the basic idea of its political system, namely to concentrate power in a strong government that is, based on a parliamentary majority, able to realise its program also against the will of an opposition.

I therefore propose a trade-off between influence by elections and direct participation. Its basic idea is: The more a political system realises high influence of voters by elections, the less it can grant influence by direct participation, and *vice versa*.[30] In the following Figure 4.2, I visualise this trade-off and locate some polities according to my theoretical expectations.

At the either end of the spectrum ranging from representative and majoritarian to direct consensus democracy, I set the cases of Great Britain and Switzerland, each of which maximises one of the forms of participation – election or votation – while offering the least influence in the other. In between I situate some intermediate types of democracy. Swiss cantons differ in their openness to direct democracy. Yet, all of them offer a higher degree of influence than elections at the federal level because the executive branch – the cantonal council – is elected by the people. The US states are situated more on the side of representative or majoritarian democracy. As in Britain the competitive and majoritarian election of state parliaments and governors provide an opportunity for political change, yet in many US states we find a frequent use of the initiative and the referendum.

My hypothesis of an institutional trade-off between elections and direct democracy is in contrast to arguments of US political scientists Tolbert and Smith, who propose the political culture of direct democracy having a positive effect on electoral participation.[31] Stadelmann-Steffen and Freitag, in their exhaustive analyses of the Swiss cantons

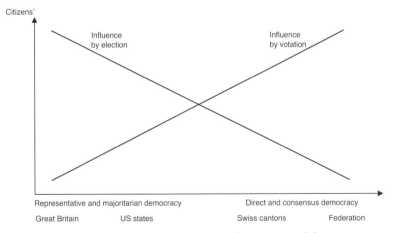

Figure 4.2 Citizens' influence in majoritarian parliamentary and direct consensus democracies: A theoretical model

however confirm the trade-off between voting and direct participation: the more open the polity of a canton to direct democracy, the less the participation of voters in elections.[32]

The trade-off means that voters in democracy cannot have the maximum of both, political influence by elections and direct participation. This leads to the second question: Which combination of both is 'best' in terms of maximum voter influence? This is not easily answered because we would have to know how citizens evaluate the two forms of influence. The fact that social movements in many European countries seek some forms of direct democracy may be a sign that majoritarian parliamentary systems today need some complement to their purely electoral democracy. It is obvious, however, that regular referenda in Britain, for instance, would weaken not only the ability of the government to achieve its programmes, but also the importance of elections, which would be a disenchantment for the British voter. Similarly, competitive elections in Switzerland could give more influence to the electorate but the same electorate would not accept cut-backs in direct democracy. There is no panacea of democracy, and in institutional reform we are therefore limited to looking for 'optimal' voters' influence. In other words: finding combinations of single-issue participation and programmatic election that in the eyes of an electorate best serve the influence in their own democracy.

4.6.3   Consensus democracy – Its past and its future

Looking at the past, we can distinguish three different features of consensus democracy. The first one is *integration,* which in the twentieth century had different meanings. In the earliest times, power-sharing helped to overcome the religious divide, and to prevent the linguistic minorities to be dominated by the German-speaking minority. Later, social partnership and participation of the political left in the government helped reduce social class conflict. In the most crucial time before World War II a high national consensus helped overcome threats to the country's independence. The second feature is *political stability and efficiency.* The perfection of power-sharing after the Second World War was undoubtedly beneficial. Switzerland passed smoothly through growing wealth to societal modernisation: the stability of its political system was an advantage for the Swiss economy in many respects. Whereas some West European democracies went from liberalism to socialism and back, Swiss politics held its middle course. The policy of integration, and of prudent adaptation rather than risky innovation, was efficient. The third one is the *development of a specific political culture.* The British scholar Clive

Church, already mentioned as a life-long observer from the outside, gives a definition that goes beyond the scope of conventional surveys (see Box 4.4). Many of the items such as 'constitutionalist, decentralist and federalist, pluralist, multiple loyalties, positive belief in compromise and cooperation, tolerance of domestic difference, willingness to accept adverse decisions, cautious attitude to policy change' have to do with power-sharing. We may leave it an open question if this political culture was influenced by the institutions or *vice versa*. The important point is that the functioning of power-sharing also depends on the cultural attitudes of political élites and citizens as well.

Box 4.4   Swiss political culture, as defined by a British scholar

Cognitive:	Limited collegiate authority
	Constitutionalist
	Decentralist and federalist
	Democratic
	Neutral
	Pluralist
	Republican
Affective:	Desire for decision to be made directly
	Enthusiastic support for federal and other institutions
	Multiple loyalties
	Positive belief in compromise and cooperation
	Strong sense of patriotism and independence
	Tolerance of domestic differences
	Willingness to accept adverse decisions
Judgemental:	Acceptance of the obligation to take part in politics
	Agreement that nation depends on acts of will
	Belief that the country is fragile
	Cautious attitude to policy change
	High levels of satisfaction with outcomes
	Positive evaluation of Swiss democracy and neutrality
	Trust in authorities

Source: Clive Church, The Politics and Government of Switzerland, Basingstoke/ New York: Palgrave Macmillan, 2004, p. 183

It would be wrong, however, to overlook the shadows of consensus democracy which began to grow longer since the 1970s. Economic recession made political consensus more difficult, and in such periods the lack of innovation and coherent government policies was particularly felt. Political power-sharing does not include immigrants who represent more than 20 per cent of the residents today, and efforts for social integration were not sufficient. Moreover, new social movements – progressive as well as conservative[33] – indicated a loss of the Swiss system's capacity to integrate all parts of society. Basic consensus amongst the political elite vanished, and the defeat of the government in the vote of 1992 on participating in the European Economic Area left a divided nation.

Since the 1990s, pressure from the outside – globalisation and Europeanisation – stimulate innovation. Power-sharing, despite growing polarisation, is working. The grand government coalition is sometimes defeated in referenda, but not more often than in earlier times. In parliament, growing antagonism between the conservative right and the welfare factions of the left is compensated for by changing issue-specific coalitions in which the political centre plays an important role. The partial break up of the bourgeois camp has made this possible. Under the conditions of a tripartite system of the right, the centre and the left, consensus democracy has the chance to work even better than in the 1980s when the bourgeois majority made the left a permanent loser. In 2007, the non re-election of a prominent member led to the biggest crisis of Swiss *concordance*. It was overcome because the institutional constraint for cooperation was stronger. Such 'crises' may be repeated in the future because already in 2003 parliament broke with the unwritten rule that members of the Federal Council in office are re-elected if they want so. Therefore, one has to expect less stability in the composition of the Federal Council in the future. This constitutes a risk and a chance. The risk is that political parties impose their pet candidates on the parliamentary majority. This could lead to a Federal Council composed of party leaders, using their office for party interests in a way that hurts trustful cooperation in the council. The chance is that more flexibility might provide parliament with wider options to elect a team of councillors being able to practice collective leadership.

Problems for the future remain, however. There are strong indications that decision-making in issues exposed to globalisation follows a different pace. Europeanisation, especially, leads to quicker and bigger innovation but is short-cutting many of the veto positions and interests relevant in domestic politics. This could lead to further polarisation between winners and losers of globalisation. Another problem is governmental reform. In globalised politics, the Federal Council and its administration have become key players, but the collegiate structure of the council – seven members with equal competencies – is still the same as in 1848. For the time being, all projects of governmental reform have failed, but the pressure for success is rising.

Institutionally, consensus democracy has proven its worth in stormy weather. Surveys show that consensus democracy gets rising popularity and is even more appreciated by the ordinary citizens than by the Swiss elites.[34] Here, however, we may identify the real weak spot of Swiss consensus democracy today. Polarisation, stimulated by the political parties of the right and of the left, leaves its traces in political culture. Pluralism, positive belief in compromise and cooperation, tolerance towards differences, willingness to accept adverse decisions, are declining among parts of the political elite, and parts of the electorate as well. With good reason, adherents of the Swiss *Konkordanz* worry about the loss of the 'spirit of accommodation'. It could paralyse power-sharing in the long run. As a strategy towards majoritarian politics, however, the politics of confrontation would not be enough. Gradual transformation towards majoritarian politics seem feasible only under electoral change which sees a leading party, capable to formulate a convincing political program but also to carry the necessary institutional reforms. And the trade-off mentioned earlier will impose limits to gradual transformation: In the near future one should not expect the Swiss to be willing to leave consensus democracy in favour of a majoritarian system with less direct democracy.

5
Comparative Perspectives

5.1 Direct democracy

5.1.1 Experiences of direct democracy compared

The first worldwide comparative study on direct democracy in 1978 produced some astonishing results: its authors, Butler and Ranney,[1] counted more than 500 nationwide referenda in countries all over the world. Their distribution, though, was uneven. Up to 1978, Butler and Ranney counted 300 referenda for Switzerland, 39 for Australia, 20 for France and 13 for Denmark. In all other countries the number was below ten. However, with the exception of the USA and the Netherlands, all countries surveyed had, prior to 1978, experimented at least once with popular votes at the national level. Fifteen years later, Butler and Ranney[2] (1994) counted already 799 popular votes. As shown in Table 5.1, more than half of these votes were held in Switzerland, followed by other European countries, the Near East, Australia and New Zealand as well as the Americas.

Table 5.1 Number of nationwide referenda up to 1993

Area	Number
Europe (excluding Switzerland)	149
Africa and Middle East	93
Asia	30
Americas	49
Australasia	64
Switzerland (up to 1996)	414

Source: David Butler and Austin Ranney (1994: 5) *op. cit.*, and *Bundesamt für Statistik* (for Switzerland).

Concerning the issues of votes, one can distinguish three general categories. The first one comprises *the establishment or secession of a state, of a new constitutional order or regime.* In these cases the principle of self-determination of a people, and the attempt to provide legitimation for fundamental changes in the political order are important motives. Some historical examples are the separation of Norway from Sweden in 1905, the vote of English Togo (under United Nations supervision) to join with Ghana, and of French Togo to become independent in 1965, as well as the more recent case of the Philippines where, in 1986 after the end of the Marcos regime, President Corazon Aquino allowed the people to ratify the new constitution. At the beginning of the 1990s, the transformation of communist regimes to democracies in Eastern Europe saw many referenda in Kyrgyzstan, Azerbaijan, Turkmenistan and in the Baltic states. In the reunion of Eastern and Western Germany, however, the peoples were not granted a say.

A second category, relatively new, comprises decisions on *membership in transnational organisations or changes of the status of membership.* In both cases, votes are held because the member states agree to share part of their sovereignty with the trans- or supranational organisation. Spanish citizens, for instance, voted to remain in the North Atlantic Treaty Organisation (NATO) in 1985. On EU issues, Denmark and Ireland held six referenda each. In 2005, France and the Netherlands voted against the EU treaty for a European Constitution, and in 2008 Ireland's referendum blocked the Lisbon treaty. Before the EU enlargement of 2004, referenda were held in nine out of ten candidate countries (Slovenia, Czech Republic, Slovakia, Estonia, Latvia, Lithuania, Hungary, Poland, Malta).[3]

A third category deals with *important national policy decisions* for which a government wants to be given additional legitimacy. In Chapter 3, I have already mentioned French president de Gaulle's plebiscite on independence for Algeria in 1962, which put an end not only to the colonial regime but also to the deep divide of the French nation on this question. In some East European countries, plebiscites were used from the very beginning of the liberalisation process. Whereas the Polish authorities failed to obtain the support of the people when trying to pass early reforms for economic liberalisation, the Hungarian opposition in 1989 won a referendum on the question of election procedure against the wishes of the still communist-controlled government.

These examples illustrate the vast variety of occasions on which people are able to express their preferences. For a better understanding of the different uses made of the devices of direct democracy, a classification according to the following criteria is useful:

Binding and non-binding referenda: It is obvious that binding referenda have a higher impact than non-binding votes which are merely consultative or advisory. In New Zealand, for instance, the referendum is non-binding and it is left to the government or legislature to interpret the results. For binding referenda the consequences depend much on the type of the popular vote.

The authority empowered to call a popular vote: With regard to who has the authority to demand that a popular vote be held, we can distinguish four basic types of participation:

1. *Government-controlled referenda.* The majority of parliament or the president have the sole power to decide whether or not a referendum should be held. They decide the subject matter and the wording of the proposition to be voted upon. It is often referred to as *plebiscite.*
2. *Constitutionally required referenda.* The constitution requires that certain decisions (constitutional amendments, ordinary laws, decisions on financial or international issues) be approved by the voters before they can take effect. In these constitutionally defined decisions, the government has a free hand when formulating the proposition, but is legally bound to a direct-democratic procedure.
3. *Referenda called by the people.* A certain number of voters are authorised to demand a popular vote to be held on specific government measures, be it before or after these have taken effect. Thus it depends on a group of citizens to decide whether a government decision has to be ratified by the people. A similar device is the *recall,* which allows a certain number of voters to demand the removal of an authority or a single person of an authority from office.
4. *Popular initiatives.* A certain number of voters are authorised to demand a popular vote to be held on broad statements of intent or specific measures which they themselves have proposed. Thus, it is a group of people who, acting as 'lawmakers', decide the subject matter and the wording of the proposition to be voted on.[4]

Most countries have only the first type of popular vote, the *plebiscite.* Under such an institutional arrangement direct democracy is limited in use and purpose. If it is left to the discretion of the government to put issues before the voters, the referendum tends to serve as an occasional device to obtain wider support for a presidential or parliamentary policy. This is especially the case with non-binding plebiscites, in which the government can realise its projects also if defeated in the vote. In the latter case, however, the government has to expect raising conflicts with the opposition or general quarrels amongst the political elites.

Types 2–4 are fundamentally different from the first type, the plebiscites. In these cases a defined class of government decision is always subject to a constitutionally required referendum, or citizens can, by petition, challenge government decisions (optional referenda) or hand in proposals for constitutional or legislative reform (popular initiatives). The difference is that all these devices sanction or correct government policies and politics. Under these institutional arrangements, direct democracy is intended to give citizens an independent voice in politics and policies. This may be in accord with governmental policies, especially in the case of constitutionally required referenda. But the voice of the citizens can be, and often is, raised against the government. To challenge government decisions in a selective way is the 'natural' use of popular referenda. The idea of 'correcting' representative democracy is further developed by the popular initiative, which gives the people the possibility not only of approving or repealing government decisions, but also offers a group of citizens the chance to have their own propositions to put a popular vote.

The list of countries where direct democracy is used to challenge or correct the parliamentary process is short. In Australia national referenda, which are required for certain constitutional amendments, are held quite frequently. The Italian constitution provides for referenda with the proviso that the citizens can challenge a parliamentary law only some time after its introduction and application. This unique 'abrogative referendum' was used in the divorce issue for instance, when part of the Catholic population wanted to abolish the secular and liberal divorce law. The Philippine constitution of 1986 has institutionalised both the initiative and the referendum. Recently, Slovakia, Hungary, Lithuania and some Caucasian states have introduced referenda on constitutional reforms.

National and sub-national referenda: While in Switzerland direct democracy is known on all federal levels, some other countries practice direct participation only on the sub-national levels. This is the case, for instance, in Germany were votes are held in some *Bundesländer* and their communes. The prominent case are the US states, where direct democracy is as widely institutionalised and used as it is in Switzerland. In all US states, with the exception of Delaware, any amendment of the constitution requires a popular vote. In about half of the states we find one or another type of referendum for parliamentary laws, often complemented by a financial referendum. Moreover, citizens in many states can propose legislation by means of the popular initiative, or initiate a 'recall', which allows voters to remove or discharge a public official from office. In no other part of the world but California have citizens had so much opportunity to express their political preferences: from 1884 to 2003, Californians voted on nearly 1800 issues.[5]

5.1.2   The practice of direct democracy in US states and Switzerland: Similarities and differences

As mentioned above, US direct democracy is fundamentally different from Switzerland's in one point: it is limited to state or local level. Populist forces in the late 1970s demanded nationwide referenda without success. They had no real chance to change the tradition of republican belief in the system of 'checks and balances', which is opposed to any form of plebiscite at national level. Yet, the US states' and Switzerland's experience of direct democracy are the richest; the instruments of the referendum and the popular initiative are practically the same, and one can find many similarities in their use. For an assessment of direct democracy, it may be most useful to compare their experiences.

In his overall assessment of direct democracy in US states, Thomas Cronin comes to the conclusion that:

> In sum, direct democracy devices have not been a cure-all for most political, social, or economic ills, yet they have been an occasional remedy, and generally a moderate remedy, for legislative lethargy and the misuse of legislative power. It was long feared that these devices would dull legislators' sense of responsibility without in fact quickening the people to the exercise of any real control in public affairs. Little evidence exists for those fears today. When popular demands for reasonable change are repeatedly ignored by elected officials and when legislators or other officials ignore valid interests and criticism, the initiative, referendum and recall can be a means by which the people may protect themselves in the grand tradition of self-government.[6]

This assessment could also be largely subscribed to in the case of Switzerland, whose ideas of popular control of representative government in fact influenced the development of direct democracy in the USA between

1890 and 1920.[7] Another common conclusion can be drawn: historically speaking, critics as well as proponents of direct democracy overestimated the power of the referendum and the initiative, whether for ill or good. Finally, even if voters in the USA and Switzerland are aware of its limited effects and deficiencies, direct democracy constitutes an element of political culture that citizens are not willing to relinquish.

Further similarities show up when comparing a number of Cronin's points on the 'general effects of direct democracy devices'.[8]

1. *Uncertainty on the question if 'Direct democracy can enhance government responsiveness and accountability'.* For Switzerland, we have noted characteristics of the public sector (the small budget of central government, limited public administration, the modification of a proposed policy programme after its defeat in the first popular vote, and so on) that indicate a high level of responsiveness to the 'will of the people'. On the other hand, the power-sharing coalition of an all-party government can also work as a political cartel and thus reduce responsiveness. Valid comparisons, though, cannot be made. In the USA, where comparison with purely representative states is possible, Cronin notes that, 'few initiative, referendum and recall states are known for corruption and discrimination. Still, it is difficult to single them out and argue persuasively that they are decidedly more responsive than those without the initiative, referendum, and recall'.

2. As in Switzerland, *'direct democratic processes have not brought about rule by the common people'.* In both systems, more than 90 per cent of important parliamentary decisions are not challenged. Popular initiatives change and influence the political agenda, but do not call into question the role of parliament as the dominant lawmaking institution. At more than 45 per cent, the rate of successful initiatives is higher in the American states than in the Swiss federation (10 per cent) and its cantons (30 per cent). But in both countries direct democracy is followed by inequalities of participation. It is the better educated, socially better-off citizen who engages and participates significantly more in direct democracy. Empirical data seem to indicate that the more complicated the procedure and the issues at stake, the more direct participation is socially discriminatory. This selective bias affects the devices of direct democracy, which are generally more complex than simply casting an election vote.[9] Finally, direct democracy requires citizens to get organised. Cronin states that 'direct democracy devices occasionally permit those who are

motivated and interested in public policy issues to have a direct personal input by recording their vote, but this is a long way from claiming that direct democracy gives a significant voice to ordinary citizens on a regular basis'.

3. *'Direct legislation does not produce unsound legislation and unwise or bad policy.'* There are strong arguments for this value judgement, despite empirical evidence in both countries that citizens are not always well informed about the issues on which they vote. For the Swiss case, Kriesi's analyses show that simplifying strategies, such as heuristic voting based on cues or party recommendations, does not lead to irrational choices.[10] For the US case, Cronin states that the contributions of direct democracy do not essentially differ from those of parliament. As with every procedure based on majority rule, minorities can lose, and this risk, according to Cronin, may be slightly greater in a direct democracy than with lawmaking through the legislative process. But voters in direct democracies 'have also shown that most of the time they too will reject measures that would diminish rights, liberties, and freedoms for the less well-represented or less-organized segments of society'.[11]

Kriesi's and Cronin's arguments, however, compare only direct and parliamentary legislation. How about the fundamental question: does direct participation lead to more or to less stability of democracy? I propose that the quality of direct democracy depends on the consolidation and on the quality of democracy as a whole. Even for the consolidated case of Switzerland there is empirical evidence that direct democracy is ambiguous. On the one hand, it has integrating effects. On the other, it allows political elites to use fundamental societal cleavages for mobilisation of the voters. The latter may be detrimental for a non-stable and non-consolidated democracy. Germany's change from a democracy to an authoritarian regime was 'legitimated' by three plebiscites in 1933–6, and Austria approved the *Anschluss* in 1938 by a popular vote. If Switzerland at that time rejected the popular initiatives of the Nazi movement, an important reason for this was that besides the people, a clear majority of political elites were also hostile to the idea of fascism.[12] These historical examples illustrate that direct democracy is vulnerable; instead of contributing to political integration, it may be a factor of de-stabilisation in deeply divided societies or in non-consolidated democracies.

4. *'Direct democracy can influence the political agenda in favour of issues important to less well organized interests.'* Environmentalists provide a

good example of this for California and Switzerland. The popular initiative widens the political agenda and the horizon in respect of what is politically conceivable. We have to note, however, that these innovative effects may become unwelcome. In California, for instance, there is criticism that direct democracy is part of the reason why the state has become 'ungovernable': An abundant number of popular initiatives is launched by a professional campaigning industry that promotes special vested interests rather than those of the ordinary citizens.[13] In Switzerland, the smaller 'political market' and lower chances for success of popular initiative may set closer limits to a professional referenda industry.

5. *'Direct democracy tends to strengthen single issue and interest groups rather than political parties with larger, general interest, programmes.'* Popular democratic rule partially loses or changes its meaning when devices of direct democracy, originally used by social movements, pass into the hands of interest groups.[14] The 'normal' form and function of direct democracy are not what they were at the beginning. This statement for Switzerland can be complemented by the US experience that 'Initial achievements or victories were won by the populists and progressives, but the very bosses or interests against whom these devices were aimed soon learn to adapt to the new rules, deflect them, or use them to advance their strategic interests'. Cronin, who partially agrees with this critique made by both Herbert Croly and Richard Hofstadter, however, makes the point that special interest and single-issue groups regularly take part in direct democracy as well as in representative democracy. If the USA has become a nation of interest groups, it is the very task of politics to blend divergent interests into great governing coalitions. This, in Cronin's view, parliament is best placed to achieve.

6. *'Money is, other things being equal, the single most important factor determining direct legislation outcomes.'* It costs money to collect signatures for a referendum or initiative petition, to create an effective organisation for a voting campaign, to formulate and pass a political message on to voters by direct mail, to finance propaganda and to attract the attention of the mass media. The frequent use of the devices of direct democracy lead to the professionalisation of campaigns, an evolution well known in the USA and observable in Switzerland, albeit with a time lag. Unequal distribution of money leads to unequal campaign spending, sometimes up to ratios of 1:20 or 1:50. In Switzerland as in the American states, the high-spending side wins in most cases. It is exceptional for underdogs to win

against 'big money'. Some American scholars speak of campaign money as the single most powerful predictor of who wins and who loses.[15] In the Swiss case, there is evidence that money cannot play the same role with all votations. In the case of pre-dispositioned issues, where citizens' preferences are related to first-hand experience and their own values, campaigning can do much less than in non-pre-dispositioned ones, mostly complex and abstract issues. Moreover, money is part of the political parties' campaigning, which induces not only influence by propaganda but also 'argument based' behaviour of the voters. Votations cannot generally 'be bought'. But in highly controversial issues with heavy campaigning because of an expected tight vote, money can be the decisive factor (see Section 3.5.5).

To a certain extent, money can be substituted by voluntary work of political activists. Together with socially unequal participation, however, the distorting effect of money rests probably one of the most serious deficiencies of direct democracy. First, unbalanced campaign spending violates the fundamental idea a democracy based on 'one person, one vote'. We could draw an analogy with a town meeting or a television debate where one side gets to speak twice, or five or 20 times more than the other side. Second, the risk of deceptive advertising can be greater if there is no counterbalance. Citizens can be prevented from making a fair judgement of the real issue. These deficiencies, however, are not specific to direct democracy – they can be observed with elections and representative systems as well. They are unresolved in Switzerland, while attempts in the USA to regulate the financing of direct-democracy campaigns have been thwarted in the courts.

After all these similarities, there are three fundamental differences.

1. *In US states, direct democracy is not an element of political power-sharing.* In the USA, with its two-party system, its winner-take-all elections and its relatively homogeneous majority which has installed a white Anglo-Saxon Protestant hegemony, the referendum is not a device that permits cultural minorities – blacks for instance – to gain better access to power or secure proportional representation. Nor do we know about negotiation processes carried out in the shadow of the referendum challenge which characterise Swiss parliamentary legislation. One reason for this might be that US interest groups find it much easier to exert their influence through parliamentary

bargaining. Lobbyists in the US legislative tradition can try to get their interests to appear in many bills by attaching their desires as 'riders' (non-germane amendments). This leads to bills that are sometimes a conglomerate of matters such as money for agriculture, schools, highway construction – and so on. Non-germane amendments facilitate the finding of 'constructive majorities' between interest groups. In Switzerland – as in other European legislative traditions – these deals would not be possible because different matters must be regulated by different bills. In the US, however, non-germane amendments allow interest groups to influence legislation in a direct way without a 'referendum threat' which is much riskier. US states' direct democracy, therefore, is neither an incentive for cooperation and power-sharing as it is in Switzerland nor has it the institutional function of political integration. Finally, direct democracy in the USA has not led to the devaluation of elections that is observable in Switzerland.

2. *Direct democracy in the USA is a complementary element of a representative polity while in Switzerland it has transformed the whole political system.* With the introduction of the referendum at the end of the nineteenth century, Swiss political institutions – which originally followed representative ideas – were completely restructured. The merely majoritarian democracy was transformed into a system of consensus democracy. Negotiated legislation and power-sharing became necessary if the government was to avoid defeat in referenda. This institutional transformation has not happened in the USA, and especially the idea of proportional representation seems to contradict American political culture which favours competitive elections and majority decision. To the Swiss observer it seems as if representative and direct democracy in the American states were much more independent of each other. As part of the political culture, the predominant idea in Switzerland is direct democracy while in the USA it is representative democracy.

3. *In one respect direct democracy is of much more consequence in Switzerland than in the USA: the referendum and the popular initiative are also used at national level.* This distinction is important. In Switzerland not only national but also foreign policy are not excluded from the devices of direct democracy. The latter is even more astonishing as the Swiss constitution was influenced by nineteenth century doctrines which put foreign policy into the hands of an executive body so that it might have complete autonomy in its negotiations with foreign powers. In practice the Federal Council is under much less

parliamentary control for its foreign policy than it is for domestic affairs.[16] Nevertheless, three constitutional amendments, passed in 1920, 1977 and 2003, introduced and even extended the people's rights in foreign policy. Today, membership in international organisations and all international treaties implying substantial unifications of law are subject to mandatory referenda.[17] If the government should want Switzerland to become a member of a supranational organisation or a system of collective security, the referendum is obligatory. The Swiss polity thus empowers the people to participate in matters which in earlier times were the sovereign right of the monarch and which have partially remained prerogatives of the executive in most democratic polities.[18]

5.1.3   The theory of direct democracy: Between ideal and reality

5.1.3.1   *Direct vs representative democracy*

In the USA, where the development of modern democracy was accompanied by theorising which influenced the framing of the constitution, the two different strands of direct and representative democracy were present from the beginning. On one side were Benjamin Franklin and Thomas Jefferson, who were suspicious of government, but confident of the common sense of the people. Jefferson, especially, held that the will of the people was the only legitimate foundation of government, and 'wished to see the republican principle of popular control pushed to its fullest exercise'.[19] On the other side, John Adams and James Madison, advocates of informed, wise and responsible decision-making by elected representatives, were sceptical about possible abuses of democracy by an ill-informed and irrational general public. The US constitution, as a purely representative system, with its checks and balances and filters of indirect election of the president, much resembles this model of prudence. Representative government, besides having become the common standard all over the world, serves as a normative reference point in much democratic theory of today. And many of the arguments against direct democracy have not changed much since Madison's times: participation beyond elections goes beyond the horizon and competence of most people, who are not willing to engage in or spend much time on the study and discussion of complex public affairs. The building of consensus, they say, should be left to political elites.

The case for direct democracy in modern theory, as represented by Benjamin Barber and others,[20] can be made on two grounds. The first argument is a critique of the deficiencies of the representative model: if representative government is more than an elitist power arrangement, its elected officials must somehow be responsive to their constituency. But on this point the theory of representative democracy was never clear. The debate between 'mandate' theorists (representatives have to present their voters views as faithfully as possible) and 'independent' theorists (the representative's duty is to deliberate free of particular interests and in the general interest of all) is still unresolved. The ambiguity and weakness of the representative model – 'thin democracy' – can be remedied only by direct participation of the people to produce a 'strong democracy'.[21] The second argument concerns the role of democracy in society. Whereas part of modern theory (especially economic theory, beginning with Joseph Schumpeter and Anthony Downs)[22] considers democracy merely as an instrument for choosing the governing elites, populist-plebiscitary proponents share the unbroken tradition of a broader normative concept: democracy has to make man and woman free. Democracy as citizens' deliberative involvement and participation in public affairs are part of an individual's development and creates citizenship and community.[23]

5.1.3.2 'Sensible' or 'semi-direct' democracy – A third model?

The sharp contrast between models of direct and representative democracy disappears when looking at actual practice. Despite the many weaknesses in the theoretical model, representative government has become the predominant type of democracy. The device of competitive elections with the possibility of a change of power seems to be responsive enough, at least in industrialised countries, to work satisfactorily for its citizens. Democratic government 'for' the people is realistic in the sense that a large majority of citizens are not – and probably will never want to be – political activists. But in some democracies, such as in the USA and in the Swiss federation and its cantons, citizens wanted more. It was the deficiencies of representative government as well as the citizens' claim for personal expression and political participation that gave populist movements their successes when introducing the devices of direct democracy into initially representative systems. The experiences of this amalgam have dashed the original hopes of the populists and contradicted most of the fears of opponents of direct democracy – at least in practice. Concerning the debate between proponents of direct and indirect democracy, the predictive value of democratic theory has been rather disappointing, except for one important point: direct democracy, by giving people the power to define when and on which issue to take things into their own hands, has always acted as a corrective to representative government.

In the view of Thomas Cronin, this amalgam of representative government and corrective direct democracy constitutes a third model, *sensible democracy*, which I have called *semi-direct democracy* for Switzerland. It combines the features of the two types:

'Sensible democracy, with its referenda, initiatives and the recalls:

1. Values representative institutions and wants legislators and other elected officials to make the vast majority of laws;
2. Values majority rule yet understands the need to protect minority rights most of the time;
3. Wants to improve legislative processes;
4. Wants occasionally to vote on public policy issues;
5. Wants safety-valve recall or vote of no confidence procedures as a last resort for inept and irresponsible public officials – but is willing to make these options difficult to use;
6. Wants to improve the ability of the ordinary person both to run for office and to use direct democracy procedures;
7. Wants to lessen the influence of secrecy, money, and single-interest groups in public decision-making processes;
8. Trusts representatives most of the time, yet distrusts the concentration of power in any one institution;
9. Trusts the general public's decision some of the time, yet distrusts majority opinion some of the time;
10. Is indifferent to most initiatives and referenda except when it comes to its own pet initiative issue;
11. Agrees with the central arguments of both the proponents and opponents of populist democracy, hence favours a number of regulating safeguards for direct democracy devices;
12. Is fundamentally ambivalent toward popular democracy – favouring it in theory and holding a more sceptical attitude toward it as it is practiced in states and localities.'[24]

This seems to be a 'realistic' normative appreciation. Taking into account the slightly different experiences of Swiss semi-direct democracy, however, I would propose four points for discussion. These all are based on the central argument that relations between direct democracy and representative government can also develop in a less harmonious way than in Cronin's perspective.

1. *Participation and the problem of social equality.* As mentioned earlier, direct democracy is particularly sensible to the unequal participation

of citizens, and to the inequality between different groups in gaining the attention of the public at large and influencing public opinion. Under these conditions, point 7 of Cronin's list may be too optimistic. As Macpherson mentions,[25] it is not easy to escape a vicious circle of the sort that better participation first needs more social equality – and that more social equality in turn requires better participation. Whenever democratic theory makes its normative point about equality in society,[26] it rests mostly on a moral appeal that is unconvincing because of its essential point that democratic procedures by themselves should have an equalising effect. In practice, sometimes they do, and sometimes they do not. Neither of the models of direct democracy nor that of sensible democracy give us a convincing answer.

2. *Normative orientation.* Cronin's model of sensible democracy does not imply that any subject or matter should be excluded from the people's vote. In his concluding remarks, however, he opposes national referenda and initiatives being held in the USA, among other reasons on the ground that 'too many issues at the national level involve national security or international economic relations'.[27] We may find here one of the discrepancies (point 12 of the model) between theory and practice. In practice, Cronin makes a good point: military power and negotiation of global terms of trade, on which the 'way of life' of US people depend, may be better left in the hands of a strong presidency and Congress. Thus, the US citizens, renouncing on direct participation at the national level, may make a rational choice as long as they prefer benefitting from international strength and supremacy. Theoretically, however, I see no argument why the model of 'sensible democracy' should not apply for the national level – at least in domestic affairs.

3. *Optimal influence of citizens' preferences.* The term 'sensible democracy' suggests that institutional arrangements should be such that the preferences of the citizens have the utmost influence on government politics and policies. Sensible democracy, complementing representative decisions with occasional popular votes, seems to meet this criterion. But it depends on additional specificities of the institutions whether the optimum influence of citizens can be realised, and sensible democracy has many forms. Taking the Swiss case first, we observe a high interdependence between representative and direct democratic procedures. The referendum challenge enforces legislation by negotiation and power-sharing. As discussed in Chapter 4, proportional representation can however devalue elections. As to the responsiveness and sensibility of government, there may be a trade-off

between elections and voting: Swiss citizens may lose in 'programmatic control' through elections what they have won in 'issue control'
through direct democracy. Thus, empirical evidence casts some doubts
on whether any combination of direct democracy and representative
government can always give citizens optimum influence. Second,
there may be other models. Fritz Scharpf, in his *Democratic Theory,* provides some strong arguments in support of the idea that enhancing
participation in practice leads to a group pluralism that favours the
status quo of the haves and eliminates basic reform issues that the
have-nots need most. He therefore proposes a model that maximises
voters' preferences through elections, the simplest and socially least-
discriminating mechanism. According to Scharpf, the system most
responsive to voters' preferences for structural reform is given by a
two-party parliamentary democracy sensitive to small electoral changes,
with enough power to overrule resistance by pluralist interest groups.
Consequently, Scharpf puts priority for enhancing participation not
in the field of political institutions but in the field of society and
economy.[28]

4. *Population size – a limiting factor for sensible democracy?* Historical
experience gives evidence that semi-direct democracy may work not
only in a small seven-million-people-country like Switzerland but
also in California with a population of more than 35 million. But
could the practice of referenda and initiatives also work nationwide
for the US with 300 million, or India with more than one billion
inhabitants? The idea may be regarded by many with scepticism. Is
direct democracy the most vulnerable part of democracy in large
countries because of increasing manipulation by big money and the
mass media? Or is direct democracy an appropriate way to make
central government more responsive? Nobody knows, but one point
seems to be clear: the political culture of direct participation is a
collective learning process that needs time to develop, as well as
possibilities to correct errors. From this perspective, bottom-up
development from the local to the national level is more appropriate than the top-down way, both in respect of democracy and
direct participation.

5.1.3.3   *Perspectives of direct participation*

Sensible or semi-direct democracy, the amalgam of parliamentary
decision-making by way of referenda and popular initiatives, is not the
only way to give people a say beyond elections. In the last decades,
direct participation has made its way in different forms from the local

up to the national level. If in the European countries nationwide plebis-cites and those on EU- affairs have become more and more frequent, this may be seen as the result of strong grass-roots movements that started half a century ago. Civil rights movements in the US, students and many other populist movements in European countries were dissatisfied with the lack of responsiveness of government, they challenged elitist politics and claimed more political participation. New social movements, grass-roots politics and non-governmental organisations have made civil society more active in daily politics. Instruments of direct participation, especially at the local and the sub-national level, developed in many forms, advocacy planning, citizens forums, panels, citizens networks, to mention just a few. With the development of the internet, the range of mobilisation has drastically increased. The local and the global are interconnected.[29]

Direct participation plays a role for young democracies. In East Euro-pean countries we find experiences of direct democracy despite a dif-ficult situation: having to walk the difficult path of developing a civic culture, democracy and a market economy all at the same time. In Brazil or South Africa, landless workers' and farmers' movements are claiming their rights through combinations of direct confrontation and negotiation with government. Decentralisation projects in sub-Saharan countries often go hand in hand with direct participation of the local people in the planning and budgeting process, including pro-cedures allowing even illiterates to participate. In these cases, direct participation allows for more than people expressing their needs. It is also a device to make people familiar with the functioning of the local state and democracy.[30]

All these experiences of direct participation, made in completely dif-ferent contexts, have some characteristics in common. They are still at an experimental stage, they are punctual if not exceptional, and they are able to influence institutional politics only in a modest way. Even so, they all are driven by the motives of people to have better voice for their values, interests and rights, which may lead to sustainable forms of participative democracy.

It would be wrong, however, to see more participation as the only means of improving democracy, or to hope that direct democracy will provide the answer to all problems of governance. Governing also always implies making decisions for groups and interests which cannot be democratically represented and which cannot adequately parti-cipate. Decisions about the education system, for instance, mostly affect young people under the age of majority but they are made by adults.

Many social reforms, such as of criminal law or psychiatry, need the advocacy of professionals, journalists and other members of an 'active public'. Most importantly, industrialised societies have to take account of future generations. People in industrialised democracies, especially, are consuming in a few decades natural resources that took millions of years to develop. Energy consumption risks destroying the natural climatic equilibrium worldwide. Such long-term effects of industrial activity are neither integrated into the price system of the market nor taken care of in today's democratic procedure. Can we think of finding democratic majorities for decisions renouncing the short-term advantages of most voters in favour of long-term advantages for a future generation? Under what kind of societal structures and values could we hope to have such communitarian and enlightened behaviour? Democratic theory and practice have to face up to such issues.

5.2 Federalism

5.2.1 The essentials of federalist institutions

We have considered federalism in Switzerland as an institutional arrangement that has enabled national unity while maintaining cantonal and regional autonomy. This may be a first approximation of most existing federal systems. Ivo Duchacek, the author of *Comparative Federalism, Nations and Men,* put it in the following words: 'What water is for fish, the federal system is for the territorial communities that desire to manage their affairs independently (near sovereignly) yet within the confines of an all-inclusive national whole'.[31] Federalism is therefore a political answer to provide a common biosphere for segmented parts of a larger population. Yet, it is an answer to *territorial* segmentation of a society, and it is responsive to the cultural autonomy of language, ethnicity and so on only to the degree that these cultures coincide with the geographical boundaries of the territorial communities. The carp swimming in a school of pike is not protected against being eaten. There is, therefore, a fundamental difference from *plural democracy*. While political pluralism also aims at respecting societal diversity and segmentation, it has no connotation for territorial boundaries.

What distinguishes federalist systems in the universe of national states, when we find a large spectrum ranging from unitary systems like that of France, to loose confederations or treaty-like federacies (USA-Puerto Rico) and leagues (the Arab League)? On the basis of his comparative work on federalism, Duchacek finds the following six yard-sticks most important:

1. Indestructible identity and autonomy of the territorial components;
2. Their residual and significant power;
3. Equal or favourably weighted representation of unequal units;
4. Their decisive participation in amending the constitution;
5. Independent sphere of central authority;
6. Immunity against secession (that is a permanent commitment to build and maintain a federal 'union' in contradistinction to a confederal system which lacks such a commitment).[32]

Commonly, the first five criteria may be realised as part of the constitutional framework. The sixth yardstick, however, tells us that federalism is more than a constitutional characteristic used to divide up governmental powers. It refers to part of the political culture, and of the political will of a society to constitute and remain a nation or state. Secessions of the Yugoslav regions and the republics of the Soviet Union show that this political commitment can evaporate if a central government loses its power and control to centrifugal forces.

Federalism is thus typical of societies where territorial segmentation has led to political division between forces preferring centralisation *or* decentralisation. In federations, therefore, we find different distributions of power between *shared rule* and *self-rule*.[33] But this dimension is not as clear and distinctive as it seems. A first ambiguity lies in the word 'federalism', which is sometimes connoted with 'centralisation', as in Anglo-Saxon cultures, but is sometimes a password for decentralising forces, as in Germany. However, it is not just a question of semantics – federalism itself is fundamentally ambiguous. At the moment, when several territorial entities create a common government they give up part of their sovereignty – and this process is not only unifying but centralising. Once the central government is created, the problem of living federalism may well be to guarantee the territorial autonomy of the components, their differences and therefore their relative independence from each other. As Daniel Elazar puts it: 'Federalizing does involve both the creation and maintenance of unity and the diffusion of power in the name of diversity'.[34]

Amongst the 192 member states of the UN, 28 are known as federations and represent about 40 per cent of the worldwide population. We find many other countries which have strong regional authorities, governments or even parliaments (such as Italy, Japan, Columbia,

France, Peru, United Kingdom).[35] Despite considerable devolution of powers and autonomy of the regional governments, these states are not federations but unitary states that – for different reasons – have undergone a process of decentralisation. What is the difference between a federation and a decentralised unitary state? Looking at Duchacek's definitions, we find that decentralised unitary states may meet yardsticks 1, 2, 5 and 6 as any federation. The decisive difference lies in yardsticks 3 and 4: Federations only let sub-national units substantially participate in the affairs of central government up to amending the constitution, and this under the rule of a favourably weighted representation of unequal units.

5.2.2   Federalism: A structure, a process and a political culture

So far we have considered federalism mainly as an institutional structure, or even as a constitutional framework. Scholars comparing different federal systems all over the world found the institutional scheme useful. But at the same time they detected its limits: 'many polities with federal structures were not at all federal in practice – the structures masked a centralised concentration of power that stood in direct contradiction to the federal principle'.[36]

Evidently federalism can be 'strong' or 'weak', and it is more than a structure. Besides varying structural settings of shared rule and self rule, the political process, too, can be organised in different ways: strong veto power of sub-national units leads to processes of co-decision in which central government must respect sub-national interests also in its own fields of competency. Conversely, weak power of sub-national units can lead to financial dependency and processes in which the central government controls the use of resources despite formal autonomy of the former. Different equilibriums of power imply different appropriate behaviour, which may crystallise into political cultures, too: high veto power of the sub-national units favours power-sharing, gentle negotiations and respectful dealing with sub-national units from the side of the central government. In the opposite case, processes between the central government and sub-national units are characterised by hierarchic subordination. Figure 5.1 illustrates the position of a series of countries on two of these unitary-federalist dimensions, constitutional structure and political process, and it includes unitary systems as well. Thus, it ranges from the most federal systems (upper right) to the most unitary countries (lower left). It presents the situation of the 1980s and is a historical document of the time before the breakdown of the Soviet Union. It illustrates, however, that some

Figure 5.1   Structure and process in federal and selected non-federal polities

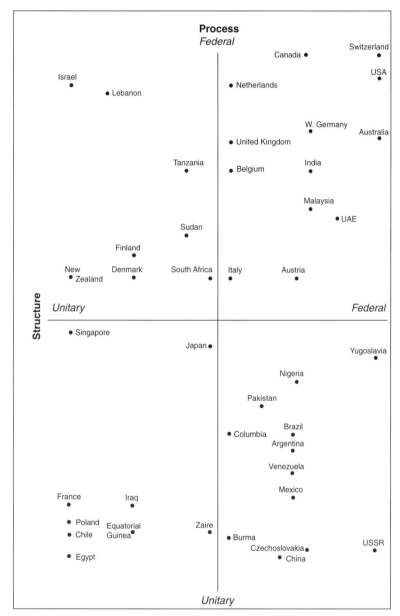

Source: D. Elazar, 'Federalism and Consociational Regimes', in: *Publius, The Journal of Federalism*, vol. 15, no. 2 (1985), pp. 17–35.

elements of federalism can be found not only in liberal democracies but also in authoritarian regimes. Moreover, the document helps to understand the nature of federalism under a strong central authority: The institutional structures of former Yugoslavia and the Soviet Union were federalist, but the central governments kept decisions on resources in their own hands, controlling the economic activities by ways of highly centralised government planning. Meanwhile, the Soviet Union and Yugoslavia have ended in implosion or civil war. Whereas the concentration of power of these one-party regimes was well known, most observers underestimated the fact that their centralised power also kept together different territorial units with different histories and cultures – artificially, we may say in retrospect, but under structures that were 'federal' in structure as those of liberal democracies.

USA and Switzerland are similar examples, being federalist both in structure and process. These two oldest federations developed by a bottom-up process, the sub-national units keeping much of their 'sovereign' rights as formerly independent states. The veto power of the sub-national units is high, especially in Switzerland. In the latter case, we have found that the cantons have a high financial autonomy and are mandated with the implementation of federal policies. Federal lawmaking is accompanied by a process of consultation with the cantons. If their reaction to a proposed bill is negative, the federal authorities drop the project or modify it until a solution satisfactory to the cantons is found. And even if the federal court has extensive constitutional power to review the law of cantons or municipalities, it is reluctant to intervene in their decisions if the latters' autonomy would thereby be restricted. The federal authorities often do not exercise all the powers they have, and when dealing with the cantons and the communes, use their competences with caution. Instead of deciding unilaterally, federal authorities negotiate, and respect the cantons or communes as equivalent partners. These non-hierarchical procedures have developed on the necessity to cooperate. The process of accommodation of the federal authorities with the sub-national units is an appropriate behaviour to find solutions under the conditions of the cantons' high veto power. It has become an element of political culture, mostly informal, and just occasionally prescribed as a legal procedure.

Taking the two dimensions of process and structure into consideration provides a preliminary picture of the variety of federalisms and decentralised polities. Elazar's comparative work showed that there are additional dimensions – such as the coincidence of social and political unity and diversity – which can further describe and help to explain the rich varieties of federalism. This coincides with the observation of the cultural differences that exist between the USA and Switzerland, even though both figure at the high end of federalism with regard to structure and processes: in Chapter 2 it was mentioned that Swiss federalism is aimed at equal opportunity in all regions and at equalising policies among the municipalities – US federalism is not but stresses federalist competition. Another cultural difference can be found in the fact that Swiss federalism was conceived to protect minorities – US federalism was not. This all explains why there is *no common model of federalism*, but a rich variety of *federalisms*.[37] They depend not only on political structures and processes but also on the history, the specific political culture and the socioeconomic challenges of a society and its polity.

5.2.3   Modern meanings of federalism

5.2.3.1   *Cultural autonomy and difference*

The case of Switzerland is instructive for the realisation of political unity whilst maintaining cultural diversity: the 26 cantons, with their different cultures, languages and religions, most of them having enjoyed centuries of political autonomy, were able to create a modern territorial state. Without federalism and its principle of dividing power between the new central government and the cantonal authorities, and without the federal promise to maintain regional differences and autonomy, this historical process of the nineteenth century would not have resulted in successful nation-building. Meanwhile, religious differences have faded. And, even if we can still distinguish German-, French- and Italian-speaking cantons, the language boundaries, which never did coincide entirely with cantonal ones have been penetrated by the electronic and print media and become more fluid. Switzerland today is a comparatively homogeneous society. But the Swiss would not dream of giving up their federalism. Despite complaints about federal particularities that may sometimes become obsolete or troublesome, the Swiss like the formal autonomy of their 26 cantons and 2600 municipalities, which in many respects may be fictive and to the foreign observer may appear to be an institutional luxury in a country of just about seven million inhabitants.

Bottom-up state-building and the federal experience itself are the historical heritage that have shaped a strong preference for 'small government' up to our days and helped to develop the idea of subsidiarity: central government should not meddle in things that the cantons are capable of doing themselves and the cantons should not bother with problems that the municipalities can handle. However, subsidiarity can lead to too small solutions, because the lowest federal level defines what the problem is. If the refusal of necessary centralisation is sometimes deplored, it offers opportunities for living 'differently'. Decentralised trial-and-error processes allow for political innovation, and successful experience can be transferred to upper levels in the sense of 'best practice'. Political institutions are not only rooted in and adapted to specific cultural needs, they are part of the social culture. Some say the Swiss feel Swiss only when abroad – when at home they are *Thurgauer, Genevois or Ticinesi*. Nationalism in the sense of exaggerated pride in a one and chosen people, its language or superiority, is not possible: between regional culture and awareness of the four linguistic groups the Swiss are part of a greater, international culture of French-, German- and Italian-speakers. Thus, the Swiss federal structures have remained, even though many of their original rationales have disappeared in the last 150 years.

Are these connotations of a federalist structure and its culture just a styled reminiscence of the past or are they meaningful beyond the case of Switzerland and in today's world? I will try to give some answers, illustrating a few of the many facets of federalism.

5.2.3.2   Federalism in times of globalisation

Today the *nation-state seems to be too small* to handle problems of national security, ecology, to guarantee human rights or to find answers with respect to growing inequalities between industrially advanced and developing countries. As part of the process of globalisation, international organisations multiplied, and nation-states conferred competencies of their own to the inter- and supra-national level. In one point, supra-national organisations resemble ideas of federalism: they decide certain affairs by majority but respect Duchacek's yardstick No. 3 of 'equally or favourably weighed representation of unequal members'. In the General Assembly of the UN, for instance, China, Liechtenstein or Switzerland are represented as equal, and each state is represented by one single seat. This gives small countries an over-proportional influence on decisions, but we also see that this advantage should not be overestimated: some big powers are permanent members of the Security Council and can veto the declarations of the General Assembly. Closer to the ideas of federalism comes the EU. Besides favourably weighed representation of its unequal members in most of its institutions, the EU Commission, EU Parliament and the Council of Ministers allow members to influence decisions in different ways, and on matters requiring unanimity every member has the right to veto the decision. We may say, therefore, that the development of the international community is to a lesser or stronger degree influenced by structural and procedural ideas of federalism. This is part of the solution to the problem of the nation-state having become too small.

Globalisation and internalisation, however, are contested on different grounds: that they widen inequalities between the first and the third world, that global capitalism is irresponsible to ecology, that policies of the international community lack democratic legitimation or destroy national structures and cultural identities – and the State, which in the high times of the neo-liberal strand was often reduced to a 'minimum state'. In the financial crisis of 2008, however, the state had to intervene as 'last resort' in order to save the financial system from a sudden break-down. This all could lead to a re-assessment of the role of the nation-state, the more so as despite globalised capitalist economy all redistribution of wealth (social security) and important collective goods (education, health) are still confined to the nation-state.

If the nation-state might be brought back in, what will be its future structure? While some scholars doubt that federalism can survive in a globalised world, others see modest impacts or even countervailing developments.[38] Indeed, in many European countries and beyond we observe some important and long lasting trends: decentralisation, the rising salience of local and regional politics, movements claiming territorial autonomy, or the growing awareness of linguistic, ethnic or cultural minorities to defend their identity or to claim new group rights. For the protagonists of all these movements, *the state is not too small but too big, and incapable of dealing with the diversity of its society*. Decentralisation or federalisation are the institutional answers to this problem. Spain or Belgium, once unitary systems, are recent cases in which federalisation took place as a reaction to claims for regional autonomy. Others may follow.

5.2.3.3   *Federalism in developing countries*

The process of international development and modernisation is, in the first instance, a clash between worldwide penetration through capitalistic enterprises seeking new markets on the one hand and subsistent indigenous economies and cultures on the other. The intermediate structures of government in many developing countries have not found solutions for dealing with inevitable conflicts. Above all, young democratic regimes, if seduced by short-term chances of centralisation or a charismatic concentration of power, fail to combine selective economic modernisation with selective backing of indigenous traditions and cultures. There are structural reasons for this. Many states were created by colonial powers, artificially uniting different ethnicities under one common roof, a problem I will take up in the next paragraph. Countries in sub-Saharan Africa, in contrast to many in Asia, lack the cultural heritage of a state overarching familistic and clan structures. Top-down state and nation-building after the end of European colonisation was a moderate success: central governments not taking ground in the periphery, abuse of political power, corruption by the political elites are keywords associated with the phenomenon of unsuccessful or even 'failed states'. Failed states, however, may be the wrong term and an episode. European countries needed centuries for their nation-building and were not exposed to a global stress of accelerated socioeconomic modernisation. Seeking for answers to improve the state structures of developing countries in the long run, decentralisation or even federalisation have become important concepts of developing agencies.[39] Decentralisation is said firstly to bring the state 'closer to the people' and giving them a better voice for their needs. Secondly, overcoming clientelism and clan politics is possible only under the condition that a non-familistic institution like the state receives trust from the citizens. People have to learn that public goods are not gifts from a Big Man but the return of their own fiscal contribution. And they must have trust in the authorities that this return will be fair and corresponding to their needs, which implies learning processes also for the political elites. Local autonomy, fiscal decentralisation or even federalism could provide better chances for this learning process than centralised government.[40] They represent an alternative to the mainstream politics of the last 50 years: strategies for a bottom-up state-building.

5.2.3.4 *Federalism as a guarantee for cultural difference and diversity*

While Belgium's, Switzerland's or Canada's federalisms try to unite the diversity of only a small number of cultural segments, Nigeria or India are much more complex: in these cases, federalism seems able to unite the cultural diversity of dozens of ethnics or hundreds of languages. Thus, federalism is sometimes used as a synonym of the guarantee for cultural difference and diversity, regardless of history or socioeconomic circumstances. But is this true, and to what degree can cultural minorities be effectively protected?

First, we have to note that not all federations are meant for cultural difference and diversity. Indigenous people in the US, for instance, are protected through reservation areas but do not benefit from political autonomy in a federal state. As a nation of immigrants, the US still favour the 'melting pot' concept: it trusts the idea that the dominating white, Anglo-Saxon and Protestant culture will assimilate all immigrants. The more important question, however, is whether federalism is really capable of protecting cultural difference and diversity, if this is the project. The experience is mixed. In South Africa, federalism seems to play an important role for the consolidation of a deeply divided society.[41] Under the common roof of India's or Nigeria's immense cultural diversity are some shadows: in-depth studies provide evidence that in situations of serious crisis federal structures in both countries are not used to ease a conflict.[42] In Canada, federalism could not prevent the French-speaking minority from calling a plebiscite for the independence of their stronghold, the Province of Quebec. In Belgium, which grants its two segments of French and Flemish-speakers utmost autonomy, national unity is said to be fading. This reminds us that federalist polities, giving too little or too much way to minorities, run a double risk of transforming themselves into unitary systems or of breaking apart. One should not confound effects and cause, however. Modest success is partly due to the fact that it is primarily divided societies trying to integrate minorities through federalism. Such is the case with three recent projects of federalisation, Ethiopia, Nepal and Sudan.

It may be useful to look at the potential and the limits of minority protection from a theoretical perspective.[43] The following conditions seem to be pertinent:

1. *Minorities not too small but sufficient in number:* It is evident that a 20 per cent minority has greater chances to benefit from federal autonomy than a minority of 2 per cent. With one single minority group, however, size alone may be of little help: it is always the same (regional) conflict which is at stake, and despite federalism the majority can decide. Conflicts may accumulate, as for instance in former Czechoslovakia, which dissolved in 1993. If federalist autonomy is claimed by several minorities and different kinds of minorities, chances of protection are better: the problem becomes more 'objective'; coalitions change and compensation between different actors and issues are possible. Too great a number of minorities divided up into many units, however, may become a disadvantage. Nigeria, for instance, started with three regions in 1960; today, not less than 36 ethnic groups of its society claim federalist autonomy. While this may be reasonable from the point of view of a single ethnic group, it may lessen the influence of the sub-national units on the central government, and the latter could use a strategy of 'divide and rule'.

2. *Cross-cutting conflict lines:* A single region may be characterised by several political cleavages: it belongs to both a religious and linguistic minority, and it is poor. In this case, conflicts may accumulate, as we have seen in the case of the Jura, the exception of failed integration in Switzerland (see Chapter 2), and chances of minority protection are less propitious than in situations of cross-cutting conflict lines. If a cultural minority region is not poorer or even wealthier than others – as for instance the Basque region in Spain – chances of autonomy being respected are favourable.

3. *Effective political majority in a sub-national unit:* As already mentioned, federalism protects only territorial segmented minorities, as in a pond which is divided into two parts for pikes and carp. This means that a carp swimming in the pikes' part is not protected against being eaten. Similarly, even a large minority cannot benefit from federalism if it is not able to constitute a political majority within the boundaries of a sub-national unit, as is the case with Muslims in Switzerland. Their number surmounts the population of an average Swiss canton, but they are dispersed over all cantons.

4. *No complete geographical division of ethno-cultural groups along borders of sub-national units*: In situations of serious conflict, federalisation is sometimes used to separate hostile ethnic groups. This was the case in Bosnia-Herzegovina, when the Dayton Agreement of 1995 cut borders of the sub-national units along the geographical borders of the Bosniac, Serb and Croatian populations. This helped peace for the moment but inadvertently continued the policy of 'ethnic cleansing'. It led to ethnic regions which bear the risk of creating their own minority problems. With ethnic political parties, the ethnic cleavage and its conflicts may remain the central concern of all politics. To a certain extent, Points 3 and 4 seem to be contradicting: Minorities should be able to constitute a majority but not be able to exclusively dominate a sub-national unit. Yet, this is not a contradiction, rather an unresolvable paradox: any minority protection through federalism creates a new minority problem. After each opening of a Russian nested doll, a smaller Matryoshka becomes the biggest one. Under inversed roles, the minority in a country, having become the majority of a sub-national unit, has to find its way to protect its own minority.

Looking at the points above, we notice that in Switzerland minority protection benefitted from favourable conditions: the number and size of minorities was not too small. Religious, cultural and social cleavages were cross-cutting, which facilitated the development of national political parties which are not confined to language or ethnicity. Cross-cutting cleavages had the side effect that every member of the political elite is somewhat part of a minority or a majority. If a radical, Catholic French-speaking candidate from Valais runs for elections to the national parliament, he has the advantage of belonging to the linguistic and religious majority but the handicap of politically representing a minority in a Christian-Democratic stronghold. Once being elected to the National Council, however, he belongs to the bourgeois and religious majority but to the linguistic minority. Being in the majority and the minority at times is the experience of most Swiss politicians and citizens.

If these favourable conditions may have helped successful dealing with minority problems, it should be noted that federalism alone would probably not have helped much in the Swiss case. Federalism is only one part of the solution for minority integration, in Switzerland or elsewhere. To achieve minority protection, federalism must be embedded in other institutional devices such as a non-religious, non-ethnic concept of the central state, a strong and effective tradition of human rights, and institutional elements of political power-sharing.[44]

5.2.3.5   *Federalism and democracy*

Democracy, basically, is majority rule founded on the number of votes cast, each vote having equal weight, whereas federalism implies equal or weighted representation of uneven units. A common pattern of institutionally combining the two modes is bicameralism: government proposals have to be voted on in two parliamentary chambers, one representing the people, the other the member states. Yet, there are many ways to proceed. While taking part in the deliberation of all federal law, Germany's *Bundesrat* has full decision-making powers only in matters which have certain consequences for its *Länder,* and it is composed of government representatives of the member states. Switzerland's polity requires double majorities in parliament and a popular vote for any amendment to the constitution, whereas ratification of amendments to the US constitution proposed by two-thirds majorities of Congress relies on individually organised procedures of the states, where a majority of three quarters is required. Yet in all cases important central government proposals have to find a double – or compound – majority.

Inevitably, the protection of territorial minorities leads to a distortion of the principle of equal rights in a democracy. The votes of individuals or representatives of member states with a small population are weighted more heavily than those of large member states. They can organise a veto to block democratic majorities. For Switzerland, where cantonal population size varies in a ratio of 1:34, we have already discussed the implications of the theoretical veto power of the smallest member-states, who represent just 9 per cent of the population (see Chapter 2). In other countries, such as the USA, with similar population differences between its units, the consequences may be less important because a divide between large and small states is unlikely to happen. But there is no doubt that federalism, with its compound majorities, implies a compromise with the democratic principle of equally weighted votes.

Federalism has, however, two main advantages that can compensate for this cost. First, when conflicts arise federalism is a constraint that 'forces' democratic majorities to bargain with federal minorities. In general, this favours the *status quo*. In practice, however, the reverse has applied in Switzerland too. Minorities of cantons may introduce innovations within their boundaries for which majorities at the federal level would not be found. Later, when the innovation proves successful at cantonal level, the innovation is accepted at central government level. Federalism is therefore not only an institution 'forcing' negotiation to take place, but one that provides opportunities for social learning by trial and error, and innovation.

Second, democratic costs of federalism at the central level can be compensated for by democratic gains in the sub-national units. In fact, democratic federations are mostly conceived as multi-level democracies whose constitution prescribes the same standards of institutional democracy for their member states and local governments. In a multi-level democracy, the political rights of the citizens – the election of officials, legislature and so on – have a much greater significance. Not only can voters elect the authorities of different levels, but they can vote for different parties at different levels. Thus a voter can express different preferences in local, sub-national and national politics. The frequency of elections provides citizens as well as authorities with permanent information on the popularity of the ruling majority. This phenomenon can be particularly well-observed in Germany, where 21 *Länder* governments are elected during one term of the federal government. Changes of power in parliamentary democracies often make their way up and down the federal levels. In a federation, not only the state but also democracy is closer to the people.

5.2.3.6   The question of secession

At a congress of East European and Swiss scholars of constitutional law held in Lausanne in 1990, one unforeseen issue dominated the discussions: how may a canton secede from the Swiss federation? Participants from Lithuania, the Ukraine, Croatia and other regions, eager to obtain advice on the then emerging desire for national autonomy, were somewhat disappointed to hear that neither the Swiss constitution nor law scholars in Switzerland had thought about the question of secession. Meanwhile, history in Yugoslavia has given a series of answers: the *de jure* recognition of the first *de facto* secession of Croatia through West European countries, the break-down of the federation in an atrocious and destructive civil war, the secession of Macedonia by popular vote, and, in the case of Kosovo, again the *de jure* recognition of a *de facto* secession by other countries and the international community. While civil war is to be rejected without discussion, the other answers leave many doubts. Should federations regulate secession? Can we think of a 'right' to secede, what should be its procedure, and what would be its consequences?

International law gives only some general and fragmentary answers. Secession is lawful under the narrow circumstances of severe violation of human rights and in cases of de-colonisation. Nothing is provided for federations and their paradoxical particularity: The federal polity gives its components 'indestructible identity and autonomy', which makes it more vulnerable to secession. At the same time, however, a federation is conceived as a permanent union – in contradistinction to a confederal system which lacks such commitment. Under this perspective, a secession clause seems to be needless: Federalism, in historical perspective, is successful when it transforms a constitutional arrangement into a commitment felt and accepted by all regions and their citizens, thus rendering the question of secession obsolete.

But this historical process can fail. Cultural segments may recall ancient dreams of independence that go beyond federal autonomy. There may be territorial segments that are systematically discriminated against. Instead of shaping a collective memory of a respectful pluralist experience, the passing of time provides undeniable 'proof' of discrimination, creating alienation and justifying hatred among different groups.[45] Behind many ethnic conflicts we find the economic question of redistribution: a region is not willing to share the wealth coming from natural resources with others, or inequalities of productivity and wealth are growing instead of diminishing. One part of the country may feel to be the permanent loser. Conflict on questions of the economy, language, religion and culture may escalate and end up in deep divides. If secession seems unavoidable, 'peaceful divorce' like the one in Czechoslovakia, with both parts in 1992 agreeing to break with their federation, is unfortunately the rare exception in the past. Rather we find a territorial minority seeking self-determination and secession against a majority of citizens who find it justified that their national government should defend the integrity of the federation. In this situation, both sides may feel the need for procedures designed to bring about a peaceful solution.

Thus, it may not be absurd to formulate future secession rules. Two questions would have to be answered. First, under what circumstances should a federation be obliged to let one of its members go? If any member is able to quit at any time, the federation cannot function. If the decision has to be made unanimously by all members, the rules may be irrelevant because secession may become impossible. Therefore, the answer must lie somewhere in between. Second, who should have the right to claim secession? This question may be crucial because within the boundaries of a secessionist member-state we may find a minority who would like to stay within the federation. Here the case of the Jura region separating from the Bern canton is instructive. As described in Chapter 2, the people of every district of the region was given the right to determine by direct vote whether to stay with the Bern canton or to become a member of the new Jura canton. Thus, it was the popular will of each minority that defined the territorial boundaries of secession. The Jura region was cut into two parts – one remaining with the old canton, the other founding its own canton. The problem remains unresolved in the eyes of the irredentist forces who wanted to unite the whole region under the new Jura canton. But the division prevented the creation of a new minority problem: the minority that wanted to stay with the old canton was not overruled and was given the same right of self-determination as the separatist majority.

This leads us to the following conclusion: in most cases, territorial secession gives rise to as many new minority problems as it claims to resolve. This is inevitable where territorial segmentation is not perfect. In the Czechoslovak 'divorce', for instance, the Slovak minority wished to free itself of Czech majority rule. But on Slovak territory today we find a minority of about 11 per cent Hungarians among the 5.3 million Slovaks, as well as other important minorities such as Czechs, Russians, Ukrainians, Romanys and so on – we are reminded by the allegory of the Russian nested doll mentioned above. Therefore, the now popular idea of a national state based on one language or culture – claimed by many secession movements – is ill-founded.

International law inadvertently may promote this problematic idea. The right to 'people's self-determination', today, is increasingly used as an argument for secession also by ethnic groups. The difficulties of definition of 'people' that should be granted 'self-determination' may lead to inconsistent interpretation and opportunistic intervention by the international community. In this respect, a look at the secession cases of Serbia's Kosovo and Georgia's Abkhazia and South Ossetia is instructive.[46]

Federations, other things being equal, are more vulnerable to secession than unitary states. Two policies may help to safeguard their unity: one, to find solutions other than secession; two, to find these solutions without interference from the outside. As to the first policy, giving problematic regions a status of special autonomy is a reasonable alternative to eventual secession. It is a compromise that may ease tensions and leave both parts better off, as in Spain's autonomous communities of Catalonia, the Basque Country and Galicia. In a more general way, special arrangements with particular sub-national units are known as 'asymmetric federalism' in the constitutions of India, Malaysia, Belgium or Canada and others.[47] Second, rules for secession should serve the one and only objective to prevent future secession. This seems paradoxical at first sight but is not. Rules of secession may change the balance of power: Openly and clearly specifying the conditions of eventual secession may strengthen the position of sensitive territorial minorities and give them more bargaining power against the central government. If installed well ahead of the time when a potential conflict breaks out, such rules may lead to more cooperative processes in the federal polity and reduce risks of secession. Two young federations, both with considerable potentials of conflict, Ethiopia and Sudan, have installed rules for secession. Future will show if their provisions work out in the proposed sense.

5.2.4 Non-territorial federalism

The idea of a territorial state that has exclusive power over all the people living within its boundaries is relatively recent. The older concept of political power was based more on the idea of personality. For instance, following the Germanic invasions of various provinces of the Roman Empire, there lived – side by side in the same territory and under the sway of the same 'barbarian' ruler – ex-Roman citizens and members of one of the Germanic tribal confederations (such as Goths, Vandals, Burgundians, Franks, and Lombards). Yet in most cases, and over a considerable period of time, the two groups remained distinct entities and, what mattered, before the law was who the defendant was, not where he was living. Usually, Romans were judged by Roman law and the new Germanic settlers by their old Germanic customary law. Both groups regarded this practice as proper and, indeed, as a precious safeguard of their respective rights and privileges'.[48]

With industrialisation and the development of bureaucratic state-hood, the West European countries led the way in becoming territorial states. Under the principle of *ius soli,* the territorial state claims all jurisdiction over its citizens – whatever their origin may be. Earlier I described part of this evolution in Switzerland. In its religiously seg-mented society of the nineteenth century marriages and education were regulated and organised separately for Protestants and Catholics by their churches. Whereas the label 'State Church' has not completely disappeared, the churches have mostly lost their status as actors in public affairs in favour of the confessionally neutral state which pro-vides for Protestant and Catholic citizens alike and under the same laws.

Yet, the principle of *ius sanguinis* has not completely disappeared. In the last days of the Austro-Hungarian Empire, Karl Renner and Otto Bauer proposed forms of non-territorial or corporate federal-ism to resolve the nationalities problem: 'Within each region of self-government, the national minorities shall form corporate entities with public judicial status, enjoying full autonomy in caring for the education of the national minority concerned, as well as in extending legal assistance to their co-nationals *vis-à-vis* the bureau-cracy and the courts'.[49] Corporate federalism was introduced for cultural minorities in Estonia in 1925, in Cyprus under the 1960 constitution and lately for Burmese minorities. The most prom-inent example, however, is Belgium where federalisation since 1970 has taken territorial and corporate forms as well. The country is divided into the regions of Flanders, Wallonia and Brussels. But Belgium is also divided into a Flemish-speaking community (com-prising both the geographically defined area of Flanders and the corporately defined group of Flemish-speakers in Brussels), a French-speaking community (comprising both the region of Wallonia and Francophone Bruxellois) and a German-speaking community (Eupen/ Malmédy).[50]

Corporate federalism allows a minority to maintain its own public institutions without territorial segmentation. This raises two questions. The first is: what are the limits of cultural minorities' right to run their own public institutions? This eventually depends on the concept of the state, of the constitution and on a society's ideas of pluralism as well. Therefore, we find different answers even for the same issue. In Switzer-land's public education, for instance, French-speaking schools in the German part of the country are well accepted as an element of multi-linguism. Religious schools, however, were declared non-constitutional by the laicist majority of the nineteenth century because in its view these schools violated the separation of state and Church. Today, schools of religious and other communities are tolerated under certain conditions but at any rate must respect constitutional freedoms, such as gender equality or freedom of speech. Constitutional law sets the principles which are to be respected by all segments of a pluralist society. But these principles and the concepts of pluralism vary considerably. The second question deals with the consequences: can non-territorial federalism keep the balance of unity and diversity, or do parallel institutions, exclusively reserved to cultural minorities, lead to deeper social divide and undermine unity? In literature, the question remains controversial: While some observers of the Belgian case fear the latter, others see non-territorial federalism as a promising approach to 'identity politics'.[51]

5.3   Power-sharing and consensus democracy

5.3.1   Majoritarian and consensus democracy: A comparison

If there is a continuous thread in Swiss political history it is probably the desire to prevent winners from taking all, leaving losers with nothing – or in other words, power-sharing. It is found in the constitution, in the federalist bargain between Protestants and Catholics, in the compromise between centralists and cantonalists, and in the development of proportional representation for the election of parliament, then of the Federal Council, of bureaucracies and commissions. All this gives minorities the opportunity to participate. The lawmaking political elites, in order to minimise referenda risks, try to arrive at a political compromise that includes all important political groups. Power-sharing provided the solution to the problem of integrating a heterogeneous, multicultural society by political means. It has led to a type of democracy different from others.

The combining of these elements of the *Swiss Concordance*, which avoids alternating government and opposition forces, may be unique but power-sharing, as a mode of democracy different from majority rule, is not. Arend Lijphart, a prominent scholar comparing political institutions, has called this 'consociational', 'power-sharing' or 'consensus' democracy, a type of democracy different from the 'majoritarian' or 'Westminster' model of democracy.[52] These two types are ideally different from each other in the following ways:

Table 5.2 Ljiphart's types of majoritarian and consensus democracy

	Majoritarian Democracy	Consensus Democracy
1. Executive	Concentration of power in one-party and bare-majority cabinet	Power-sharing in broad coalition cabinet
2. Relations executive/ parliament	Cabinet dominance	Balance of power
3. Political parties	Two-party system	Multi-party system
4. System of elections	Majoritarian and disproportional	Proportional representation
5. Influence of interest groups	Pluralism	Corporatism
6. Government structure	Unitary and centralised	Federal and decentralised
7. Parliament	Concentration of legislative power in unicameral legislature	Strong bicameralism
8. Type of constitution	Flexibility, simple procedure of amendment, or unwritten constitution	Rigidity, complex procedure of amendment
9. Judicial review	Absent or weak	Strong
10. Central bank	Controlled by executive	High degree of autonomy

Source: Lijphart (1999), 9ff., 31ff.

These two types of democracy represent coherent and therefore ideal polities maximising the basic ideas of either majoritarian or power-sharing politics. It is easy, however, to identify Switzerland and Great Britain as two polities that correspond to most criteria of one of the models, distinct by their basic ideas. Great Britain systematically favours the logic of majority rule. Competitive elections between only two parties based on one major political division lead to clear parliamentary majorities. The winner-takes-all rule makes parliamentary majorities sensitive to even small changes in the electorate's preferences, and favours alternating government and opposition roles if the two major parties are of similar size. Because of its parliamentary majority the executive cabinet is empowered to realise its policy programme, as long as there is no vote of no confidence, which may necessitate resignation or a new election. Power is concentrated among the parliamentary majority and the cabinet. The House of Lords has few competencies; almost all legislative power belongs to the House of Representatives. The latter may change constitutional documents in the same way as any other laws, which cannot be overridden by judicial review. One may speak of a nearly 'sovereign' parliament, with the main exceptions of devolution of power to Scotland and Wales, and of more independence given to the Bank of England. A similar coherence of elements, but with the opposite goal of power-sharing and negotiating politics, is found in the consensus model of Switzerland.

Majoritarian and consensus democracy are more than descriptions of two special cases in abstract terms. Lijphart's typology was particularly seminal in a comparative perspective. His latest study of 1999 shows how 36 countries can be situated on a continuum from majoritarian to

Figure 5.2 Majoritarian and consensus democracy: A two-dimensional conceptual map of 18 countries

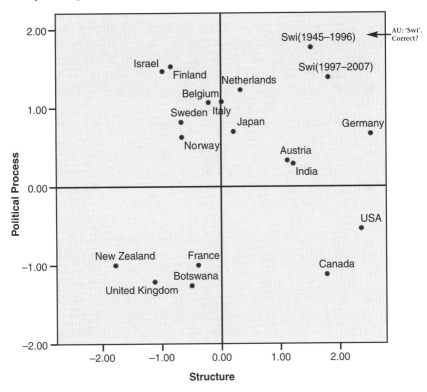

Source: Own calculations, using Lijphart's (1999) data from 18 countries.

consensus democracy. Using Lijphart's concept and taking half of his sample, we present a map of 18 countries (Figure 5.2).

In the two-dimensional Figure 5.2, Lijphart's ten criteria are divided into two groups. The vertical dimension sums up all indicators of the political process of parliament and government that lead to majoritarian or power-sharing politics (characteristics 1–5 in Table 5.2). On the horizontal dimension, we find the aggregate indicators of majoritarian or consensus structures of the polity, which include characteristics 5–10 and essentially represent a unitary-federal dimension. Not surprisingly, almost all federations – Canada, the US, Austria, Germany, India and Switzerland – are placed at the right side of the map. Federalism therefore shows up as an important structural element of consensus democracy but is not as decisive as one could expect: Canada and the US are two countries combining federalism with majoritarian processes of politics. In the Scandinavian countries, Lijphart found only these characteristics of power-sharing which are not related to federalism: multiparty systems, proportional representation, grand coalition cabinets designed to integrate different political forces, corporatism, and balances of power between cabinet and parliament. We note that Great Britain and Switzerland, as mentioned above, end up as 'purely' majoritarian or consensual because their logics of structure and process coincide. In the case of Switzerland, we observe a phenomenon that could be illustrated also for other cases: countries, in a lapse of time, may change their consensual or majoritarian character. This has to do primarily with the political process: the volatility of elections, especially, may lead to more or less power-sharing and coalitions in all countries. It shows, however, that the consensual mode of democracy is present in many democracies, both in unitary and federalist systems, and that there is a 'finely graded continuum from amicable agreement to majority rule'.[53]

Does power-sharing make a difference? Yes, says Lijphart. In many of his comparative studies he found evidence for a different performance of politics in majoritarian and consensus democracies. Consensus democracies, he summed up, demonstrate 'kinder and gentler qualities in the following ways: they are more likely to be welfare states; they have a better record with regard to the protection of the environment, they put fewer people into prison and are less likely to apply the death penalty; and consensus democracies in the developed world are more generous with their economic assistance to the developing world'.[54] With regard to the developing world, I add a further point: power-sharing helps democratisation. Drawing from Lijphart, we developed a concept of power-sharing allowing use also for non-consolidated democracies or even authoritarian regimes. In a comparative study of 62 countries from Africa and Asia, we found that between 1965 and 1995 power-sharing and the cultural element of low familism turned out to be the strongest predictors of democratisation, while economic factors – often viewed as the most important variables for shaping democratisation – have only limited effects.[55]

5.3.2 Democratic power-sharing: A key to resolving conflicts in multicultural societies

The first three chapters of this book illustrated what political power-sharing has done for Switzerland: complementing federalism, it became the key element in integrating a people following two religions and speaking four languages. Later it provided the Swiss with a collective identity strong enough to defend their political independence in periods of war in Europe, and it helped to overcome some economic class struggles. Power-sharing – considered by political scientists as the most appropriate form of democracy for pluralist or segmented societies – has even turned Switzerland into a relatively homogeneous society, in spite of its different languages. From such a perspective, the 'paradigmatic case of political integration'[56] of Switzerland has been an undeniable success. Can power-sharing and consensus democracy be used by other countries facing the problem of multicultural integration?[57]

The question is pertinent. The integration of different cultures through political institutions has become an important issue, worldwide, in much larger scales, and with more difficult problems than in the case of Switzerland. I have already mentioned India with its many hundred languages and idioms; some of Africa's Sub-Saharan young states are faced with the challenge of forming conglomerates of dozens of ethnic tribes which never before in history had been united together under a common political regime. In the new order of worldwide liberalisation and open markets, if the money does not go to the poor, the poor will go where the money is. Millions of people are migrating within the Third World or from the Third World to the industrialised countries. This has also led to the intertwining and confrontation of different cultures which once had been quite separated. Great Britain and other European countries are experiencing growing immigration from overseas. In California or New Mexico, US states with strong immigration, a considerable part of the population have become Spanish-speakers. They do not identify with the culture of white Anglo-Saxon Protestants, and the melting pot idea of assimilation is fading.

Today, a large majority of the countries considered as sovereign states constitute multicultural societies. Yet, conflicts between different groups of language, religion, or ethnicity are salient in all regions of the world. Historical minority problems in industrialised democracies have not faded away, and in Europe immigration has led to new social tensions. Gurr[58] estimated that at the beginning of the millennium about 275 minority groups from 100 countries, representing one seventh of the world population, are politically endangered. Instead of classical war between states, we increasingly find armed conflict between different groups of deeply divided societies – such as in Kenya, Sri Lanka or Pakistan, to mention just a few. In many cases, causes of internal conflict boil down to conflict about resources, but political escalation, alienation and mass mobilisation are often based on cultural difference or are intertwined with discrimination against cultural minorities.[59]

In order to prevent minority problems becoming salient or even escalating to violent forms of ethno-politics, more, or better, political integration is needed. But is power-sharing or consensus democracy appropriate for the problems of multicultural coexistence or integration, and why?

To begin with, we notice that the predominant model of democracy is majoritarian. Before spreading all over the world, majoritarian democracy was invented and first practised by white Anglo-Saxon Protestants. They shared common cultural values and beliefs and spoke a common language. On this basis Westminster democracy is an adequate decision-making procedure for the solution of social conflict in Britain's industrial society. Part of the voters, not being tied to an ideological position, are open to the question of whether the country needs more liberties for entrepreneurs or more social equality for workers. According to the economic situation and the performance of the last government, the British may vote in a pragmatic way: at first for the conservatives, then for labour, and eventually again for the conservatives. This change of individual preferences sums up to changing political majorities and to turning roles of government and opposition.

In multicultural societies, however, majoritarian democracy may encounter serious difficulties. Cultural values, beliefs and languages are not only heterogeneous, but may lead to different political preferences that do not change: parents can not opt out of sending their children to schools held in their own language, or discard their religious beliefs, without giving up part of their cultural identity. Individuals or groups cannot 'free' themselves from their cultural heritage. In many such situations cultural minorities cannot put much hope in majoritarian democracy. Catholics in Northern Ireland, for instance, are not likely to become a majority. If the predominant cultural majority is large enough, it will not have to take into account the preferences of the minority. In the worst case, government's chances of re-election under the winner-takes-all rule may even increase if it offers special advantages to its own cultural group while discriminating against the minority. If majoritarian democracy does not offer a regular change of power it may suffer from three deficiencies: One is that despite elections the political majority becomes 'eternal', which is against the basic idea of majoritarian democracy. The second one is that such an 'eternal' government has no incentives to take into account the needs and preferences of the minorities. It can afford not to learn which is the pathologic use of power. The third one is that majority rule may be alienating for those cultural segments which find themselves always in a minority position.

Tocqueville's, Madison's or J.S. Mill's criticism of democracy as a 'tyranny of the majority' is therefore well founded. It led to corrective institutions, such as fundamental rights for individuals, federalism or particular autonomy rights for regions and for minority groups. A further corrective element is political power-sharing. Lijphart, already in the first versions of his theory, proposed that consensus democracy is better suited for multiculturally segmented societies than majoritarian institutions. The theoretical reason is obvious: consensus democracy gives societal minorities a chance to participate in political power and have a voice in the policies of the government which cannot be overheard. By mutual agreement and compromise, societal divides may be eased or even overcome. Looking at the classical power-sharing democracies of Switzerland, Belgium or the Netherlands, Lijphart's proposition makes sense. The case of Northern Ireland, where elements of power-sharing were introduced as part of the peace-making process between Protestants and Catholics, is at least promising. Finally, India shows that elements of power-sharing can be useful also for developing countries and under conditions fundamentally different from small states in Europe. On the African continent, however, we find contradictory experiences: In South-Africa, power-sharing allowed the passage from Apartheid to a democratic regime, allowing the white minority as well as different black ethnicities to participate. The power-sharing pact in Rwanda 1993, however, could neither outweigh conflicts on resources nor put an end to the historical hostilities between Hutu and Tutsi, once influenced by the colonial powers. An atrocious civil war followed. Moreover, peace agreements in divided societies, often arranged by the international community such as in Bosnia, Cambodia, Burundi or East Timor proved to be of moderate success despite provisions for political power-sharing.[60] Against this background, one is not surprised to find a controversial academic debate. Critics of Lijphart proposed that power-sharing is not helpful with peace-making or that it even undermines democratisation.[61]

Much of this academic critique takes a wrong point, as it does not compare majoritarian with consensus democracy as a sustainable institutional arrangement under equal conditions. Rather, it evaluates the short-term success of power-sharing agreements as part of the peace-making process. It is obvious that the transformation of peace-making treaties into stable democratic institutions bears high risks and can fail for many reasons. From a vast literature, one can learn that the consolidation of democracy entails a long process also under conditions more favourable than war-torn societies. In developing countries, it depends on the existence of a consolidated state, of chances of economic development, and of the compatibility of the cultural heritage with social modernisation.[62]

Power-sharing peace arrangements after armed conflicts in deeply divided societies may be the beginning but are not the same as an established constitutional order, and only part of a consensus democracy yet to be developed. So, when it boils down to the relevant question of comparing majoritarian or power-sharing institutions and their long-time effect, empirical evidence suggests the latter.[63] From this perspective, I propose the following points:

1. *Proportional representation has a high symbolic value favouring mutual respect between different cultural groups.* Self esteem and political recognition of minority groups are essential and a precondition for any rational political discourse or accommodation amongst political elites. To promote this objective, proportional representation can be practised in any institution: in the electoral system, in parliament, in the executive, in all branches of the administration or in police and armed forces. Of course, proportional representation has some pitfalls. Under the conditions of one single minority or of one single cleavage, there is a risk that proportional representation perpetuates societal conflict instead of cooling down the divide. With more than one minority or more cross-cutting cleavages, however, political competition may favour the development of non-ethnic or non-regional political parties, elites and cultures. The evolution from a

divided to a pluralist society lets old cleavages fade into the background.

2. *The rule of proportional representation favours negotiation and accommodation of conflict solution in which minorities have an effective voice.* Proportional representation introduces veto power for minorities but does not suspend the formal rule of majority decision. Yet, where minorities are permanently participating in decisions, formal decisions imply negotiation and accommodation, avoiding 'the winner takes all' situations. The effective voice of minorities depends on two conditions. The first is mutual recognition of the different parts of the political elite. This opens the doors for cooperation on a rational discourse. On such a basis, solutions turning zero-sum games into positive-sum games become feasible. Cooperation then is more advantageous than non-cooperation because it leaves all parts better off. The second condition is turning issue-specific coalitions. If today's opponent is tomorrow's coalition partner, both actors are partly dependent on each other. This favours a political culture of mutual respect. Empirical evidence is found that under power-sharing conditions politicians listen more to each other and give more weight to arguments of their opponents than in majoritarian situations. Thus, proportional representation and power-sharing realise more of the ideal of 'deliberative democracy'.[64]

3. *Political cooperation between political elites may favour general patterns of intracultural relations.* Cooperation in parliamentary and executive decisions not only promotes compromise in political issues. It may also lead to a better understanding between different cultural segments, their mutual respect and the development of common values. This process may at first be limited to the political elites, but it may be followed by a trickle-down to larger segments of society.

4. *Federalism or decentralisation, if combined with other elements of power-sharing, may be more effective for multicultural co-existence.* Federalism may be considered a structural element of power-sharing. While restricting the power of the central government, it can guarantee autonomy for different cultural segments in territorial sub-divisions. Like basic individual rights or statutory minority rights and vetoes, federalism is an institutional mechanism restricting majority rule and majority politics. Federalism as a 'vertical' dimension of power-sharing has its deficiencies, however, as we have discussed in the previous part of this chapter. In combination with the 'horizontal' elements of political power-sharing, federalism and decentralisation may become more effective for minority voice and protection.[65]

5. *Consensus democracy rejects hegemonic claims of one single group and avoids the fallacy of a monocultural 'nation-state'.* Consensus democracy is possible only under the conditions of recognition of equality of all societal cultures and their groups before the state. Thus, political power-sharing requires a certain acceptance of societal and cultural pluralism. This pluralism must be installed in the basic concept of the state: the latter must guarantee equal rights to all its citizens and renounce on undue privileges for a specific culture discriminating against other groups. In contrast to the 'cultural concept', this means a political concept of the state, in which citizenship is the only qualification of the rights of individuals. Such a concept is basically indifferent to religion, language or ethnicity of its different groups. Of course, every constitutional order, to a certain degree, is characterised by the heritage of a specific culture and its predominant values. The idea of separation of religion and the state, for instance, is realised in different ways and to different degrees in industrialised Western democracies.[66] These differences may be greater even in developing societies where ligatures of religion are much stronger. Non-industrialised, traditional societies exposed to outside pressure of accelerating modernisation are sometimes even pushed towards relying on religion and other cultural traditions. However values that symbolise a precious good for one cultural segment may be threatening for another segment. Such divides can be overcome only by the development of equal rights, of mutual respect among all cultural groups and the development of common intercultural values. Such a collective identity or political culture requires a high degree of indifference or impartiality on the part of state authorities with respect to particular cultural segments.

6. *The development of a political culture of power-sharing takes time.* A new constitution can be enshrined in a few weeks, political parties founded, elections held, a parliament and a government installed in a few years. Successful democratisation, however, may take much longer because the consolidation of the institutions, the functioning of the political process, or the appropriate behaviour of actors all need the development of a democratic political culture. In times of global pressure towards accelerated modernisation and quick conflict intervention by the international community it should not be forgotten that changes in social values, the development of common values between different cultures and cultural pluralism are processes of social integration that take time. Even more patience

is needed when it comes to power-sharing as a means to overcome societal divide or to accommodate deep social conflict. The wounds of discrimination or of civil war take generations to heal.[67] More than majoritarian settings, power-sharing institutions incite a 'spirit of accommodation',[68] respect, trust or even 'deliberative potentials'.[69] But these incentives cannot be accelerated, are weak and vulnerable. While trust in consensus democracy may take a long time to develop, it may quickly be destroyed by a hegemonic use of power.

7. *Consensus democracy provides better chances for, but not a guarantee of peaceful solution of conflict in multicultural societies.* Peaceful solution of conflict in divided societies depends on many circumstances: on economy and resources, on the countries' exposure to neighbours and foreign interests, on a societies' culture and history – and the political institutions. The latter are therefore just one of many factors. The only proposition is made with regard to the type of democracy: if the choice is between majoritarian and consensus institutions, the latter provides better chances for the solution of multicultural conflict. In theory there are two major arguments against the consensus model. First, it is said that the political will to share power depends to a great extent on political elites, and that power-sharing can turn into an elitist model of democracy. Second, consensus democracy can be used by hegemonic groups as a veil to hid the real power processes when giving minorities the opportunity to participate but no substantial influence.[70] In this case, which can be observed for instance in the relations between the Jewish majority and the Arab minority in Israel, Ian Lustick speaks of a 'control model' with different characteristics from the consensus model.[71] However, neither argument devalues the consensus model as such but illustrates its limits: the consensus model offers more chances or opportunities than majoritarian democracy for peaceful conflict resolution in multicultural societies, but there is no guarantee for successful integration through mutual adjustment.

5.4 Epilogue

5.4.1 Switzerland's future in the process of globalisation

In the epilogue of the first version of 'Swiss Democracy', written in 1994, I noted: On 6 December 1992 the Swiss people, in a popular vote, turned down membership of the European Economic Area (EEA). Whereas the other members of the European Free Trade Association

(EFTA) – Austria, Finland, Iceland, Norway, Sweden and Liechtenstein – have decided to become integrated into the EC market and may soon become full EC members, Switzerland, for the time being, has chosen to remain outside. No other political decision since the Second World War has been of such crucial importance to Switzerland than this decision.

This policy change was highly controversial, and the popular vote of December 1992 left behind a divided nation. Whereas the treaty was of immediate economic importance, its significance for many people went far beyond economics. The referendum, therefore, was a vote on Switzerland's political future and national identity, and it is this question that is now dividing the country.

On one hand, there were those who saw the decline of the *Sonderfall Schweiz* (Special Case of Switzerland). Indeed, with the fundamental political changes in Central and Eastern Europe, Switzerland has lost many of the economic privileges of its former neutral *Sonderfall* position. Moreover, the EC's offer for an EEA treaty seemed to be a good opportunity to take a first step towards integration: the treaty promised intense economic cooperation without political responsibilities as a full member of the EC. Culturally, many Swiss feel 'European' and therefore want to participate in the process of integration. For them the EEA treaty signalled a more open Swiss society.

On the other hand there were those who still placed great store in Switzerland's *Sonderfall*. Sceptical about 'big government', foreign influence, international bureaucracies and foreign political commitment, they believed that the country was still strong enough to stay on its own. Whilst some businessmen saw economic opportunities in the fact that Switzerland, by remaining outside the EC, could be attractive for US or Japanese capital, ecologists wanted to preserve Switzerland's higher environmental standards. Conservatives feared losing political neutrality, federalism and direct democracy, as well as a genuine Swiss culture being free from foreign influence. They fiercely opposed the idea that Switzerland, one day, could become a member of the EC.

For the moment Swiss consensus is shaken, also on several domestic issues such as economic and social policy. This could lead to a polarisation of political parties in Switzerland, to changes in executive power-sharing or even an end to consensus democracy at large. Some observers do not rule out the possibility of a realignment of the Swiss party system into three main forces: a new national conservative party could draw members from all governmental parties and seek a new clientele with populist preferences; liberal Christian democrats and radicals could merge into a new centre force; social democrats, including the greens, could represent the political left. Switzerland, as Karl Deutsch put it 20 years ago, is in a critical situation between 'innovation and stagnation'.[72] The country's future is less certain and political compromise less easy than for a long time in the past.

Fifteen years later, I could still subscribe to these comments. The divide of Swiss society on its future has not disappeared. Admittedly, the Swiss government, in the meantime, has managed to find a way to deal with the EU: the 'bilateral way' has led to a number of treaties, regulating the important economic relations with the EU market. They were accepted by the EU members and by the Swiss people as well. Nobody knows, however, how long this way may be open. It may become more costly, and lead into a dead end. Step by step, the Swiss government might have to adopt all EU legislation. Would then the Swiss be willing to join the EU in order to participate in the development of European integration or still try to defend an autonomy which risks to become an empty pocket? Neither government nor political parties like to discuss the question because it still divides Swiss society. Despite its 'No' to the EEA treaty, Switzerland is fully exposed to the dynamics of Europeanisation and globalisation as well. It not only creates winners and losers but widens the divide between pro-Europeans and national autonomists. The national conservatives have gained political ground. Their belief in Swiss strength to maintain utmost autonomy and sovereignty has been shaken neither by the increasing vulnerability of Switzerland to external pressure nor by the dwindling acceptance of the Swiss *Sonderfall* by the international community. Scepticism is nourished also by the fact that *de facto* Swiss politics follow the path of liberalisation and globalisation quicker than many EU members.

Pressure from the outside has led to a two-speed political process: accelerated in internationalised affairs, incremental in domestic politics. Liberalising forces use globalisation as their tool; the traditional balance between the interests of the domestic and the internationalised economy has changed. Globalisation weakens many of the traditional veto points; federalist autonomy of the cantons, similar to national autonomy, has lost significance in economy, in policies and beyond.

No wonder that Swiss politics have become much more polarised. The old cleavages between capital and labour, and between urban and rural regions, are rising. The system of the political parties has been transformed: The people's party is driving the national-conservative road and has become the biggest governmental party at the cost of the centre parties of the radicals and the Christian democrats. The bourgeois block is often split, which leads to a tri-partite system of left, centre and right. Polarisation, the strategy of both the right and the left, makes consensus more difficult and is detrimental to the spirit of accommodation. The rules of the *arithmetic concordance* of the government have become blurred. Some speak of a 'crisis of concordance'.

'Switzerland is on its way of becoming a divided society rather than the paradigm of cohesion claimed by Deutsch in the 1970s' is the verdict of the British scholar Clive Church, the most reliable outside observer of Swiss politics for decades. And, before a clear majority commitment for European integrations would ever be possible, he adds, 'Europe may do damage to Swiss political integration'.[73] For the moment, this outlook is realistic rather than pessimistic. But other scenarios are possible, too. As long as the EU rests an elitist project, bureaucratic and with little democratic legitimation, Swiss voters will not accept to join. Direct democracy, while being the main obstacle for membership, is at the same time the most robust political institution that holds the Swiss together. It forces the political elite to share power, maintain cooperation, negotiation and compromise despite all other transformations of the Swiss polity, despite growing divides, and despite the ongoing difficulties induced by globalisation. In this sense, Deutsch's paradigm of integration through political institutions is still true.

5.4.2 Swiss democracy: Export model or subject of dialogue?

In 1926, Gazi Mustafa Kemal Atatuerk, the Father of the modern Republic of Turkey, adopted the codification of Swiss civil law for his country. After the fall of the USSR, many Islamic countries in the south of the Soviet Union, now independent, adopted the Turkish code of civil law. Today, over 350 million people live under direct or indirect influence of Swiss civil law. Should and could the Swiss similarly try to export their 'Swiss model of democracy'? My first answer is no.

The first reason is that political institutions have a different cultural context even amongst countries of similar socioeconomic level. For Great Britain, which had to contend with secessionist forces in Scotland and Wales, a Swiss mediator proposing federalist institutions would certainly not have been welcomed. For the British, the word 'federalism' often has connotations of centralisation, and would have been in contradiction to any project of devolution of power. Or, if direct democracy would be introduced in the EU, one could not expect the peoples of the EU countries to behave like the peoples of the Swiss cantons because the common interests are much stronger for the latter.[74] While 'difference of culture' as an obstacle to direct export of institutions is obvious in these cases, it is often not respected with regard to developing countries. The agenda of big powers of the First World and their agencies is full of democratisation, governance or even human right programs lacking respect and empathy for the societal context of countries in transition. Their numerous failures can be explained by several factors: many of them are ethnocentric, blind for the socio-cultural particularities of the addressed countries. Few of them take into consideration that before democratisation is feasible, the state as well as the economy must have reached a certain degree of consolidation first, and that in traditional societies Western institutions of democracy cannot immediately take ground.[75] Finally, democratisation is abused as a geopolitical strategy. The lesson is that all these forms of 'export of democracy' are not recommendable and do not help.

So I come to my second answer to the 'export' question: If the Swiss want to aid democracy, they should choose other ways, *the way of dialogue*. No matter whether in academic discussion, in expertise, or official cooperation, such a dialogue on democracy has to meet some common criteria. Democracy is not a negotiation chip but an issue of dialogue and cooperative learning amongst equals. The Swiss when finding partners interested in the *Helvetic* model of democracy should be prepared for a double translation. The Swiss case, first of all, is not an ideal model but a historical experience. The narrative of its wars, conflicts, failures and success shows the peculiarities of Swiss institutions and their context. Yet, while the Swiss system is unique as every other, federalism, power-sharing or direct democracy are not. This leads to the first translation: putting these institutions in an abstract or comparative perspective which highlights their functioning in different contexts. In a dialogue of equals, this should be followed by the narrative of the partner. He gives an account on his own history, its conflicts, failures and success, and then passes to the second translation: Trying to find out if, on the basis of his cultural heritage, there are elements of own institutions that can be developed and combined with modern concepts of federalism, power-sharing or direct participation – and trying to evaluate their chances for the solution of the problems of institution-building at stake. Having listened to the other's narrative, both partners learn in the double translation process. One side may learn, for instance, that the Swiss are not peaceful by nature but because of their institutions, while the other side becomes aware that direct participation is practised in many local societies of Asia or Africa. In such mutual learning processes, which I have experienced in many countries in Eastern Europe, the Near East, Asia and Africa, Swiss democracy was not used as an export model but proved to be a most precious subject for a credible, respectful and open dialogue. In the course of such dialogues, I became more and more impressed by the well known but not always heard insight: democracy cannot be imposed but must develop on the political will of a people, on its socioeconomic conditions, and on a country's own cultural heritage.

Notes

Chapter 1

1 H.U. Jost writes that the division between French- and German-speaking Swiss was mainly a matter of the political elites and their activist press, whereas at the level of the common people relations seemed to be much more unconstrained. See Hans Ulrich Jost, 'Menace et repliement (1914–1945)', in: *Nouvelle histoire de La Suisse et des Suisses* (Lausanne: Payot, 1986).

2 For a comprehensive discussion see Clive Church (ed.), *Switzerland and the European Union* (London and New York: Routledge, 2007).

3 Karl Deutsch, *Die Schweiz als paradigmatischer Fall politischer Integration* (Bern: Haupt, 1976).

4 Tobias Kästli, *Die Schweiz – eine Republik in Europa* (Zurich: Verlag Neue Zürcher Zeitung, 1998), pp. 17–44.

5 Andreas Ernst, Albert Tanner and Matthias Weishaupt (eds), *Revolution und Innovation – Die konfliktreiche Entstehung des schweizerischen Bundesstaats von 1948* (Zurich: Chronos, 1998).

6 Alfred Kölz, *Neuere Schweizerische Verfassungsgeschichte* (Bern: Stämpfli, 1992), pp. 608–610 and Roland Ruffieux, 'La Suisse des radicaux (1848–1914)', in: *Nouvelle histoire de la suisse et des Suisses,* vol. II (Lausanne: Payot, 1983), pp. 10–11.

7 In 1830 Basel Country demanded proportional representation in the cantonal parliament, that is, a number of seats according to the size of population. After Basel City refused this proposition, a civil war broke out in which people were wounded and killed. Finally the Swiss confederation approved in 1833 the separation between Basel City and Basel Country in two semi-cantons and brought the conflict to an end. See Georges Andrey, 'Auf der Suche nach dem neuen Staat', in: *Geschichte der Schweiz und der Schweizer,* vol. II (Basel and Frankfurt am Main: Helbing und Lichtenhahn, 1983), pp. 247–249.

8 William E. Rappard, *Le facteur économique dans l'avénement de la démocratie moderne en Suisse* (Genéve: Georg, 1912).

9 Alois Riklin 'Neutralität am Ende? 500 Jahre Neutralität der Schweiz', *Zeitschrift für Schweizerisches Recht*, vol. 125, Issue 1 5 (December 2006), pp. 583–597.

10 Alois Riklin, *Funktionen der schweizerischen Neutralität* (St. Gallen: Institut für Politikwissenschaft, 1991), p. 6. Riklin, *op. cit.*, quotes three additional functions: (a) the free-trade function, (b) the function of maintaining political equilibrium in Europe, (c) the function of offering 'good offices' in international relations. For Swiss foreign policy from 1848 to 1991 see Georg Kreis, Jean-Claude Favez and Urs Altermatt, 'Geschichte der schweizerischen Aussenpolitik 1848–1991', in: Alois Riklin *et al.* (eds), *Neues Handbuch der schweizerischen Aussenpolitik* (Bern: Haupt, 1992), pp. 27–78 and Laurent Goetschel, 'Foreign policy', in: Ulrich Klöti *et al.* (eds), *Handbook of Swiss Politics* (Zurich: Neue Zürcher Zeitung Publishing, 2007), pp. 571–591.

11 For new perspectives on Swiss neutrality and foreign policy see: Stephan Kux (ed.), *Zukunft Neutralität?* (Bern: Haupt, 1994); Jürg Martin Gabriel, *Die Neutralität auf dem Prüfstand* (St. Gallen: Institut für Politikwissenschaft, 1995); and Jürg Martin Gabriel and Thomas Fischer (eds), *Swiss foreign policy, 1945–2002* (Basingstoke: Palgrave, 2003).

12 According to James H. Huston, *The Sister Republics* (Washington: Library of Congress, 1991), there were several periods of mutual influence. Especially important were three periods: (a) in the debate between American federalists and anti-federalists, the latter took the model of the old Swiss confederation as their reference; (b) the Swiss, in 1848, had the American constitution very much in their minds when combining the principles of federalism and democracy; (c) towards the end of the nineteenth century the institutions of Swiss direct democracy were taken as a point of reference.

13 Arnold Niederer, *Gemeinwerk im Wallis: bäuerliche Gemeinschaftsarbeit in Vergangenheit und Gegenwart* (Basel: Krebs, 1965).

14 Rolf Soland, *Joachim Leonz Eder und die Regeneration im Thurgau 1830–1831: Ein Kapitel aus der thurgauischen Verfassungsgeschichte* (Weinfelden: Mühlemann, 1980).

15 François Masnata and Claire Rubattel, *Le pouvoir Suisse: 1291–1991. Séduction démocratique et répression suave* (Lausanne: Editions de l'aire, 1991).

16 Karl Deutsch, *The Nerves of Government: Models of Political Communication and Control* (New York: Free Press, 1967), pp. 214–243.

17 Ulrich Im Hof, *Mythos Schweiz. Identität-Nation-Geschichte* (Zurich: Verlag Neue Zürcher Zeitung, 1991).

18 Brigitte Ruckstuhl, 'Die Schweiz – ein Land der Bauern und Hirten', in: Silvia Ferrari *et al.*, *Auf wen schoss Wilhelm Tell?* (Zurich: Rotpunktverlag, 1991), p. 136. For the role of language in modern notions of Swiss identity: Christof Demont-Heinrich, 'Language and National Identity in the Era of Globalization: The Case of English in Switzerland', *Journal of Communication Inquiry*, vol. 29, no. 1 (2005), pp. 66–84.

19 In the years after the foundation of the federal state the Catholics were going to extend their educational system step by step (establishing new schools, founding of a university). See Urs Altermatt, *Katholizismus und Moderne* (Zurich: Benziger, 1991), p. 147.

20 See Kenneth D. McRae, *Switzerland: Example of Cultural Coexistence* (Toronto: The Canadian Institute of International Affairs, 1964); Uli Windisch, *Les relations quotidiennes entre Romands et Alémaniques* (Lausanne: Editions Payot, 1992) and Pierre du Bois, *Alémaniques et Romands entre unité et discorde: histoire et actualité* (Lausanne: Favre, 1999).

21 If the total population, including the 16 per cent made up of foreigners, is taken into consideration, the proportion of Italian speakers increases, whereas the proportion of German speakers decreases. See also Table 1.1.

22 In 1938 Article 116 of the constitution was amended to include Romansh as the fourth national language of Switzerland. This was the result of a request of the executive of the Grisons in 1935 at the time of Italian fascism under Mussolini. The initiators understood the request 'primarily as an aid to Romansh in its uphill struggle for survival against the inroads of modern communications and tourism'. See McRae (1964), *op. cit.*, p. 9. With an amendment to the constitution in 1996, Romansh has become an official language.

23 Despite limits of multilingualism the Swiss seem to have a better knowledge of English than people in most continental countries. In a comparative survey, Switzerland ranks second behind Sweden, followed by Germany, Belgium, France and Spain. See: Iwar Werlen, 'Englisch als Fremdsprache bei Erwachsenen in der Schweiz', in: Sandro Moraldo, *Sprachkontakt und Mehrsprachigkeit* (Heidelberg: Winter, 2008), pp. 211f. and Iwar Werlen, *Sprachkompetenzen der erwachsenen Bevölkerung in der Schweiz. Schlussbericht Nationales Forschungsprogramm 56* (Bern: Institut für Sprachwissenschaft, 2008).

24 As a comparison of the Canada, the US and Switzerland see: Carol L. Schmid, *The politics of language: Conflict, identity, and cultural pluralism in comparative perspective* (New York: Oxford University Press, 2001).

25 Windisch (1992), *op. cit.*

26 Richard J. Watts, 'Linguistic minorities and language conflict in Europe: Learning from the Swiss experience', in: Florian Coulmas (ed.), *Language Policy for the EC* (Berlin: Mouton de Gruyter, 1991), Schmid (2001), *op. cit.* and Windisch (1992), *op. cit.*

27 See also: Jürg Steiner, 'Power-sharing: Another Swiss "Export-Product"?', in: Joseph V. Montville, *Conflict and Peacemaking in Multiethnic Societies* (Massachusetts and Toronto: Lexington Books, 1990).

28 See Erich Gruner, *Arbeiterschaft und Wirtschaft in der Schweiz 1880–1914*, vol. I–III (Zurich: Chronos, 1988).

29 Erich Gruner, '100 Jahre Wirtschaftspolitik, Etappen des Staatsinterventionismus in der Schweiz', *Schweizerische Zeitschrift für Volkswirtschaft und Statistik* (1964), pp. 34–70.

30 Peter Farago, *Verbände als Träger öffentlicher Politik* (Grüsch: Rüegger, 1987); Clive Church, *The Politics and Government of Switzerland* (Basingstoke and New York: Palgrave-Macmillan, 2004), pp. 71–81; André Mach, 'Interest Groups', in: Ulrich Klöti *et al.* (2007), *op. cit.*, pp. 359–380.

31 Farago (1987), *op. cit.*; Hanspeter Kriesi, *Entscheidungsstrukturen und Entscheidungsprozesse in der Schweizer Politik* (Frankfurt and New York: Campus Verlag, 1980).

32 Gruner (1988), *op. cit.*; Hans Ulrich Jost, *Die reaktionäre Avantgarde: Die Geburt der neuen Rechten in der Schweiz um 1900* (Zurich: Chronos, 1992).

33 Wolf Linder, 'Entwicklung, Strukturen und Funktionen des Wirtschafts- und Sozialstaats in der Schweiz', in: Alois Riklin, *Handbuch Politisches System der Schweiz*, Band I (Bern and Stuttgart: Haupt, 1983), pp. 255–382.

34 Christine Trampusch, 'The Welfare State and Trade Unions in Switzerland. A Historical Reconstruction of the Shift from a Liberal to a Post-Liberal Welfare Regime', *Journal of European Social Policy* (2009), forthcoming.

35 Otto K. Kaufmann, 'Frauen, Italiener, Jesuiten, Juden und Anstaltsversorgte. Vorfragen eines Beitritts der Schweiz zur Europäischen Menschenrechtskonvention', *St. Galler Festgabe zum Schweizerischen Juristentag 1965* (Bern: Stämpfli, 1965), pp. 245–262.

36 Eidgenössische Kommission für Frauenfragen, *Berichte; Die Stellung der Frau in der Schweiz/Gleiche Rechte für Mann und Frau/Die politische Repräsentation der Frauen in der Schweiz/Viel erreicht – wenig verändert?/Frauen Macht Geschichte* (Bern: Eidg. Kommission für Frauenfragen, 1980–1999). Thanh-Huyen Ballmer-Cao, *Changement social et rapport entre hommes et femmes* (Lausanne: Editions

Payot, 2000). For the role of women in Swiss politics: Thanh-Huyen Ballmer-Cao and Manon Trembley (eds), 'Modes de scrutin, partis politiques et élection des femmes', *Swiss Political Science Review*, vol. 14, no. 4 (2008), pp. 609–630. For the success of gender politics: Martin Senti, *Geschlecht als politischer Konflikt* (Bern: Haupt, 1995).
37   Bundesamt für Statistik, *Statistik des Freiheitsentzugs* (2008).

Chapter 2

1   Edgar Bonjour, *Die Gründung des schweizerischen Bundesstaates* (Basel: Schwabe, 1948), *Kapitel VII: Das Zustandekommen der Bundesverfassung*; Tobias Kästli, *Die Schweiz – eine Republik in Europa* (Zurich: Verlag Neue Zürcher Zeitung, 1998), pp. 23–176.
2   Andreas Ernst, Albert Tanner and Matthias Weishaupt (eds), *Revolution und Innovation – Die konfliktreiche Entstehung des schweizerischen Bundesstaats von 1848* (Zurich: Chronos, 1998).
3   See: Alfred Kölz, *Neuere schweizerische Verfassungsgeschichte. Ihre Grundlinien vom Ende der Alten Eidgenossenschaft bis 1848* (Bern: Stämpfli, 1992), pp. 301–540.
4   For an overview see: Adrian Vatter, 'Federalism', in: Ulrich Klöti *et al.* (eds), *Handbook of Swiss Politics* (Zurich: Neue Zürcher Zeitung Publishing, 2007), pp. 197–225.
5   For institutional development and dimensions of the constitutions of 1848 and 1874, see Jean Francois Aubert, *Traité du droit constitutionnel suisse, Troisième partie: La structure fédérale* (Neuchâtel: Ides et Calendes, 1967), pp. 510–894. For the constitution revised 1999, see Jean Francois Aubert and Pascal Mahon, *Petit commentaire de la Constitution fédérale de la Confédération suisse du 18 avril 1999* (Zurich: Schulthess, 2003), pp. 379–455.
6   Wolf Linder, 'Verfassung als politischer Prozess', in: Beat Sitter (ed.), *Herausgeforderte Verfassung: Die Schweiz im globalen Kontext* (Freiburg: Universitätsverlag, 1997a).
7   For a substantive analysis of the intergovernmental relations see: Wolf Linder and Adrian Vatter, 'Institutions and Outcomes of Swiss Federalism: The Role of the Cantons in Swiss Politics', in: *West European Politics* 24 (2001), pp. 95–122.
8   Ruth Lüthi, 'The Parliament', in: Ulrich Klöti *et al.* (2007), *op. cit.*, pp. 121–142.
9   Ruth Lüthi, *Die Legislativkommissionen der Schweizerischen Bundesversammlung: Institutionelle Veränderungen und das Verhalten von Parlamentsmitgliedern* (Bern: Haupt, 1997).
10   Adrian Vatter, 'Bicameralism and Policy Performance: The Effects of Cameral Structure in Comparative Perspective', *Journal of Legislative Studies*, vol. 11 (2) (2005), pp. 194–215; George Tsebelis and Jeannette Money, *Bicameralism* (Cambridge: Cambridge University Press, 1997).
11   Reto Wiesli and Wolf Linder, *Repräsentation, Artikulation und Durchsetzung kantonaler Interessen im Ständerat und im Nationalrat: Studie im Auftrag der Parlamentsdienste der Schweizerischen Bundesversammlung* (Bern: Institut für Politikwissenschaft, 2000).
12   Katia Horber-Papazian, 'The Municipalities', in: Klöti *et al.* (2007), *op. cit.*, pp. 227–250.

13 Hans Geser, Andreas Ladner, Roland Schaller and Thanh-Huyen Ballmer-Cao, *Die Schweizer Lokalparteien* (Zurich: Seismo, 1994) and Andreas Ladner, *Verbreitung und Bedeutung der Lokalparteien in den Gemeinden* (Zurich: Soziologisches Institut, 2003) (http://socio.ch/par/ladner/lad_03.pdf).

14 See Arnold Niederer, *Gemeinwerk im Wallis: bäuerliche Gemeinschaftsorbeit in Vergangenheit und Gegenwart* (Basel: Krebs, 1965).

15 Hans Geser, Peter Farago, Robert Fluder and Ernst Gräub, *Gemeindepolitik zwischen Milizorganisation und Berufsverwaltung* (Bern: Haupt, 1987) and Andreas Ladner, *Die Schweizer Gemeinden im Wandel: Politische Institutionen und lokale Politik* (Lausanne: Cahier de l'IDHEAP Nr. 237, 2008).

16 Raimund E. Germann, *Ausserparlamentarische Kommissionen, Die Milizverwaltung des Bundes* (Bern: Haupt, 1981).

17 Frédéric Varone, 'The Federal Administration', in: Klöti *et al.* (2007), *op. cit.*, pp. 281–308.

18 For an overview of the implementation process of different federal policies see: part 7 of Ulrich Klöti *et al.* (eds), *Handbook of Swiss Politics* (Zurich: Neue Zürcher Zeitung Publishing, 2007), pp. 569–841.

19 For details of the process see: *Année politique Suisse,* Annual political journal (Bern: Institute of Political Science, University of Bern 1990–2008).

20 For other compensating effects of federal policy weakness see Fritz Sager, 'Kompensationsmöglichkeiten föderaler Vollzugsdefizite. Das Beispiel der kantonalen Alkoholpräventionspolitiken', *Swiss Political Science Review* 9(1) (2003), pp. 309–333.

21 Brigitte Schwab and Muriel Surdez, 'Education and Cultural Policy', in: Klöti *et al.* (2007), *op. cit.*, pp. 788–798.

22 Maja Coradi Vellacot and Stefan Wolter, *Equity in the Swiss Education System: dimensions, causes and policy responses. National Report* (Aarau: Swiss Coordination Centre for Educational Research, 2004).

23 The use of the term 'region' is ambiguous in Switzerland. It can designate (a) the geographical boundaries of the four languages, or other geographical subdivisions of the country with a number of common characteristics (mountain, urban, rural, suburban regions); (b) the geographic boundaries of several communes, belonging sometimes to different cantons, defined for the purpose of a specific federal policy programme, as in the case of the development of the mountain regions; (c) administrative organisations, formed by several communes, for regional land-use planning and economic development. None of these regions are political organisations representing a 'fourth tier' in the federal system. In cases (b) and (c) we could speak of administrative organisations that are confined to one specific function.

24 Michel Bassand and François Hainard, 'Dynamique socio-culturelle régionale', PNR, vol. 35.5, *Synthèse des problèmes régionaux* (Lausanne: Presses Polytechniques Romandes, 1985).

25 Adrian Vatter and Markus Freitag, 'Political Institutions and the Wealth of Regions: Swiss Cantons in Comparative Perspective', *European Urban and Regional Studies,* vol. 11 (4), 2004, pp. 227–241.

26 See Gaston Gaudard and Catherine Cudré-Mauroux, *Une nouvelle inégalité interrégionale en Suisse* (Fribourg: Imprimerie St-Paul, 1997) and Paul Messerli, 'Regionalpolitik zwischen Theorie und Praxis', in: Christoph A. Schaltegger *et al.* (eds), *Perspektiven der Wirtschaftspolitik* (Zurich: vdf, 2004), pp. 435–450.

27   Adrian Vatter (ed.), *Föderalismusreform, Wirkungsweise und Reformansätze föderativer Institutionen in der Schweiz* (Zurich: Verlag Neue Zürcher Zeitung, 2006); René Frey (ed.), *Föderalismus – zukunftstauglich?!* (Zurich: Verlag Neue Zürcher Zeitung, 2005).

28   See Michel Bassand *et al.*, *Les Suisses entre la mobilité et la sédentarité* (Lausanne: Presses polytechniques romandes, 1985).

29   Albert O. Hirschman, *Exit, Voice and Loyalty: Responses to Decline in Firms, Organizations, and States* (Cambridge, Mass: Harvard University Press, 1970).

30   For more details of historical events see Jean-François Aubert, *Exposé des institutions politiques de la Suisse à partir de quelques affaires controversées* (Lausanne: Payot, 1983); J.R.G. Jenkins, *Jura Separatism in Switzerland* (Oxford [England]; New York: Clarendon Press, 1986) and Gilbert Ganguillet, *Le conflit jurassien: genèse et trajectoire d'un conflit ethno-régional* (Zurich: bokos druck, 1998).

31   Jean-Daniel Delley *et al.*, *Le droit en action, Etude de mise en oeuvre de la loi Furgler* (St. Saphorin: Editions Georgi, 1982).

32   For an overview: Ingrid Kissling-Näf and Sonja Wälti, 'The implementation of Public Policies', in: Klöti *et al.* (2007), *op. cit.*, pp. 502–524. For an in-depth-study: Christian Rüfli and Fritz Sager, 'Public Health, Prävention und Föderalismus: Erkenntnisse aus der Umsetzung des Bundesgesetzes über die Krankenversicherung', Sozial- und Präventivmedizin. *International Journal of Public Health* 49(3) (2004), pp. 216–223.

33   Michel Bassand, Gerard Chevalier and Erwin Zimmermann, *Politique et logement* (Lausanne: Presses Polytechniques Romandes, 1984).

34   Wolf Linder, *Politische Entscheidung und Gesetzesvollzug in der Schweiz* (Bern: Haupt, 1987), pp. 224–227.

35   For the early politics of Swiss women's organisations, see Beatrix Mesmer, *Ausgeklammert-Eingeklammert. Frauen und Frauenorganisationen der Schweiz des 19. Jahrhunderts* (Basel and Frankfurt am Main: Helbing und Lichtenhahn, 1988).

36   The first comprehensive sociological report on the position of women in Swiss society dates from 1974 (Thomas Held and René Levy, *Die Stellung der Frau in Familie und Gesellschaft: Eine soziologische Analyse am Beispiel der Schweiz* (Frauenfeld: Huber, 1974)).

37   Iris von Roten, *Frauen im Laufgitter* (Zurich and Dortmund: Efef, 1991 [1958]); for the response to the book see the politically illustrative biography of Iris von Roten: Yvonne-D. Köchli, *Eine Frau kommt zu früh* (Zurich: Weltwoche-ABC, 1992).

38   This interpretation is not at odds with Lee Ann Banaszak, 'The Influence of the Initiative on the Swiss and American Women's Suffrage Movements', *Schweizerisches Jahrbuch für Politische Wissenschaft*, no. 31 (Bern: Haupt, 1991), pp. 187–207. She compares not only the influence of the initiative but also the 'various dimensions of the political opportunity structure' and finds that the Swiss women's suffrage movement lacked the support of other movements and parties. The reason for this was weak, and in many cantons non-existent, party competition.

39   While the cantons of Appenzell Ausserrhoden, Nidwalden and Obwalden have abandoned, Appenzell Innerrhoden as well as Glarus still hold an annual assembly of all citizens, the *Landsgemeinde,* where the election of authorities

and ballots on some important issues take place. See Silvano Möckli and Peter Stahlberger, 'Die schweizerischen Landsgemeinde-Demokratien', *Staat und Politik*, vol. 34 (Bern: Haupt 1987), pp. 237–260 and Felix Helg, *Die schweizerischen Landsgemeinden: ihre staatsrechtliche Ausgestaltung in den Kantonen Appenzell Ausserrhoden, Appenzell Innerrhoden, Glarus, Nidwalden und Obwalden* (Zurich: Schulthess, 2007).

40 Decision of the Federal Court no. lb/294/1990 of 27 November 1990.

41 Walter Kälin, *Verfassungsgerichtsbarkeit in der Demokratie. Funktionen der staatsrechtlichen Beschwerde* (Bern: Stämpfli, 1987), pp. 187–200.

42 The following paragraphs are based on Raimund E. Germann, 'Die Europatauglichkeit der direktdemokratischen Institutionen in der Schweiz', *Schweizerisches Jahrbuch für politische Wissenschaft*, no. 31: *Direkte Demokratie* (Bern: Haupt, 1991), pp. 257ff. and Wolf Linder, *Schweizerische Demokratie, Institutionen, Prozesse, Perspektiven* (Bern: Haupt, 2005), pp. 184–195.

43 Among others, Germann (1991), *op. cit.*, p. 269, predicted a majority of the cantons for the EEA treaty only if 57 per cent of the people voted for it.

44 Martina Koll-Schretzenmayr/Willy Schmid, Agglomerations-politik in der Schweiz, DISP 152 (2003), pp. 4–14.

45 See for instance: Fritz Sager, *Vom Verwalten des urbanen Raums. Institutionelle Bedingungen von Politikkoordination am Beispiel der Raum – und Verkehrsplanung in städtischen Gebieten* (Bern: Haupt, 2002).

46 Districts (German, *Bezirke;* French, *districts*) are subdivisions of cantons, comprising a number of communes. Originally, the districts were created to decentralise cantonal power and cantonal authorities, an idea that was mostly substituted by direct delegation of cantonal tasks to the communes. Today, the responsibilities of districts are limited to judicial organisation and some police tasks. Furthermore, they serve as constituencies for the election of the members of cantonal parliaments.

47 Bericht der Arbeitsgruppe *'Zusammenarbeit in den Agglomerationen'* (Bern: Forschungszentrum für schweizerische Politik, 1992) and Luzia Lehmann, Stefan Rieder and Stefan Pfäffli, 'Zusammenarbeit in Agglomerationen: Anforderungen – Modelle – Erfahrungen', *Luzerner Beiträge zur Gemeindeentwicklung und zum Gemeindemanagement*, Bd. 9 (Luzern: Verlag IBR, 2003).

48 For Swiss foreign policy since the 1990s see: Laurent Goetschel, Magdalena Bernath and Daniel Schwarz (eds), *Swiss Foreign Policy: Foundations and Possibilities* (London and New York: Routledge, 2005).

49 For a general view see: Pascal Sciarini, Alex Fischer and Sarah Nicolet, 'How Europe Hits Home: Evidence from the Swiss Case', *Journal of European Public Policy* 11 (3) (2004), pp. 353–378. For a perspective from the outside: Clive Church (ed.), *Switzerland and the European Union* (New York and London: Routledge, 2007).

50 André Mach, Silja Häusermann and Yannis Papadopoulos, 'Economic Regulatory Reforms in Switzerland: Adjustment without European Integration or How Rigidities Become Flexible', *Journal of European Public Policy*, vol. 10, no. 2

(2003), pp. 301–318 and Christine Trampusch, 'The Politics of Institutional Change. Transformative and Self-Preserving Change in the Vocational Education and Training System in Switzerland', *Comparative Politics*, vol. 41 (2009).

Chapter 3

1 For a concise description of the legal institutions: Jean Francois Aubert and Pascal Mahon, *Petit Commentaire de la Constitution Fédérale de la Confédération Suisse* (Zurich: Schulthess, 2003), pp. 1061–1116. Direct democracy institutions from a political science perspective: Wolf Linder, *Schweizerische Demokratie, Institutionen, Prozesse, Perspektiven* (Bern: Haupt, 2005), pp. 241–283.

2 Georg Lutz and Dirk Strohmann. *Wahl- und Abstimmungsrecht in den Kantonen* (Bern: Haupt, 1998).

3 Adrian Vatter, *Kantonale Demokratien im Vergleich: Entstehungsgründe, Interaktionen und Wirkungen politischer Institutionen in den Schweizer Kantonen* (Opladen: Leske + Budrich, 2002), pp. 219ff.; Alexander Trechsel and Uwe Serdült, *Kaleidoskop Volksrechte: Die Institutionen der Direkten Demokratie in den Schweizerischen Kantonen (1970–1996)* (Basel: Helbing und Lichtenhahn; Genève: Faculté de droit, 1999).

4 Patricia Lafitte, *Les Institutions de DéMocratie Directe en Suisse au Niveau Local* (Lausanne: Cahiers de l'IDHEAP no. 34, 1987) and Philipp Karr, *Institutionen Direkter Demokratie in den Gemeinden Deutschlands und der Schweiz: Eine Rechtsvergleichende Untersuchung* (Baden-Baden: Nomos, 2003).

5 Christian Moser, 'Erfolge kantonaler Volksinitiativen nach formalen und inhaltlichen Gesichtspunkten', in: *Schweizerisches Jahrbuch für Politische Wissenschaft*, no. 27 (Bern: Haupt, 1987), pp. 59–188 and Vatter (2002), *op. cit.*, pp. 330ff.

6 Alfred Kölz, *Neuere Schweizerische Verfassungsgeschichte Ihre Grundlinien vom Ende der Alten Eidgenossenschaft bis 1848* (Bern: Stämpfli, 1992), pp. 615–620.

7 Karl Bürkli, *Direkte Gesetzgebung Durch das Volk* (Zurich and Geneva: 1869).

8 I will therefore use the term 'semi-direct democracy' when referring to the Swiss political system and its elements of representative and direct democracy as a whole, and 'direct democracy' when referring to the two instruments of the referendum and the initiative, as well as to their use.

9 On the cantonal level, we find similar procedures for cantonal initiatives, with the difference that the final decision on the validity of a popular initiative may be demanded from the Federal Court.

10 Peter Bachrach and Morton S. Baratz, 'Decisions and Nondecisions: An Analytical Framework', *American Political Science Review*, vol. 57 (September, 1963), pp. 632–642.

11 Jean-François Aubert, *Petite Histoire Constitutionnelle de la Suisse* (Bern: Francke, 1974), pp. 43–44.

12 See Jürg Steiner, *European Democracies* (London: Longman, 1991), p. 139.

13 The exception was Ireland, where an obligatory referendum had to be held – and failed in 2008.

14 See Jean-Daniel Delley, *L'initiative populaire en Suisse. Mythe et Réalité de la Démocratie Directe* (Lausanne: L' Age d'Homme, 1978); Oswald Sigg, *Die eid-*

genössischen Volksinitiativen 1892–1939 (Bern: Francke, 1978); Hans Werder, *Die Bedeutung der volksinitiative in der Nachkriegszeit* (Bern: Francke, 1978); Yannis Papadopoulos (ed.), *Elites Politiques et Peuple en Suisse, Analyse des Votations Fédérales 1970–1987* (Lausanne: Réalités sociales, 1994), p. 260.

15 This ended in the 1990s, when the People's Party got engaged in the immigration issue and took over the small anti-immigration parties and their protest voters.

16 One of the deputies in 1850 explained his motive as follows: 'If we have to allow citizens of other cantons to vote on national issues, there is no reason why French or Italians should not have this same right'. See Pierre-André Schmitt, 'Neuenburg ist allen andern hundertvierzig Jahre voraus', in: *Die Weltwoche*, 13 July, 1989.

17 See Schattschneider's earlier criticism of Dahl: 'The flaw in the pluralist heaven is that the heavenly chorus sings with a strong upper-class accent', E.E. Schattschneider, *The Semisovereign People. A Realist View of Democracy in America* (Hinsdale: Dryden Press, 1960), p. 35 and Georg Lutz, *Participation, Information and Democracy: The Consequences of Low Levels of Participation and Information for the Functioning of Democracy* (Hamburg: Lit, 2006), pp. 114ff.

18 For an overview on current research, see Hanspeter Kriesi, *Direct Democratic Choice: The Swiss Experience* (Lanham, Md.: Lexington Books, 2005); Yannis Papadopoulos, *Démocratie Directe* (Paris: Economica, 1998) or: Alexander Trechsel, 'Popular votes', in: Ulrich Klöti *et al.* (eds), *Handbook of Swiss Politics* (Zurich: Neue Zürcher Zeitung Publishing, 2007), pp. 405–434.

19 VOX no. 32, July 1987.

20 See Alex Fischer, Sarah Nicolet and Pascal Sciarini, 'Europeanisation of a Non-EU Country: The Case of Swiss Immigration Policy', in: *West European Politics*, vol. 25 (4) (2002), pp. 143–170; Gerald Schneider and Thomas Holzer, *Asylpolitik auf Abwegen. Nationalstaatliche und Europäische Reaktionen auf die Globalisierung der Flüchtlingsströme* (Opladen: Leske + Budrich, 2002), or Wolf Linder, 'Migrationswirkungen, institutionelle Politik und politische Öffentlichkeit', in: W. Kälin and R. Moser (eds), *Migrationen aus der Dritten Welt* (Bern: Haupt, 1991) (2), pp. 152–155.

21 Giovanni Sartori, *The theory of democracy revisited* (Chatham, N.J.: Chatham House, 1987), p. 120, or: Ian Budge, *The New Challenge of Direct Democracy* (Cambridge Mass.: Polity Press, 1996), p. 69.

22 Arthur Lupia and Mathew D. McCubbins, *The Democratic Dilemma: Can Citizens Learn What They Need to Know?* (Cambridge: University Press, 1998) and Kriesi (2005), *op. cit.*, p. 9.

23 Kriesi (2005), *op. cit.*

24 Papadopoulos (1994), *op. cit.*, p. 137.

25 Kriesi (2005), *op. cit.*, pp. 82–83.

26 Hanspeter Hertig, 'Werbebudget und Abstimmungsergebnis: Sind Abstimmungserfolge käuflich', in: Erich Gruner and Hanspeter Hertig, *Der Stimmbürger und die Neue Politik* (Bern: Haupt, 1983), pp. 130–137.

27 See Thomas E. Cronin, *Direct Democracy. The Politics of Initiative, Referendum, and Recall* (Cambridge, Mass. and London: Harvard University Press, 1989), pp. 99–113.

28 Hans Hirter, *Die Werbung der Printmedien zu den Volksabstimmungen vom 4.12.88 und 26.11.89* (Bern: Forschungszentrum für schweizerische Politik, 1989 and 1990); Claude Longchamp, 'Herausgeforderte politische Öffentlichkeit', *Schweizerisches Jahrbuch für Politische Wissenschaft*, vol. 31 (Bern: Haupt, 1991), pp. 303–326.

29 Hanspeter Kriesi, 'Sind Abstimmungsergebnisse käuflich?' in: Adrian Vatter *et al.* (eds), *Demokratie als Leidenschaft* (Bern: Haupt, 2009), pp. 83–106 and Chapter 4.

30 Wolf Linder, Regula Zürcher and Christian Bolliger, *Gespaltene Schweiz – Geeinte Schweiz: Gesellschaftliche Spaltungen und Konkordanz bei den Volksabstimmungen seit 1874* (Baden: hier + jetzt, 2008).

31 For a rather pessimistic outlook on this topic: Yannis Papadopoulos, 'Démocratie Suisse et idéologie populiste: Quand on récolte ce qu'on a semé', in: Adrian Vatter *et al.* (eds), *Demokratie als Leidenschaft* (Bern: Haupt, 2009), pp. 107–117.

Chapter 4

1 Jean-François Aubert, *Petite histoire constitutionnelle de la suisse* (Bern: Francke, 1974), pp. 43–44.

2 For the impact of proportional election of the Federal Council on the *Konkordanz* from a historical perspective: Urs Altermatt, Konkordanz im Spiegel der Bundesratswahlen, in: Adrian Vatter *et al.* (eds), *Demokratie als Leidenschaft* (Bern: Haupt, 2009), pp. 247–270.

3 Andreas Auer, 'Les detours du "retour a la democratic directe". Le droit fédéral d'urgence 1971–1975', in: *Mémoires Publiés par la Faculté de Droit Genève*, Mélanges offerts à la Société Suisse des Juristes (Genève: 1976).

4 For a comprehensive study of the development of the pre-parliamentary procedures and the indirect effects of the referendum, see Leonhard Neidhart, *Plebiszit und Pluralitäre Demokratie* (Bern: Francke, 1970); Yannis Papadopoulos, *Les Processus de Decicion Federaux en Suisse* (Paris: L'Harmattan, 1999), pp. 69–96 and Jeremias Blaser, *Das Vernehmlassungsverfahren in der Schweiz: Organisation, Entwicklung und Aktuelle Situation* (Opladen: Leske and Budrich, 2003).

5 For extensive accounts see: Pascal Sciarini, 'The Decision-Making Process', in: Ulrich Klöti *et al.* (eds), *Handbook of Swiss Politics* (Zurich: Neue Zürcher Zeitung Publishing, 2007), pp. 465–524 and Wolf Linder, *Schweizerische Demokratie, Institutionen, Prozesse, Perspektiven* (Bern: Haupt, 2005), pp. 301–332.

6 Ruth Lüthi, *Die Legislativkommissionen der Schweizerischen Bundesversammlung: Institutionelle Veränderungen und das Verhalten von Parlamentsmitgliedern* (Bern: Haupt, 1997) and Annina Jegher, *Der Einfluss von Institutionellen, Entscheidungspolitischen und Inhaltlichen Faktoren auf die Gesetzgebungstätigkeit der Schweizerischen Bundesversammlung* (Bern: Haupt, 1999).

7 Pascal Sciarini and Alexandre Trechsel, 'Démocratie directe en Suisse: l'élite victime des droits populaires?', in: *Revue Suisse de Science Politique* 2 (2) (1996), pp. 201–232.

8 *Année Politique Suisse 1969* (Bern: Forschungszentrum für schweizerische Politik, 1969).

9 For an overview see: Frédéric Varone, 'The Federal Administration', and Ingrid Kissling-Näf and Sonja Wälti, 'The Implementation of Public Policies', both in: Klöti *et al.* (2007), *op. cit.*, pp. 281–308 and pp. 501–524.

10 Christine Trampusch, The Welfare State and Trade Unions in Switzerland. A Historical Reconstruction of the Shift from a Liberal to a Post-Liberal Welfare Regime. In: *Journal of European Social Policy*, vol. 20 (1) (2010), pp. 58–73.

11 See Robert Jörin and Peter Rieder, *Parastaatliche Organisationen im Agrarsektor* (Bern: Haupt, 1985).

12 See André Mach: 'Interest Groups', in: Klöti *et al.* (2007), *op. cit.*, pp. 359–380.

13 Enid Kopper, 'Swiss and Germans: Similarities and Differences in Work-Related Values, Attitudes, and Behaviour', *International Journal of Intercultural Relations*, vol. 17 (1993), pp. 167–184.

14 Andre Bächtiger, Markus Spörndli, Marco Steenbergen and Jürg Steiner, 'The Deliberative Dimension of Legislatures', *Acta Politica* 40 (2) (2005), pp. 225–238.

15 Karl Deutsch, *The Nerves of Government. Models of Political Communication and Control* (New York: Free Press, 1967).

16 Arend Lijphart, 'Consociational Democracy', *World Politics* 21 (2) (1969), pp. 207–225.

17 Hans Huber, 'Staat und Verbände', in: *Rechtstheorie, Verfassungsrecht, Völkerrecht, Ausgewählte Aufsätze 1950–70* (Bern: Stämpfli, 1971).

18 See Mancur Olson, *The Logic of Collective Action* (Cambridge: Harvard University Press, 1965).

19 Fritz Scharpf, *Demokratietheorie Zwischen Utopie und Anpassung* (Konstanz: Universitätsverlag, 1970); Huber (1971), *op. cit.*, pp. 589–630; Linder (2005), *op. cit.*, pp. 120–125.

20 Heidrun Abromeit and W. Pommerehne (eds), *Staatstätigkeit in der Schweiz* (Bern: Haupt, 1992) and Klaus Armingeon, 'Konzertierung in der Schweiz', in: Sven Jochem and Nico A. Siegel (eds), *Konzertierung, Verhandlungsdemokratie und Reformpolitik im Wohlfahrtsstaat – Das Modell Deutschland im Vergleich* (Opladen: Leske + Budrich, 2003), pp. 311–330. In a comparative perspective: Heidrun Abromeit, *Interessenvermittlung zwischen Konkurrenz und Konkordanz* (Opladen: Leske, 1993). To the time-management of the process of mutual adjustment: Alain Poitry, *La fonction d'ordre de l'Etat. Analyse des mécanismes et des déterminants sélectifs dans le processus législatif suisse* (Bern: Lang, 1989).

21 Raimund E. Germann, *Politische Innovation und Verfassungsreform* (Bern: Haupt, 1975).

22 Raimund E. Germann, 'Bundesverfassung und "Europafähigkeit" der Schweiz', in: *Schweizerisches Jahrbuch für Politische Wissenschaft,* 30 (Bern: Haupt, 1990), pp. 17–28.

23 Silvio Borner, Aymo Brunetti and Thomas Straubhaar, *Schweiz AG: vom Sonderfall zum Sanierungsfall* (Zurich: Verlag Neue Zürcher Zeitung, 1990), pp. 153ff., 169ff. and Silvio Borner and Hans Rentsch (eds), *Wieviel direkte Demokratie verträgt die Schweiz?* (Chur: Verlag Rüegger, 1997).

24 Wolf Linder, 'Schweizerische Konkordanz im Wandel', *Zeitschrift für Staats- und Europawissenschaften,* vol. 7 (2) (2009), pp. 209–230.

25 Oscar Mazzoleni, *Nationalisme et Populisme en Suisse – La Radicalisation de la 'Nouvelle' UDC* (Lausanne: Presses Polytechniques et Universitaires, 2003).

26 Daniel Schwarz and Wolf Linder, *Fraktionsgeschlossenheit im Schweizerischen Nationalrat 1996–2005: Studie im Auftrag der Parlamentsdienste der Schweizerischen Bundesversammlung* (Bern: Institut für Politikwissenschaft, 2007).

27   See: Alex Fischer, 'Internationalisation of Swiss Decision-Making Processes', in: Klöti *et al.* (2007), *op. cit.*, pp. 547–568.
28   André Mach, Silja Häusermann and Yannis Papadopoulos, 'Economic Regulatory Reforms in Switzerland: Adjustment without European Integration, or How Rigidities Become Flexible', *Journal of European Public Policy*, vol. 10, no. 2 (2003), pp. 301–318.
29   Wolf Linder, Regula Zürcher and Christian Bolliger, *Gespaltene Schweiz – Geeinte Schweiz: Gesellschaftliche Spaltungen und Konkordanz bei den Volksabstimmungen seit 1874* (Baden: hier + jetzt, 2008).
30   Earlier versions of this trade off in: Linder (2005), *op. cit.*, pp. 320–323; Wolf Linder, 'Repräsentative und direkte Demokratie, Systeme im Spannungsverhältnis', in: Eugen Antalovsky (ed.), *Die Bürger und ihre Stadt* (Wien: Magistrat der Stadt Wien, 1991).
31   Caroline Tolbert and Daniel Smith, 'The Educative Effects of Ballot Initiatives on Voter Turnout in the United States', *American Politics Research* 33 (2) (2005), pp. 283–309.
32   Isabelle Stadelmann-Steffen and Markus Freitag, 'Abstimmung – oder Wahldemokratie? Zum Einfluss der direkten Demokratie auf die Wahlbeteiligung in den Kantonen', in: Adrian Vatter *et al.* (eds), *Demokratie als Leidenschaft* (Bern: Haupt, 2009), pp. 157–182.
33   In a comparative perspective: Hanspeter Kriesi, 'Bewegungen auf der Linken, Bewegungen auf der Rechten: Die Mobilisierung von zwei neuen Typen von sozialen Bewegungen in ihrem politischen Kontext', *Schweizerische Zeitschrift für Politische Wissenschaft*, vol. 1, Summer (1995), pp. 9–52.
34   M.I.S. Trend/L'hebdo, *Die Schweizer und die Globalisierung. Die Meinungen der Leader und der Bevölkerung* (Lausanne, May 2008). (http://www.mistrend.ch/articles/Sophia%202008_D.pdf), pp. 4–7.

Chapter 5

1   David Butler and Austin Ranney (eds), *Referendums. A Comparative Study of Practice and Theory* (Washington, DC: American Enterprise Institute for Public Policy Research, 1978), p. 7.
2   David Butler and Austin Ranney, *Referendums around the World. The Growing Use of Direct Democracy* (London: Macmillan, 1994), p. 5.
3   Aleks Szczerbiak and Paul Taggard (eds), 'Choosing Union: The 2003 EU Accession Referendums', *West European Politics*, Special Issue vol. 27 (4) (2004).
4   I suggest not to mix up the four types of polls with questions of quorum and binding force. In fact, all four types may exist with or without a quorum, and with binding or merely advisory effects on government.
5   Thomas E. Cronin, *Direct Democracy, The Politics of Initiative, Referendum, and Recall* (Cambridge, Mass. and London: Harvard University Press, 1989). For a systematic comparison of US and Swiss direct democracy see: Silvano Möckli, *Direkte Demokratie: Ein Vergleich der Einrichtungen und Verfahren in der Schweiz und Kalifornien: unter Berücksichtigung von Frankreich, Italien, Dänemark, Irland, Österreich, Liechtenstein und Australien* (Bern: Haupt, 1994) and Nicolas von Arx, *Ähnlich, aber anders: die Volksinitiative in Kalifornien und in der Schweiz* (Genève: Helbing und Lichtenhahn, 2002).

6   Cronin (1989), *op. cit.*, p. 222.
7   Andreas Auer, *Le Référendum et L'initiative Populaire Aux Etats-Unis* (Basel: Helbing und Lichtenhahn, 1989).
8   Cronin (1989), *op. cit.*, pp. 224–232.
9   For empirical evidence for Switzerland see Chapter 3 Table 3.3; for the US, Cronin (1989), *op. cit.*, p. 76.
10 Hanspeter Kriesi (2005), *Direct Democratic Choice: The Swiss Experience* (Lanham, Md.: Lexington Books), as discussed in Chapter 3, 3.5.3.
11 Cronin (1989), *op. cit.*, p. 123.
12 See: Leonhard Neidhart, *Plebiszit und pluralitäre Demokratie* (Bern: Francke, 1970), pp. 238–243.
13 *The Economist*, May 15, 2009.
14 Cronin, citing Richard Hofstadter, *The Age of Reform* (New York: Vintage Books, 1955) and Herbert Croly, *Progressive Democracy* (New York: Macmillan, 1914). For recent studies on voting participation and behaviour see: Marc Bühlmann and Hanspeter Kriesi, *Political Participation. Quantity versus Quality* (University of Zurich, 2007). With regard to problems on foreign policy: Gerald Schneider and Cyrill Hess, 'Die innenpolitische Manipulation der Aussenpolitik: Die Logik von Ratifikationsdebatten in der direkten Demokratie', *Schweizerische Zeitschrift für Politische Wissenschaft*, vol. 1, Issue 2–3 (1995), pp. 93–111 and Gerald Schneider and Patricia Weitsman, 'The Punishment Trap, Integration Referendums as Popularity Tests', *Comparative Political Studies*, vol. 28, no. 4 (1996), pp. 582–607.
15 Betty H. Zisk, *Money, Media and the Grass Roots: State Ballot Issues and the Electoral Process* (Newbury Park, California: Sage Publications, 1987), pp. 90–137; Daniel H. Loewenstein, 'Campaign Spending and Ballot Propositions: Recent Experience, Public Choice Theory, and the First Amendment', *UCLA Law Review*, vol. 29 (February 1982), pp. 505–641; Hanspeter Kriesi, 'Sind Abstimmungsergebnisse käuflich?', in: Adrian Vatter *et al.* (eds), *Demokratie als Leidenschaft* (Bern: Haupt, 2009), pp. 83–106.
16 See: Walter Kälin, 'Verfassungsgrundsätze der schweizerischen Aussenpolitik', *Zeitschrift für Schweizerisches Recht* (1986) zweiter Halbband, pp. 269–272.
17 For details see Jean-François Aubert and Pascal Mahon, *Petit commentaire de la Constitution Fédérale de la Confédération Suisse du 18 Avril 1999* (Zurich: Schulthess 2003), pp. 1102–1120; Ulrich Häfelin and Walter Haller, *Schweizerisches Bundesstaatsrecht* (Zurich: Schulthess, 2005), pp. 564f.
18 Jean-Daniel Delley, *Démocratie Directe et Politique Étrangère en Suisse* (Genève: Helbing und Lichtenhahn, 1999).
19 Cronin (1989), *op. cit.*, p. 13.
20 Benjamin R. Barber, *Strong Democracy. Participatory Politics for a New Age* (Berkeley, Los Angeles and London: University of California Press, 1984); Kriesi (2005) *op. cit.*
21 Barber (1984), *op. cit.*
22 Joseph Schumpeter, *Capitalism, Socialism, and Democracy* (New York: Harper and Brothers, 1942); Anthony Downs, *An Economic Theory of Democracy* (New York: Harper and Row, 1957).
23 Barber (1984), *op. cit.*, pp. 179ff.; Shawn W. Rosenberg (ed.), *Deliberation, Participation and Democracy: Can the People Govern?* (Basingstoke, Hants: Palgrave Macmillan, 2007); John S. Dryzek, *Deliberative Democracy and*

Beyond: Liberals, Critics, Contestations (Oxford: Oxford University Press, 2002).

24 Cronin (1989), *op. cit.*, pp. 249–251.
25 Crawford B. Macpherson, *The Life and Times of Liberal Democracy* (London/ New York: Oxford University Press, 1977).
26 Robert A. Dahl, *Democracy and its Critics* (New Haven and London: Yale University Press, 1989), pp. 323ff.
27 Cronin (1989), *op. cit.*, p. 251.
28 Fritz Scharpf, *Demokratietheorie Zwischen Utopie und Anpassung* (Konstanz: Universitätsverlag, 1970), pp. 54ff.
29 Sidney Tarrow and Donatella della Porta, *Transnational Protest and Global Activism* (Lanham: Rowman and Littlefield, 2005).
30 Wolf Linder, 'On the Merits of Decentralization in Young Democracies', *Publius, The Journal of Federalism* (2009), forthcoming.
31 Ivo Duchacek, 'Consociational Cradle of Federalism', *Publius, The Journal of Federalism,* vol. 15, no. 2 (1985), p. 42.
32 Duchacek (1985), *op. cit.*, p. 44. Contrary to his earlier work, he finds two criteria marginal (two sets of courts and judicial review), and two criteria controversial (clear division of power and exclusive national control over foreign relations).
33 See: Ronald L. Watts, *Comparing Federal Systems* (Montreal: McGill-Queens, 2008), pp. 35ff.
34 Daniel J. Elazar, 'Federalism and Consociational Regimes', *Publius, The Journal of Federalism,* vol. 15, no. 2 (1985), p. 23.
35 George Anderson, *Federalism: An Introduction* (Oxford: Oxford University Press, 2008).
36 Elazar (1985), *op. cit.*, p. 22.
37 For an exhaustive presentation of the contemporary world of 'federalisms', analysing their constitutional structures, distribution of powers, governance, fiscal systems, local government and foreign relations see: *A Global Dialogue on Federalism,* 6 volumes, published for the 'Forum of Federations' and the 'International Association of Centers for Federal Studies' (Montreal: Mc Gill-Queens University Press, 2005–2009).
38 Daniel Kelemen, 'Globalization, Federalism and Regulation', in: *Dynamics of Regulatory Change: How Globalization Affects National Regulatory Policies* (UCIAS Edited vol. 1, Article 8, 2002).
39 Walter Kälin, 'Decentralisation – Why and how?' in: *Decentralization and Development* (Berne: Swiss Agency for Development and Cooperation: Publications on Development, 1999); Jennie Litvack, Ahman Junaid and Richard Bird, *Rethinking Decentralization in Developing Countries* (Washington DC: The World Bank, 1998); Wolf Linder, *Political Challenges of Decentralisation* (Washington DC: The World Bank Institute, 2002).
40 Dele Oluvu and James Wunsch, *Local Governance in Africa – The Challenges of Decentralisation* (Boulder and London: Lynne Rienner Publications, 2004); Linder (2009), *op. cit.*
41 René Lemarchand, 'Ethnic Conflict in Contemporary Africa. Four Models in Search of Solution', in: Günther Bächler (ed.), *Federalism Against Ethnicity? Institutional, Legal and Democratic Instruments to Prevent Violent Minority Conflicts* (Chur: Rüegger, 1997), pp. 95–106.

42 Andrea Iff, *Peace Preserving Federalism – Making Sense of India and Nigeria* (Bern: Haupt, 2009).

43 Walter Kälin, 'Federalism and the Resolution of Minority Conflicts', in: Gunther Bächler (1997), *op. cit.*, pp. 169–183 and Wolf Linder, 'Federalism and Power-Sharing as a Means to Prevent Internal Conflict', in: Gunther Bächler (1997), *op. cit.*, pp. 185–193.

44 Thomas Fleiner, Walter Kälin, Wolf Linder, Cheryl Saunders, Federalism, Decentralisation and Conflict Management in Multicultural Societies. In: Raoul Blindenbacher and Arnold Koller, *Federalism in a Changing World – Learning from Each Other* (Montreal/Kingston: McGill-Queens, 2002), pp. 197–215.

45 For the interdependence of individual and collective aspects of such conflicts, especially ethnic conflicts, see Milton J. Esman, 'Political and Psychological Factors in Ethnic Conflict', in: Joseph V. Montville (ed.), *Conflict and Peacemaking in Multiethnic Societies* (Lexington and Toronto: Lexington Books, 1990), p. 14.

46 Aidan Hehir, 'Independence, Intervention and Great Power Patronage: Kosovo, Georgia and the Contemporary Self-determination Penumbra', *Amsterdam Law Forum*, 1 (2) (2009), pp. 88–100; Christian Axboe Nielsen, 'The Kosovo precedent and the rhetorical deployment of former Yugoslav analogies in the cases of Abkhazia and South Ossetia', *Southeast European and Black Sea Studies*, 9:1 (2009), pp. 171–189.

47 Douglas Brown, 'Who's Afraid of Asymmetrical Federalism? A Summary Discussion', *2005 Special Series on Asymmetric Federalism* (Institute of Intergovernmental Relations, Queens University, 2005) and Watts (1999), *op. cit.*, 63ff.

48 Uri Ra'anan, 'The Nation-State Fallacy', in: Montville (1990), *op. cit.*, p. 14.

49 Otto Bauer, *Die Nationalitätenfrage und die Sozialdemokratie,* cited in: Uri Ra'anan (1990), *op. cit.*

50 On the Belgian experience, see: Maarten Theo Jans, 'Personal federalism: a solution to ethno-national conflicts? What it has meant in Brussels and what it could mean in Abkhazia', in: Bruno Coppieters *et al.* (eds), *Federal Practice. Exploring Alternatives for Georgia and Abkhazia.* (Brussels: Vub Press, 2000), pp. 215–229.

51 Peter G. White, 'Non-Territorial Federalism: A New Approach to Identity Politics', *The James R. Mallory Annual Lecture in Canadian Studies* (McGill University, Montreal, Quebec, 2000).

52 For the development of the theory see Arend Lijphart, 'Consociational Democracy', *World Politics* 21(2) (1969), pp. 207–225; Arend Lijphart, *Democracy in Plural Societies: A Comparative Exploration* (New Haven/London: Yale University Press, 1977); Arend Lijphart, *Democracies, Patterns of Majoritarian and Consensus Government in Twenty-One Countries* (New Haven/London: Yale University Press, 1984) and Arend Lijphart, *Patterns of Democracy. Government Forms and Performances in Thirty-Six Countries* (New Haven: Yale University Press, 1999).

53 Jürg Steiner, *Amicable Agreement Versus Majority Rule: Conflict Resolution in Switzerland* (Chapel Hill: UNC Press, 1974), p. 6.

54 Lijphart (1999), *op. cit.*, 275f.

55 Wolf Linder and André Bächtiger, 'What Drives Democratisation in Africa and Asia?', *European Journal of Political Research* 44 (2005), pp. 861–880.

56 Karl Deutsch, *Die Schweiz als Paradigmatischer Fall Politischer Integration* (Bern: Haupt, 1976).

57 For a positive yet prudent answer to this question see Andrea Iff and Nicole Töpperwien, 'Power Sharing – The Swiss Experience', *Politorbis, Zeitschrift zur Aussenpolitik* (Bern: Federal Department of Foreign Affairs 2/2008).

58 Ted R. Gurr, *Peoples versus States. Minorities at Risk in the New Century* (Washington DC: United States Institute of Peace, 2000).

59 David Lake and Donald Rothchild (eds), *The International Spread of Ethnic Conflict* (Princeton: Princeton University Press, 1998).

60 Bumba Mukherjee, 'Why Power-Sharing Agreements Lead to Enduring Peaceful Resolution of Some Civil Wars, But Not Others?', *International Studies Quarterly* 50, pp. 479–504, 2004.

61 For main positions on the debate see: Timothy D. Sisk, *Power Sharing and International Mediation in Ethnic Conflicts* (Washington DC: US Institute of Peace, 1996); Philip Roeder and Donald Rothchild (eds), *Sustainable Peace, Power and Democracy after Civil Wars* (Ithaca and London: Cornell University Press, 2005); Pippa Norris, *Driving Democracy: Do Power-Sharing Institutions Work?* (Cambridge, New York: Cambridge University Press, 2008) and Arend Lijphart, *Thinking about Democracy, Power Sharing and Majority Rule in Theory and Practice* (London: Routledge, 2008).

62 Dieter Senghaas, 'Frieden – Ein mehrfaches Komplexprogramm', in: Dieter Senghaas (ed.), *Frieden machen* (Frankfurt: Suhrkamp, 1997), pp. 560–574; Thomas Carothers, *Aiding Democracy Abroad* (Washington DC: Carnegie Endowment for International Peace, 1999); Adrian Leftwich, 'On the primacy of politics in development', in: Adrian Leftwich (ed.), *Democracy and Development: Theory and Practice* (Cambridge: Polity Press, 1996); Mick Moore, 'Political Underdevelopment. What causes "bad government"', *Public Management Review* 3 (3) (2001), pp. 385–418; Adam E. Przeworski, Michael Alvarez, José Antonio Cheibub and Fernando Limongi, *Democracy and Development. Political Institutions and Well-Being in the World, 1950–1990* (Cambridge: Cambridge University Press, 2000) and Linder and Bächtiger (2005), *op. cit.*

63 Lijphart (2008), *op. cit.* and Norris (2008), *op. cit.*

64 Andre Bächtiger, Markus Spörndli, Marco Steenbergen and Jürg Steiner, 'The Deliberative Dimension of Legislatures', *Acta Politica* 40 (2) (2005), pp. 225–238; Marco Steenbergen, 'Deliberative Politics in Switzerland', in: Vatter *et al.* (2009), *op. cit.*, pp. 283–301.

65 Linder (2009), *op. cit.*

66 John Madeley and Zsolt EnYedi, 'Church and State in Contemporary Europe', in: *West European Politics* (Special Issue), vol. 26, no.1 (2003).

67 Esman (1990), *op. cit.*, 14ff.

68 Arend Lijphart, *The Politics of Accommodation: Pluralism and Democracy in the Netherlands* (Berkeley; Los Angeles: University of California Press, 1968), p. 104.

69 Steenbergen (2009), *op. cit.*, 287.

70 Kenneth D. McRae, 'Theories of Power-Sharing and Conflict Management', in: Montville (1990), *op. cit.*

71 Ian Lustick, *Arabs in the Jewish State: Israel's Control of a National Minority* (Austin: University of Texas Press, 1980).

72 Deutsch (1976), *op. cit.*

73 Clive Church, *The Politics and Government of Switzerland* (Basingstoke and New York: Palgrave Macmillan, 2004), p. 223.

74 Klaus Armingeon, 'Direkte Demokratie als Exportartikel?', in: Vatter *et al.* (2009), *op. cit.*, pp. 433–442.
75 Carothers (1999), *op. cit.* and Wolf Linder, André Bächtiger and Georg Lutz, 'Democratisation, rule of law and development', *Swiss Development Cooperation Paper* (Bern: Swiss Agency for Development and Cooperation, 2008).

Bibliography

A *Global Dialogue on Federation (2005–2009)*, 6 volumes, published for the Forum of Federations and the International Association of Centers for Federal Studies (Montreal: McGill-Queens University Press).

Abromeit, Heidrun (1993), *Interessenvermittlung zwischen Konkurrenz und Konkordanz* (Opladen: Leske).

Abromeit, Heidrun and W. Pommerehne (eds) (1992), *Staatstätigkeit in der Schweiz* (Bern: Haupt).

Altermatt, Urs (1991), *Katholizismus und Moderne* (Zürich: Benziger).

Altermatt, Urs (2009), 'Konkordanz im Spiegel der Bundesratswahlen', in: Adrian Vatter *et al.* (eds), *Demokratie als Leidenschaft* (Bern: Haupt), pp. 247–270.

Anderson, George (2008), *Federalism: An Introduction* (Oxford: Oxford University Press).

Andrey, Georges (1983), 'Auf der Suche nach dem neuen Staat', in: *Geschichte der Schweiz und der Schweizer*, vol. II (Basel and Frankfurt am Main: Helbing und Lichtenhahn), pp. 177–288.

Année politique suisse/Politik im Jahre, Annual political journal published by the Institute of Political Science at the University of Bern (Bern: 1965 ff.).

Armingeon, Klaus (2003), 'Konzertierung in der Schweiz', in: Sven Jochem and Nico A. Siegel (eds), *Konzertierung, Verhandlungsdemokratie und Reformpolitik im Wohlfahrtsstaat – Das Modell Deutschland im Vergleich* (Opladen: Leske + Budrich), pp. 311–330.

Armingeon, Klaus (2009), 'Direkte Demokratie als Exportartikel?', in: Adrian Vatter *et al.* (eds), *Demokratie als Leidenschaft* (Bern: Haupt, 2009), pp. 433–442.

Aubert, Jean-François (1967), *Traite du Droit Constitutionnel Suisse, Troisième partie: La Structure fédérale* (Neuchâtel: Ides et Calendes).

Aubert, Jean-François (1974), *Petite Histoire Constitutionnelle de la Suisse* (Bern: Francke).

Aubert, Jean-François (1983), *Exposé des Institutions Politiques de la Suisse à Partir de Quelques Affaires Controversées* (Lausanne: Payot).

Aubert, Jean-François and Pascal Mahon (2003), *Petit Commentaire de la Constitution Fédérale de la Confédération Suisse du 18 avril 1999* (Zürich: Schulthess).

Auer, Andreas (1976), 'Les detours du "retour a la démocratie directe". Le droit federal d'urgence 1971–1975', in: *Mémoires Publiés par la Faculté de Droit Genéve*, Mélanges offerts à la Société Suisse des Juristes (Genéve).

Auer, Andreas (1989), *Le référendum et L'initiative Populaire Aux Etats-Unis* (Basel: Helbing and Lichtenhahn).

Bachrach, Peter and Morton S. Baratz (1963), 'Decisions and Nondecisions: An Analytical Framework', *American Political Science Review*, vol. 57, pp. 632–642.

Bächtiger, André, Markus Spörndli, Marco Steenbergen and Jürg Steiner (2005), 'The Deliberative Dimensions of Legislatures', *Acta Politica* 40 (2), pp. 225–238.

Ballmer-Cao, Thanh-Huyen (2000), *Changement Social et Rapport Entre Hommes et Femmes* (Lausanne: Editions Payot).

Ballmer-Cao, Thanh-Huyen and Manon Trembley (eds) (2008), 'Modes de scrutin, partis politiques et élection des femmes', *Swiss Political Science Review,* vol. 14, no. 4, pp. 609–630.

Banaszak, Lee Ann (1991), 'The Influence of the Initiative on the Swiss and American Women's Suffrage Movements', *Schweizerisches Jahrbuch für Politische Wissenschaft,* no. 31 (Bern: Haupt), pp. 187–207.

Barber, Benjamin R. (1984), *Strong Democracy. Participatory Politics for a New Age* (Berkeley, Los Angeles and London: University of California Press).

Bassand, Michel and Francois Hainard (1985), 'Dynamique socio – culturelle régionale', PNR, vol. 35.5, *Synthèse des Problèmes Régionaux* (Lausanne: Presses Polytechniques Romandes).

Bassand, Michel, Gerard Chevalier and Erwin Zimmermann (1984), *Politique et logement* (Lausanne: Presses Polytechniques Romandes).

Bassand, Michel *et al.* (1985), *Les Suisses Entre la Mobilité et la Sédentarité* (Lausanne: Presses Polytechniques Romandes).

Bericht der Arbeitsgruppe (1992), *Zusammenarbeit in den Agglomerationen* (Bern: Forschungszentrum für schweizerische Politik).

Blaser, Jeremias (2003), *Das Vernehmlassungsverfahren in der Schweiz: Organisation, Entwicklung und Aktuelle Situation* (Opladen: Leske + Budrich).

Bonjour, Edgar (1948), *Die Gründung des schweizerischen Bundesstaates* (Basel: Schwabe).

Borner, Silvio and Hans Rentsch (eds) (1997), *Wieviel direkte Demokratie verträgt die Schweiz?* (Chur: Verlag Rüegger).

Borner, Silvio, Aymo Brunetti and Thomas Straubhaar (1990), *Schweiz AG: Vom Sonderfall zum Sanierungsfall?* (Zürich: Verlag Neue Zürcher Zeitung).

Brown, Douglas (2005), 'Who's Afraid of Asymmetrical Federalism? A Summary Discussion', *2005 Special Series on Asymmetric Federalism* (Institute of Inter-governmental Relations, Queens University).

Budge, Ian (1996), *The New Challenge of Direct Democracy* (Cambridge, Mass.: Polity Press).

Bühlmann, Marc and Hanspeter Kriesi (2007), *Political Participation. Quantity versus Quality* (University of Zürich).

Bundesamt für Statistik (2003), *Volkszählung 2000* (Neuchâtel: Bundesamt für Statistik).

Bundesamt für Statistik (2006), *Ausländerinnen und Ausländer in der Schweiz, Bericht 2006* (Neuchâtel: Bundesamt für Statistik).

Bundesamt für Statistik (2008), *Statistik des Freiheitsentzugs* (Neuchâtel: Bundesamt für Statistik).

Bundesamt für Statistik, *Statistisches Jahrbuch* (1989, 1990, 1991, 2007) (Zürich: Verlag Neue Zürcher Zeitung).

Bürkli, Karl (1869), *Direkte Gesetzgebung durch das Volk* (Zürich and Geneva).

Butler, David and Austin Ranney (1994), *Referendums Around the World. The Growing Use of Direct Democracy* (London: Macmillan).

Butler, David and Austin Ranney (eds) (1978), *Referendums. A Comparative Study of Practice and Theory* (Washington, DC: American Enterprise Institute for Public Policy Research).

Butler, Michael, Malcolm Pender and Charnley, Joy (2000) (eds), *The Making of Modern Switzerland* (Basingstoke: Macmillan).

Carothers, Thomas (1999), *Aiding Democracy Abroad* (Washington DC: Carnegie Endowment for International Peace).

Church, Clive (2004), *The Politics and Government of Switzerland* (Basingstoke and New York: Palgrave Macmillan).

Church, Clive (ed.) (2007), *Switzerland and the European Union* (New York and London: Routledge).

Coradi Vellacott, Maja and Stefan Wolter (2004), *Equity in the Swiss Education System: Dimensions, Causes and Policy Responses. National Report* (Aarau: Swiss Coordination Centre for Educational Research).

Croly, Herbert (1914), *Progressive Democracy* (New York: Macmillan).

Cronin, Thomas E. (1989), *Direct Democracy. The Politics of Initiative, Referendum, and Recall* (Cambridge and London: Harvard University Press).

Dahl, Robert A. (1989), *Democracy and its Critics* (New Haven and London: Yale University Press).

De Beauvoir, Simone (1961), *Le Deuxième Sexe* (Paris: Gallimard).

Delley, Jean Daniel (1978), *L'initiative Populaire en Suisse. Mythe et Réalité de la Démocratie Directe* (Lausanne: L'Age d'Homme).

Delley, Jean-Daniel (1999), *Démocratie Directe et Politique étrangère en Suisse.* (Genève: Helbing and Lichtenhahn, 1999).

Delley, Jean-Daniel *et al.* (1982), *Le Droit en Action: Etude de Mise en Oeuvre de la loi Furgler* (St Saphorin: Editions Georgi).

Demont-Heinrich, Christof (2005), 'Language and National Identity in the Era of Globalization: The Case of English in Switzerland', *Journal of Communication Inquiry*, vol. 29, no. 1, pp. 66–84.

Deutsch, Karl (1967), *The Nerves of Government: Models of Political Communication and Control* (New York: Free Press).

Deutsch, Karl (1976), *Die Schweiz als Paradigmatischer Fall Politischer Integration* (Bern: Haupt).

Downs, Anthony (1957), *An Economic Theory of Democracy* (New York: Harper and Row).

Dryzek, John S. (2002), *Deliberative Democracy and Beyond: Liberals, Critics, Contestations* (Oxford: Oxford University Press).

Du Bois, Pierre (1999), *Alémaniques et Romands entre unité et Discorde: Histoire et Actualité* (Lausanne: Favre).

Duchacek, Ivo (1985), 'Consociational Cradle of Federalism', *Publius, The Journal of Federalism*, vol. 15, no. 2, pp. 35–48.

Eidgenössische Kommission für Frauenfragen (1980–1999) *Berichte; Die Stellung der Frau in der Schweiz/Gleiche Rechte für Mann und Frau/Die politische Repräsentation der Frauen in der Schweiz/Viel erreicht – wenig verändert?/ Frauen Macht Geschichte* (Bern: Eidgenössische Kommission für Frauenfragen).

Eidgenössisches Personalamt (2000), *Bericht an den Bundesrat über die Erste Umsetzungsperiode der Weisungen über die Förderung der Mehrsprachigkeit in der allgemeinen Bundesverwaltung 1996–1999* (Bern: Eidgenössisches Personalamt).

Elazar, Daniel J. (1985), 'Federalism and Consociational Regimes', *Publius, The Journal of Federalism*, vol. 15, no. 2, pp. 17–35.

Ernst, Andreas, Albert Tanner and Matthias Weishaupt (eds) (1998), *Revolution und Innovation – Die konfliktreiche Entstehung des Schweizerischen Bundesstaats von 1848* (Zürich: Chronos).

Esman, Milton J. (1990), 'Political and Psychological Factors in Ethnic Conflict', in: Joseph V. Montville (ed.), *Conflict and Peacemaking in Multiethnic Societies* (Lexington and Toronto: Lexington Books).

Farago, Peter (1987), *Verbände als Träger Öffentlicher Politik* (Grüsch: Rüegger).

Fischer, Alex (2007), 'Internationalisation of Swiss Decision-Making Processes', in: Ulrich Klöti *et al.* (eds), *Handbook of Swiss Politics* (Zürich: Neue Zürcher Zeitung Publishing), pp. 547–568.

Fischer, Alex, Sarah Nicolet and Pascal Sciarini (2002), 'Europeanisation of a Non-EU Country: The Case of Swiss Immigration Policy', in: *West European Politics*, vol. 25 (4), pp. 143–170.

Fleiner, Thomas, Walter Kälin, Wolf Linder and Cheryl Saunders (2002), Federalism Decentralisation and Conflict Management in Multicultural Societies. In: Raoul Blindenbacher and Arnold Koller, *Federalism in a Changing World – Learning from Each Other*, Montreal/Kingston: McGill-Queens, pp. 197–215.

Frey, Rene (ed.) (2005), *Föderalismus – Zukunftstauglich?!* (Zürich: Verlag Neue Zürcher Zeitung).

Friedan, Betty (1963), *The Feminine Mystic* (New York: W.W. Norton).

Gabriel, Jürg Martin (1995), *Die Neutralität auf dem Prüfstand* (St. Gallen: Institut für Politikwissenschaft).

Gabriel, Jürg Martin and Thomas Fischer (eds) (2003), *Swiss Foreign Policy, 1945–2002* (Basingstoke: Palgrave).

Ganguillet, Gilbert (1998), *Le conflit jurassien: genèse et trajectoire d'un conflit ethno-régional* (Zürich: bokos druck).

Gaudard, Gaston and Catherine Cudré-Mauroux (1997), *Une nouvelle inégalité interrégionale en Suisse* (Fribourg: Imprimerie St-Paul).

Germann, Raimund E. (1975), *Politische Innovation und Verfassungsreform* (Bern: Haupt).

Germann, Raimund E. (1981), *Ausserparlamentarischen Kommissionen, Die Miliz-verwaltung des Bundes* (Bern: Haupt).

Germann, Raimund E. (1990), 'Bundesverfassung und "Europafähigkeit" der Schweiz', in: *Schweizerisches Jahrbuch für Politische Wissenschaft*, 30 (Bern: Haupt), pp. 17–28.

Germann, Raimund E. (1991), 'Die Europatauglichkeit der direkt-demokratischen Institutionen der Schweiz', *Schweizerisches Jahrbuch für politische Wissenschaft*, no. 31: *Direkte Demokratie* (Bern: Haupt).

Geser, Hans, Andreas Ladner, Roland Schaller and Thanh-Huyen Ballmer-Cao (1994), *Die Schweizer Lokalparteien* (Zürich: Seismo).

Geser, Hans, Peter Farago, Robert Fluder and Ernst Gräub (1987), *Gemeindepolitik zwischen Milizorganisation und Berufsverwaltung* (Bern: Haupt).

Global Dialogue on Federalism (2005–2009), 6 volumes, published for the '*Forum of Federations*' and the '*International Association of Centers for Federal Studies*' (Montreal: Mc Gill-Queens University Press, 2005–2009).

Goetschel, Laurent (2007), 'Foreign policy', in: Ulrich Klöti *et al.* (eds), *Handbook of Swiss Politics* (Zürich: Neue Zürcher Zeitung Publishing), pp. 571–591.

Goetschel, Laurent, Magdalena Bernath and Daniel Schwarz (eds) (2005), *Swiss Foreign Policy: Foundations and Possibilities* (London and New York: Routledge).

Gruner, Erich (1964), '100 Jahre Wirtschaftspolitik, Etappen des Staatsintervention-ismus in der Schweiz', *Schweizerische Zeitschrift für Volkswirtschaft und Statistik*, pp. 34–70.

Gruner, Erich (1988), *Arbeiterschaft und Wirtschaft in der Schweiz 1880–1914*, vol. I–III (Zürich: Chronos).

Gurr, Ted R. (2000), *Peoples versus States. Minorities at Risk in the New Century* (Washington DC: United States Institute of Peace).

Häfelin, Ulrich and Walter Haller (2005), *Schweizerisches Bundesstaatsrecht* (Zürich: Schulthess).

Haller, Walter (2009), 'The Swiss Constitution' (Zurich and St. Giall: Dike).

Hehir, Aidan (2009), 'Independence, Intervention and Great Power Patronage: Kosovo, Georgia and the Contemporary Self-determination Penumbra', *Amsterdam Law Forum*, 1(2) (2009), pp. 88–100.

Held, Thomas and René Levy (1974), *Die Stellung der Frau in Familie und Gesellschaft: Eine soziologische Analyse am Beispiel der Schweiz* (Frauenfeld: Huber).

Helg, Felix (2007), *Die schweizerischen Landsgemeinden: Ihre Staatsrechtliche Ausgestaltung in den Kantonen Appenzell Ausserrhoden, Appenzell Innerrhoden, Glarus, Nidwalden und Obwalden* (Zürich: Schulthess).

Hertig, Hanspeter (1983), 'Werbebudget und Abstimmungsergebnis: Sind Abstimmungserfolge käuflich', in: Erich Gruner and Hanspeter Hertig, *Der Stimmbürger und die neue Politik* (Bern: Haupt).

Hirschman, Albert O. (1970), *Exit, Voice and Loyalty: Responses to Decline in Firms, Organizations, and States* (Cambridge, Mass.: Harvard University Press).

Hirter, Hans (1989 and 1990), *Die Werbung der Printmedien zu den Volksabstimmungen vom 4.12.88 und 26.11.89* (Bern: Forschungszentrum für schweizerische Politik).

Hofstadter, Richard (1955), *The Age of Reform* (New York: Vintage Books).

Horber-Papazian, Katia (2007), 'The Municipalities', in: Ulrich Klöti *et al.* (eds), *Handbook of Swiss Politics* (Zürich: Neue Zürcher Zeitung Publishing, 2007), pp. 227–250.

Huber, Hans (1971), 'Staat und Verbände', in: *Rechtstheorie, Verfassungsrecht, Völkerrecht, Ausgewählte Aufsätze 1950–70* (Bern: Stämpfli).

Huston, James H. (1991), *The Sister Republics* (Washington: Library of Congress).

Iff, Andrea (2009), *Peace Preserving Federalism – Making Sense of India and Nigeria* (Bern: Haupt).

Iff, Andrea and Nicole Töpperwien (2008), 'Power Sharing – The Swiss Experience', *Politorbis, Zeitschrift zur Aussenpolitik* (Bern: Federal Department of Foreign Affairs).

Im Hof, Ulrich (1991), *Mythos Schweiz. Identität-Nation-Geschichte* (Zürich: Verlag Neue Zürcher Zeitung).

Jans, Maarten Theo (2000), 'Personal federalism: A solution to ethno-national conflicts? What it has meant in Brussels and what it could mean in Abkhazia', in: Bruno Coppieters *et al.* (eds), *Federal Practice. Exploring Alternatives for Georgia and Abkhazia* (Brussels: Vub Press), pp. 215–229.

Jegher, Annina (1999), *Der Einfluss von institutionellen, entscheidungspolitischen und inhaltlichen Faktoren auf die Gesetzgebungstätigkeit der Schweizerischen Bundesversammlung* (Bern: Haupt).

Jenkins, J.R.G (1987), *Jura Separatism in Switzerland* (Oxford: University Press).

Jörin, Robert and Peter Rieder (1985), *Parastaatliche Organisationen im Agrarsektor* (Bern: Haupt).

Jost, Hans Ulrich (1986), 'Menace et repliement (1914–1945)', *Nouvelle histoire de la Suisse et des Suisses* (Lausanne: Payot).

Jost, Hans Ulrich (1992), *Die reaktionäre Avantgarde: Die Geburt der neuen Rechten in der Schweiz um 1900* (Zürich: Chronos).

Kälin, Walter (1986), 'Verfassungsgrundsätze der schweizerischen Aussenpolitik', *Zeitschrift für schweizerisches Recht*, zweiter Halbband, pp. 269–272.

Kälin, Walter (1987), *Verfassungsgerichtsbarkeit in der Demokratie. Funktionen der staatsrechtlichen Beschwerde* (Bern: Stämpfli).

Kälin, Walter (1997), 'Federalism and the Resolution of Minority Conflicts', in: Günther Bächler (ed.), *Federalism against Ethnicity? Institutional, Legal and Democratic Instruments to Prevent Violent Minority Conflicts* (Chur: Rüegger), pp. 169–183.

Kälin, Walter (1999), 'Decentralisation – Why and how?', in: *Decentralization and Development* (Berne: Swiss Agency for Development and Cooperation: Publications on Development).

Karr, Philipp (2003), *Institutionen direkter Demokratie in den Gemeinden Deutschlands und der Schweiz: eine rechtsvergleichende Untersuchung* (Baden-Baden: Nomos).

Kästli, Tobias (1998), *Die Schweiz – eine Republik in Europa* (Zürich: Verlag Neue Zürcher Zeitung).

Kaufmann, Otto K. (1965), 'Frauen, Italiener, Jesuiten, Juden und Anstaltsver-sorgte. Vorfragen eines Beitritts der Schweiz zur Europäischen Menschen-rechtskonvention', *St. Galler Festgabe zum Schweizerischen Juristentag 1965* (Bern: Stämpfli).

Kelemen, Daniel (2002), 'Globalization, Federalism and Regulation', in: *Dynamics of Regulatory Change: How Globalization Affects National Regulatory Policies* (UCIAS Edited volume 1, Article 8).

Kissling-Näf, Ingrid and Sonja Wälti (2007), 'The Implementation of Public Policies', in: Ulrich Klöti *et al.* (eds), *Handbook of Swiss Politics* (Zürich: Neue Zürcher Zeitung Publishing), pp. 501–524.

Klöti, Ulrich *et al.* (2007) (eds), *Handbook of Swiss Politics* (Zürich: Neue Zürcher Zeitung Publishing).

Koll-Schretzenmayr, Martina/Schmid, Willy, Agglomerationspolitik in der Schweiz, DISP 152 (2003), pp. 4–14.

Köchli, Yvonne-D. (1992), *Eine Frau kommt zu früh* (Zürich: Weltwoche-ABC).

Kölz, Alfred (1992), *Neuere schweizerische Verfassungsgeschichte. Ihre Grundlinien vom Ende der Alten Eidgenossenschaft bis 1848* (Bern: Stämpfli).

Kopper, Enid (1993), 'Swiss and Germans: Similarities and Differences in Work-Related Values, Attitudes, and Behaviour', in: *International Journal of Intercultural Relations*, vol. 17, pp. 167–184.

Kreis, Georg, Jean-Claude Favez and Urs Altermatt (1992), 'Geschichte der schweizerischen Aussenpolitik 1848–1991', in: Alois Riklin *et al.* (eds), *Neues Handbuch der schweizerischen Aussenpolitik* (Bern: Haupt), pp. 27–78.

Kriesi, Hanspeter (1980), *Entscheidungsstrukturen und Entscheidungsprozesse in der Schweizer Politik* (Frankfurt and New York: Campus Verlag).

Kriesi, Hanspeter (1995), 'Bewegungen auf der Linken, Bewegungen auf der Rechten: Die Mobilisierung von zwei neuen Typen von sozialen Bewegungen in ihrem politischen Kontext', *Schweizerische Zeitschrift für politische Wissenschaft*, vol. 1, Summer 1995, pp. 9–52.

Kriesi, Hanspeter (2005), *Direct Democratic Choice: The Swiss Experience* (Lanham, Md.: Lexington Books).

Kriesi, Hanspeter (2009), 'Sind Abstimmungsergebnisse käuflich?', in: Adrian Vatter *et al.* (eds), *Demokratie als Leidenschaft* (Bern: Haupt), pp. 83–106.

Kriesi, Hanspeter and Alexander H. Trechsel (2008), *The Politics of Switzerland: Continuity and Change in a Consensus Democracy* (Cambridge: Cambridge University Press).

Kux, Stephan (1994) (ed.), *Zukunft Neutralität?* (Bern: Haupt).

Ladner, Andreas (2003), *Verbreitung und Bedeutung der Lokalparteien in den Gemeinden* (Zürich: Soziologisches Institut) (http://socio.ch/par/ladner/lad_03.pdf).

Ladner, Andreas (2008), *Die Schweizer Gemeinden im Wandel: Politische Institutionen und lokale Politik* (Lausanne: Cahier de l'IDHEAP no. 237).

Lafitte, Patricia (1987), *Les Institutions de Démocratie Directe en Suisse au Niveau Local* (Lausanne: Cahiers de l'IDHEAP no. 34).

Lake, David and Donald Rothchild (1998) (eds), *The International Spread of Ethnic Conflict* (Princeton: Princeton University Press).

Lane, Jan Erik (2001), *The Swiss Labyrinth, Institutions, Outcomes and Redesign* (London, Frank Cass) or as a special volume of *West European Politics*, vol. 24, no. 2.

Leftwich, Adrian (1996), 'On the primacy of politics in development', in: Adrian Leftwich (ed.), *Democracy and Development: Theory and Practice* (Cambridge: Polity Press).

Lehmann, Luzia, Stefan Rieder and Stefan Pfäffli (2003), 'Zusammenarbeit in Agglomerationen: Anforderungen – Modelle – Erfahrungen', *Luzerner Beiträge zur Gemeindeentwicklung und zum Gemeindemanagement*, Bd. 9 (Luzern: Verlag IBR).

Lemarchand, René (1997), 'Ethnic Conflict in Contemporary Africa. Four Models in Search of Solution', in: Günther Bächler (ed.), *Federalism against Ethnicity? Institutional, Legal and Democratic Instruments to Prevent Violent Minority Conflicts* (Chur: Rüegger, 1997), pp. 95–106.

Lijphart, Arend (1968), *The Politics of Accommodation: Pluralism and Democracy in the Netherlands* (Berkeley; Los Angeles: University of California Press).

Lijphart, Arend (1969), 'Consociational Democracy', *World Politics* 21(2) (1969), pp. 207–225.

Lijphart, Arend (1977), *Democracy in Plural Societies: A Comparative Exploration* (New Haven/London: Yale University Press).

Lijphart, Arend (1984), *Democracies, Patterns of Majoritarian and Consensus Government in Twenty-One Countries* (New Haven/London: Yale University Press).

Lijphart, Arend (1999), *Patterns of Democracy. Government Forms and Performances in Thirty-Six Countries* (New Haven: Yale University Press).

Lijphart, Arend (2008), *Thinking about Democracy, Power Sharing and Majority Rule in Theory and Practice* (London: Routledge).

Linder, Wolf (1983), 'Entwicklung, Strukturen und Funktionen des Wirtschafts – und Sozialstaats in der Schweiz', in: Alois Riklin, *Handbuch Politisches System der Schweiz*, Band I. (Bern and Stuttgart: Haupt), pp. 255–382.

Linder, Wolf (1987), *Politische Entscheidung und Gesetzesvollzug in der Schweiz* (Bern: Haupt).

Linder, Wolf (1991), 'Migrationswirkungen, institutionelle Politik und politische Öffentlichkeit', in: W. Kälin and R. Moser (eds), *Migrationen aus der Dritten Welt* (Bern: Haupt) (2), pp. 152–155.

Linder, Wolf (1991a), 'Repräsentative und direkte Demokratie, Systeme im Spannungsverhältnis', in: Eugen Antalovsky (ed.), *Die Bürger und ihre Stadt* (Wien: Magistrat der Stadt Wien).

Linder, Wolf (1997), 'Federalism and Power-Sharing as a Means to Prevent Internal Conflict', in: Günther Bächler (ed.), *Federalism against Ethnicity? Institutional, Legal and Democratic Instruments to Prevent Violent Minority Conflicts* (Chur: Rüegger), pp. 185–193.

Linder, Wolf (1997a), 'Verfassung als politischer Prozess', in: Beat Sitter (ed.), *Herausgeforderte Verfassung: Die Schweiz im globalen Kontext* (Freiburg: Universitätsverlag).

Linder, Wolf (2002), *Political Challenges of Decentralisation* (Washington DC: The World Bank Institute).

Linder, Wolf (2005), *Schweizerische Demokratie, Institutionen, Prozesse, Perspektiven* (Bern: Haupt).

Linder, Wolf (2010), 'On the Merits of Decentralization in Young Democracies', *Publius, The Journal of Federalism*, vol. 40, no. 1, pp. 1–30.

Linder, Wolf (2009a), 'Schweizerische Konkordanz im Wandel', *Zeitschrift für Staats – und Europawissenschaften*, vol. 7 (2), pp. 209–230.

Linder, Wolf and Adrian Vatter (2001), 'Institutions and Outcomes of Swiss Federalism: The Role of the Cantons in Swiss Politics', in: *West European Politics* 24, pp. 95–122.

Linder, Wolf and André Bächtiger (2005), 'What Drives Democratisation in Africa and Asia?', *European Journal of Political Research* 44, pp. 861–880.

Linder, Wolf, André Bächtiger and Georg Lutz (2008), 'Democratisation, rule of law and development', *Swiss Development Cooperation Paper* (Bern: Swiss Agency for Development and Cooperation).

Linder, Wolf, Regula Zürcher and Christian Bolliger (2008), *Gespaltene Schweiz – geeinte Schweiz: Gesellschaftliche Spaltungen und Konkordanz bei den Volksabstimmungen seit 1874* (Baden: hier and jetzt).

Litvack, Jennie, Ahman Junaid and Richard Bird (1998), *Rethinking Decentralization in Developing Countries* (Washington DC: The World Bank).

Loewenstein, Daniel H. (1982), 'Campaign Spending and Ballot Propositions: Recent Experience, Public Choice Theory, and the First Amendment', *UCLA Law Review*, 29, pp. 505–641.

Longchamp, Claude (1991), 'Herausgeforderte politische Öffentlichkeit', *Schweizerisches Jahrbuch für politische Wissenschaft*, vol. 31, pp. 303–326 (Bern: Haupt).

Lupia, Arthur and Mathew D. Mccubbins (1998), *The Democratic Dilemma: Can citizens Learn What They Need to Know?* (Cambridge: University Press).

Lustick, Ian (1980), *Arabs in the Jewish State: Israel's Control of a National Minority* (Austin: University of Texas Press).

Lüthi, Ruth (1997), *Die Legislativkommissionen der schweizerischen Bundesversammlung: Institutionelle Veränderungen und das Verhalten von Parlamentsmitgliedern* (Bern: Haupt).

Lüthi, Ruth (2007) 'The Parliament', in: Ulrich Klöti *et al.* (eds), *Handbook of Swiss Politics* (Zürich: Neue Zürcher Zeitung Publishing), pp. 121–142.

Lutz, Georg (2006), *Participation, Information and Democracy: The Consequences of Low Levels of Participation and Information for the Functioning of Democracy* (Hamburg: Lit).

Lutz Georg and Dirk Strohmann (1998), *Wahl-und Abstimmungsrecht in den Kantonen* (Bern: Haupt).

M.I.S. Trend/L'hebdo (2008), *Die Schweizer und die Globalisierung. Die Meinungen der Leader und der Bevölkerung*, May 2008 (Lausanne) (http://www.mistrend.ch/articles/Sophia%202008_D.pdf), pp. 4–7.

Mach, André (2007), 'Interest Groups', in: Ulrich Klöti *et al.* (eds), *Handbook of Swiss Politics* (Zürich: Neue Zürcher Zeitung Publishing), pp. 359–380.

Mach, André, Silja Häusermann and Yannis Papadopoulos (2003), 'Economic Regulatory Reforms in Switzerland: Adjustment without European Integration, or How Rigidities Become Flexible', *Journal of European Public Policy*, vol. 10, no. 2, pp. 301–318.

Macpherson, Crawford B. (1977), *The Life and Times of Liberal Democracy* (London/ New York: Oxford University Press).

Madeley, John, and Zsolt Enyedi (2003), 'Church and State in Contemporary Europe', in: *West European Politics* (Special Issue) vol. 26, no. 1.

Masnata, François and Claire Rubattel (eds) (1991), *Le Pouvoir Suisse 1291–1991. Seduction Démocratique et Repression Suave* (Lausanne: Editions de l'aire).

Mazzoleni, Oscar (2003), *Nationalisme et Populisme en Suisse – La Radicalisation de la 'Nouvelle' UDC* (Lausanne: Presses polytechniques et universitaires).

Mcrae, Kenneth D. (1964), *Switzerland: Example of Cultural Coexistence* (Toronto: The Canadian Institute of International Affairs).

Mcrae, Kenneth D. (1990), 'Theories of Power-Sharing and Conflict Management', in: Joseph V. Montville (ed.), *Conflict and Peacemaking in Multiethnic Societies* (Massachusetts and Toronto: Lexington Books).

Mesmer, Beatrix (1988), *Ausgeklammert-Eingeklammert. Frauen und Frauenorganisationen der Schweiz des 19. Jahrhunderts* (Basel and Frankfurt am Main: Helbing and Lichtenhahn).

Messerli, Paul (2004), 'Regionalpolitik zwischen Theorie und Praxis', in: Christoph A. Schaltegger *et al.* (eds), *Perspektiven der Wirtschaftspolitik* (Zürich: vdf), pp. 435–450.

Möckli, Silvano (1994), *Direkte Demokratie: Ein Vergleich der Einrichtungen und Verfahren in der Schweiz und Kalifornien: unter Berücksichtigung von Frankreich, Italien, Dänemark, Irland, Österreich, Liechtenstein und Australien* (Bern: Haupt).

Möckli, Silvano and Peter Stahlberger (1987), 'Die schweizerischen Landsgemeinde-Demokratien', *Staat und Politik*, vol. 34 (Bern: Haupt), pp. 237–260.

Moore, Mick (2001), 'Political Underdevelopment. What causes "bad government"' *Public Management Review* 3 (3), pp. 385–418.

Moser, Christian (1987), 'Erfolge kantonaler Volksinitiativen nach formalen und inhaltlichen Gesichtspunkten', in: *Schweizerisches Jahrbuch für Politische Wissenschaft*, no. 27 (Bern: Haupt).

Mukherjee, Bumba (2004), 'Why Power-Sharing Agreements Lead to Enduring Peaceful Resolution of Some Civil Wars, But Not Others?', *International Studies Quarterly*, 50, pp. 479–504.

Neidhart, Leonhard (1970), *Plebiszit und Pluralitäre Demokratie* (Bern: Francke).

Niederer, Arnold (1965), *Gemeinwerk im Wallis: Bäuerliche Gemeinschaftsarbeit in Vergangenheit und Gegenwart* (Basel: Krebs).

Nielsen, Christian Axboe (2009), 'The Kosovo precedent and the rhetorical deployment of former Yugoslav analogies in the cases of Abkhazia and South Ossetia', *Southeast European and Black Sea Studies*, 9:1, pp. 171–189.

Norris, Pippa (2008), *Driving Democracy: Do Power-Sharing Institutions Work?* (Cambridge; New York: Cambridge University Press).

OECD (1997/2000/2005), *Revenue Statistics* (Paris: OECD).

OECD (2008), *National Accounts of OECD Countries: General Government Account*, vol. IV, 1995–2006 (Paris: OECD).

OECD (2008), *OECD Factbook: Economic, Environmental and Social Statistics* (Paris: OECD).

Olson, Mancur (1965), *The Logic of Collective Action* (Cambridge: Harvard University Press).

Oluvu, Dele and Wunsch, James (2004), *Local Governance in Africa – The Challenges of Decentralisation* (Boulder and London: Lynne Rienner Publications).

Papadopoulos, Yannis (1998), *Démocratie Directe* (Paris: Economica).

Papadopoulos, Yannis (1999), *Les Processus de Decicion Federaux en Suisse* (Paris: L'Harmattan), pp. 69–96.

Papadopoulos, Yannis (2009), 'Démocratie Suisse et idéologie populiste: Quand on récolte ce qu'on a semé', in: Adrian Vatter *et al.* (eds), *Demokratie als Leidenschaft* (Bern: Haupt, 2009), pp. 107–117.

Papadopoulos, Yannis (ed.) (1994), *Elites Politiques et Peuple en Suisse, Analyse des Votations Fédérales 1970–1987* (Lausanne: Réalités sociales).

Poitry, Alain (1989), *La Fonction D'ordre de l'Etat. Analyse des Mécanismes et des Déterminants Sélectifs dans le Processus Législatif Suisse* (Bern: Lang).

Przeworski, Adam E., Michael Alvarez, José Antonio Cheibub and Fernando Limongi (2000), *Democracy and Development. Political Institutions and Well-Being in the World, 1950–1990* (Cambridge: Cambridge University Press).

Ra'anan, Uri (1990), 'The Nation-State Fallacy', in: Joseph V. Montville (ed.), *Conflict and Peacemaking in Multiethnic Societies* (Massachusetts and Toronto: Lexington Books).

Rappard, William E. (1912), *Le Facteur Économique dans L'avènement de la Démocratie Moderne en Suisse* (Genève: Georg).

Riklin, Alois (1991), *Funktionen der Schweizerischen Neutralität* (St Gallen: Institut für Politikwissenschaft der Hochschule St Gallen).

Riklin, Alois (2006), 'Neutralität am Ende? 500 Jahre Neutralität der Schweiz', *Zeitschrift für Schweizerisches Recht*, vol. 125, Issue 1 5, pp. 583–597.

Roeder, Philip and Donald Rothchild (eds) (2005), *Sustainable Peace, Power and Democracy after Civil Wars* (Ithaca and London: Cornell University Press).

Rosenberg, Shawn W. (ed.) (2007), *Deliberation, Participation and Democracy: Can the People Govern?* (Basingstoke, Hants: Palgrave Macmillan).

Ruckstuhl, Brigitte (1991), 'Die Schweiz – ein Land der Bauern und Hirten', in: Silvia Ferrari *et al.*, *Auf wen Schoss Wilhelm Tell?* (Zürich: Rotpunktverlag).

Ruffieux, Roland (1983), 'La Suisse des radicaux (1848–1914)', in: *Nouvelle Histoire de la Suisse et des Suisses* (Lausanne: Payot).

Rüfli, Christian and Fritz Sager (2004), 'Public Health, Prävention und Föderalismus: Erkenntnisse aus der Umsetzung des Bundesgesetzes über die Krankenversicherung', Sozial-und Präventivmedizin. *International Journal of Public Health* 49(3), pp. 216–223.

Sager, Fritz (2002), *Vom Verwalten des urbanen Raums. Institutionelle Bedingungen von Politikkoordination am Beispiel der Raum-und Verkehrsplanung in städtischen Gebieten* (Bern: Haupt).

Sager, Fritz (2003), 'Kompensationsmöglichkeiten föderaler Vollzugsdefizite. Das Beispiel der kantonalen Alkoholpräventionspolitiken', *Swiss Political Science Review* 9(1), pp. 309–333.

Sartori, Giovanni (1987), *The Theory of Democracy Revisited* (Chatham (N.J.): Chatham House).

Scharpf, Fritz (1970), *Demokratietheorie Zwischen Utopie und Anpassung* (Konstanz: Universitätsverlag).

Schattschneider, E.E. (1960), *The Semisovereign People: A Realist View of Democracy in America* (Hinsdale: Dryden Press).

Schmid, Carol L. (2001), *The Politics of Language: Conflict, Identity, and Cultural Pluralism in Comparative Perspective* (New York: Oxford University Press).

Schmitt, Pierre-André (1989), 'Neuenburg ist allen andern hundertvierzig Jahre voraus', *Die Weltwoche*, 13 July.

Schneider, Gerald and Cyrill Hess (1995), 'Die innenpolitische Manipulation der Aussenpolitik: Die Logik von Ratifikationsdebatten in der direkten Demokratie', *Schweizerische Zeitschrift für Politische Wissenschaft*, vol. 1, Issue 2–3, pp. 93–111.

Schneider, Gerald and Patricia Weitsman (1996), 'The Punishment Trap, Integration Referendums as Popularity Tests', *Comparative Political Studies*, vol. 28, no. 4, pp. 582–607.

Schneider, Gerald and Thomas Holzer (2002), *Asylpolitik auf Abwegen. Nationalstaatliche und Europäische Reaktionen auf die Globalisierung der Flüchtlingsströme* (Opladen: Leske + Budrich).

Schumpeter, Joseph (1942), *Capitalism, Socialism, and Democracy* (New York: Harper & Brothers).

Schwab, Brigitte and Muriel Surdez (2007), 'Education and Cultural Policy', in: Ulrich Klöti *et al.* (eds), *Handbook of Swiss Politics* (Zürich: Neue Zürcher Zeitung Publishing), pp. 788–798.

Schwarz, Daniel and Wolf Linder (2007), *Fraktionsgeschlossenheit im schweizerischen Nationalrat 1996–2005: Studie im Auftrag der Parlamentsdienste der schweizerischen Bundesversammlung* (Bern: Institut für Politikwissenschaft).

Schweizerische Studiengesellschaft für Raumordnung und Regionalpolitik (ROREP) (1988), *Agglomerationsprobleme in der Schweiz* (Bern: Peter Lang).

Sciarini, Pascal (2007), 'The Decision-Making Process', in: Ulrich Klöti *et al.* (eds), *Handbook of Swiss Politics* (Zürich: Neue Zürcher Zeitung Publishing), pp. 465–499.

Sciarini, Pascal and Alexandre Trechsel (1996), 'Démocratie directe en Suisse: l'élite victime des droits populaires?', in: *Revue Suisse de Science Politique* 2(2) (1996), pp. 201–232.

Sciarini, Pascal, Alex Fischer and Sarah Nicolet (2004), 'How Europe Hits Home: Evidence from the Swiss Case', *Journal of European Public Policy* 11 (3), pp. 353–378.

Senghaas, Dieter (1997), 'Frieden – Ein mehrfaches Komplexprogramm', in: Dieter Senghaas (ed.), *Frieden machen* (Frankfurt: Suhrkamp), pp. 560–574.

Senti, Martin (1995), *Geschlecht als Politischer Konflikt* (Bern: Haupt).

Sigg, Oswald (1978), *Die eidgenössischen Volksinitiativen 1892–1939* (Bern: Francke).

Sisk, Timothy D. (1996), *Power Sharing and International Mediation in Ethnic Conflicts* (Washington DC: US Institute of Peace).

Soland, Rolf (1980), *Joachim Leonz Eder und die Regeneration im Thurgau 1830–1831: Ein Kapitel aus der thurgauischen Verfassungsgeschichte* (Weinfelden: Mühlemann).

Stadelmann-Steffen, Isabelle and Markus Freitag (2009), 'Abstimmungs-oder Wahldemokratie? Zum Einfluss der direkten Demokratie auf die Wahlbeteiligung in den Kantonen', in: Adrian Vatter *et al.* (eds), *Demokratie als Leidenschaft* (Bern: Haupt), pp. 157–182.

Steenbergen, Marco (2009), 'Deliberative Politics in Switzerland', in: Adrian Vatter *et al.* (eds), *Demokratie als Leidenschaft* (Bern: Haupt), pp. 283–301.

Steiner, Jürg (1974), *Amicable Agreement Versus Majority Rule: Conflict Resolution in Switzerland* (Chapel Hill: UNC Press).

Steiner, Jürg (1990), 'Power-sharing: Another Swiss "Export-Product"?', in: Joseph V. Montville (ed.), *Conflict and Peacemaking in Multiethnic Societies* (Massachusetts and Toronto: Lexington Books).

Steiner, Jürg (1991), *European Democracies* (London: Longman).

Szczerbiak, Aleks and Paul Taggard (eds) (2004), 'Choosing Union: The 2003 EU Accession Referendums', *West European Politics*, Special Issue vol. 27 (4).

Tarrow, Sidney and Donatella Della Porta (2005), *Transnational Protest and Global Activism* (Lanham: Rowman and Littlefield).

Tolbert, Caroline and Daniel Smith (2005), 'The Educative Effects of Ballot Initiatives on Voter Turnout in the United States', *American Politics Research* 33, 2, pp. 283–309.

Trampusch, Christine (2009), 'The Politics of Institutional Change. Transformative and Self-Preserving Change in the Vocational Education and Training System in Switzerland', *Comparative Politics*, vol. 41, forthcoming.

Trampusch, Christine (2010), 'The Welfare State and Trade Unions in Switzerland. A Historical Reconstruction of the Shift from a Liberal to a Post-Liberal Welfare Regime', *Journal of European Social Policy*, vol. 20 (1), pp. 58–73.

Trechsel, Alexander (2007), 'Popular votes', in: Ulrich Klöti *et al.* (eds), *Handbook of Swiss Politics* (Zürich: Neue Zürcher Zeitung Publishing), pp. 405–434.

Trechsel, Alexander and Uwe Serdült (1999), *Kaleidoskop Volksrechte: die Institutionen der direkten Demokratie in den schweizerischen Kantonen (1970–1996)* (Basel: Helbing and Lichtenhahn; Genève: Faculté de droit).

Tsebelis, George and Jeannette Money (1997), *Bicameralism* (Cambridge: Cambridge University Press).

Varone, Frédéric (2007), 'The Federal Administration', in: Ulrich Klöti *et al.* (eds), *Handbook of Swiss Politics* (Zürich: Neue Zürcher Zeitung Publishing), pp. 281–308.

Vatter, Adrian (2002), *Kantonale Demokratien im Vergleich: Entstehungsgründe, Interaktionen und Wirkungen politischer Institutionen in den Schweizer Kantonen* (Opladen: Leske and Budrich).

Vatter, Adrian (2005), 'Bicameralism and Policy Performance: The Effects of Cameral Structure in Comparative Perspective', *Journal of Legislative Studies*, vol. 11 (2), pp. 194–215.

Vatter, Adrian (2007), 'Federalism', in: Ulrich Klöti *et al.* (eds), *Handbook of Swiss Politics* (Zürich: Neue Zürcher Zeitung Publishing), pp. 197–225.

Vatter, Adrian (ed.) (2006), *Föderalismusreform, Wirkungsweise und Reformansätze föderativer Institutionen in der Schweiz* (Zürich: Verlag Neue Zürcher Zeitung).

Vatter, Adrian and Markus Freitag (2004), 'Political Institutions and the Wealth of Regions: Swiss Cantons in Comparative Perspective', in: *European Urban and Regional Studies*, vol. 11 (4), 2004, pp. 227–241.

Vatter, Adrian, Varone, Frédéric and Sager, Fritz (eds) (2009), *Demokratie als Leidenschaft,* Planung, Entscheidung und Vollzug in der schweizerischen Demokratie, Festschrift für Wolf Linder (Bern: Haupt).

Von Arx, Nicolas (2002), *Ähnlich, aber anders: die Volksinitiative in Kalifornien und in der Schweiz* (Genève: Helbing and Lichtenhahn).

Von Roten, Iris (1991 [1958]), *Frauen im Laufgitter* (Zürich and Dortmund: Efef).

Vox, *Analysen der eidgenössischen Abstimmungen und Wahlen* (1977ff.), Schweizerische Gesellschaft für praktische Sozialforschung, Forschungszentrum für schweizerische Politik der Universität Bern, Forschungsstelle für politische Wissenschaft der Universität Zürich, Département de science politique, Université de Genève (Zürich, Bern and Genève).

Watts, Richard J. (1991), 'Linguistic minorities and language conflict in Europe: Learning from the Swiss experience', in: Florian Coulmas (ed.), *Language Policy for the EC* (Berlin: Mouton de Gruyter).

Watts, Ronald L. (2008), *Comparing Federal Systems* (Montreal: McGill-Queens).

Werder, Hans (1978), *Die Bedeutung der Volksinitiative in der Nachkriegszeit* (Bern: Francke).

Werlen, Iwar (2008), 'Englisch als Fremdsprache bei Erwachsenen in der Schweiz', in: Sandro Moraldo, *Sprachkontakt und Mehrsprachigkeit* (Heidelberg: Winter).

Werlen, Iwar (2008), *Sprachkompetenzen der erwachsenen Bevölkerung in der Schweiz. Schlussbericht Nationales Forschungsprogramm 56* (Bern: Institut für Sprachwissenschaft).

White, Peter G. (2000), 'Non-Territorial Federalism: A New Approach to Identity Politics', *The James R. Mallory Annual Lecture in Canadian Studies* (Montreal, Quebec: McGill University).

Wiesli, Reto and Wolf Linder (2000), *Repräsentation, Artikulation und Durchsetzung kantonaler Interessen im Ständerat und im Nationalrat: Studie im Auftrag der Parlamentsdienste der Schweizerischen Bundesversammlung* (Bern: Institut für Politikwissenschaft).

Windisch, Uli (1992), *Les relations quotidiennes entre Romands et Alémaniques* (Lausanne: Editions Payot).

Zisk, Betty H. (1987), *Money, Media and the Grass Roots: State Ballot Issues and the Electoral Process* (Newbury Park, California: Sage Publications).

Index

Page numbers in **bold** refer to figures, page numbers in *italic* refer to tables, page numbers in ***bold italic*** refer to boxes

240   *Index*